The Transformation
of American Religion

The Transformation of American Religion

THE STORY OF A LATE-TWENTIETH-CENTURY AWAKENING

Amanda Porterfield

OXFORD
UNIVERSITY PRESS

2001

OXFORD

UNIVERSITY PRESS

Oxford   New York

Athens   Auckland   Bangkok   Bogotá   Bombay   Buenos Aires
Calcutta   Cape Town   Chennai   Dar es Salaam   Delhi   Florence   Hong Kong
Istanbul   Karachi   Kuala Lumpur   Madras   Madrid   Melbourne
Mexico City   Nairobi   Paris   Singapore   Taipei   Tokyo   Toronto

and associated companies in
Berlin   Ibadan

Published by Oxford University Press, Inc.
198 Madison Avenue, New York, New York 10016

Oxford is a registered trademark of Oxford University Press

Library of Congress Cataloging-in-Publication Data
Porterfield, Amanda, 1947–
The transformation of American religion : the story of a late-
twentieth-century awakening / Amanda Porterfield.
p. cm.   Includes bibliographical references and index.
ISBN 0-19-513137-1
1. United States—Religion—1960–   I. Title.
BL2525 .P669 2000
200'.973'09045—dc21   00-036758

2 4 6 8 9 7 5 3 1

Printed in the United States of America
on acid-free paper

To my excellent colleagues at the
University of Wyoming, with
gratefulness for their inspiration and
support.

Table of Contents

5
Gender Consciousness, Body Awareness, and the Humanization of Religion

6
The Pragmatic Role of Religious Studies

CONCLUSION
The Great Awakening of the Late Twentieth Century

Notes

Index

Acknowledgments

This book began with an essay that Peter W. Williams invited me to include in his edited volume *Perspectives on American Religion and Culture* (1999). That essay enabled me to begin to pull together a set of ideas I had been thinking about for years. After reading a version of that essay on a visit to Laramie, I became a visiting professor at the University of Wyoming and worked on this book for a year before taking up a full-time appointment. For providing such a congenial environment for writing it, this book is dedicated to my colleagues at the University of Wyoming. I am especially grateful to Paul Flesher, Ollie Walter, Janet Constantinades, Keith Hull, and Tom Buchanan for making a place for me. I would also like to thank Carolyn Anderson, Gladys Crane, Lewis Dabney, John Dorst, Kent Drummond and Susan Aronstein, Phil and Lisa Dubois, Susan Frye, Janice and Duncan Harris, Robert Hinton and Annie Sailer, Malcolm Holmes, Jeanne Holland and Cliff Marks, Phil Holt, Caroline McCracken-Flesher, Richard Machalek and Donna Barnes, Larry and Mary Lynne Munn, Eric Nye, Ric Reverand, Roger Schmit, Eric Sandeen, and Bob Torry for making life at the University of Wyoming so stimulating and enjoyable.

Scott Appleby and Tom Tweed provided helpful analyses of the book proposal. Mary Bednarowski and Paul Flesher read a draft of the

ix

manuscript and gave good encouragement and comment. Paul Courtright urged me to write about Matthew Shepard's death and its importance for the study of American religion. Charles Aho advanced my understanding of Thomas Merton's influence. Bob Torry helped me think about connections between psychoanalytic theory and Buddhist philosophy. At Oxford University Press, Cynthia Read gave the manuscript a careful and insightful reading that improved it considerably. Mark and Nick Kline made home a great place to be.

Laramie, Wyoming   Amanda Porterfield

INTRODUCTION

᭶

Post-Protestant America

In the suburban village where I grew up in the late 1950s and early
1960s, the geography of the village helped to create a closely knit community joined together in deference to Protestant values and authority.
Situated on a hill at the intersection known as the Four Corners, the
massive stone edifice of the Reformed church overlooked a cluster of
civic institutions. Down the hill and diagonally across the intersection
was the brick colonial public library. The village hall, another brick
colonial, stood on the corner between the library and the church. On
the fourth corner, the K-through-12 public school with its memorial
flagpole and double lawn faced out across the street to the church
above.

Not everyone who lived in the village attended the Reformed
church, but its importance in the village landscape contributed to the
sense of village identity that locals shared. This sense of identity was
manifest just after nightfall on Christmas Eve, when the streets inter-
secting the Four Corners were closed to traffic and families assembled
at the foot of the Reformed church lawn for the annual Nativity pageant. Each year a civic leader was appointed to the role of Joseph and
a high school senior was selected to be Mary. As the high school band
led the crowd in multiple verses of "O Little Town of Bethlehem,"
"Silent Night," and "Hark! The Herald Angels Sing," pastors from

various churches offered prayers of peace and thanksgiving. Joseph came out of the shadows leading the donkey (borrowed from the local zoo) carrying Mary to the manger in the center of the hill below the church. When Mary dismounted and took her place at the manger, a light came on in the crib, signifying the birth of Jesus. Then the Three Wise Men (village fathers dressed in exotic hats and robes) crossed the hill bearing gifts while floodlights illuminated an angel (another high school senior) on the church roof, dressed in white robes, holding a trumpet to her lips. With actors and audience drawn from the village and not just from the membership of the Reformed church, this pageant represented the integration of civic and religious values. In hosting the enactment of the Christmas story, the Reformed church provided space for the village to come together to celebrate not only the Holy Family but also the ordinary families who contributed to village life.

Commanding the pulpit of the Reformed church when I was a child was Lowell R. Ditzen, a compassionate and forceful preacher whose sweeping robes, elegant bearing, and ruggedly handsome face defined my image of God. Dr. Ditzen was an admirer of Harry Emerson Fosdick, the liberal preacher and religious writer famous for arguing that real human problems had priority over hoary theological ones and that, to better address these real problems, Christianity should be translated into modern terminology. Interpreting the meaning of Christian life in light of contemporary ideas from psychology and other social sciences, Fosdick and his younger colleague Lowell Ditzen turned away from narrow interpretations of Protestant doctrine to work with people from various denominations and faiths and to focus on managing the problems of life in ethical, effective, and emotionally satisfying ways. With their idealism about the progressive synthesis of Protestant Christianity and modern culture, these accomplished and genial men embodied the authority of the liberal Protestant establishment in America and its claim on the larger culture.[1]

Like other liberal Protestant clerics in other American cities and suburbs, Fosdick and Ditzen preached to business and professional people who exerted a disproportionate amount of influence on the larger culture and who, in many cases, took the rightness of their own worldview pretty much for granted. While disputes might arise over particular issues, this influential cohort of Protestant Americans shared many underlying assumptions about the importance of individual conscience, civic responsibility, hard work, investment capitalism, marital fidelity, child nurture, and gender role differentiation. In worship services, in Sunday school classes, and especially in fellowship activities that merged with a broad range of civic and social events, liberal Protestant churches and their members worked to protect and legitimate these underlying values and to extend their influence throughout the larger culture and the world.

At the level of national theological debate, this culture-affirming Christianity did not go uncontested. Alarmed by the looseness of liberal interpretations of the atonement, resurrection, virgin birth, and miracles of Jesus, fundamentalists and other conservative Christians insisted on strict adherence to the literal and supernatural understanding of these points of faith and on the consequent difference between themselves and religious liberals. As the evangelical conservative Carl F. H. Henry argued, "The New Testament upholds specific doctrinal affirmations as indispensable to genuine Christian confession." From this perspective, "[t]he modernist tendency to link Christian love, tolerance and liberty with theological inclusivism is therefore discredited." In other words, "[m]odernist pleas for religious tolerance were basically a strategic device for evading the question of doctrinal fidelity." Motivated by strong religious feeling, the conservative argument for strict theology was a form of resistance against the openness and tolerance of liberal Protestantism. To some extent, it was also a protest against liberal Protestants themselves and their privileged place within American culture. Henry claimed that in the process of diverging from strict interpretation of Christian doctrine, Fosdick's autobiography, *The Living of These Days* (1955), "spins a halo of self-justification."[2]

While contending with dissension from conservative Protestants such as Carl Henry, liberal Protestants also faced criticism and disaffection from within their own ranks. Liberal optimism about modernity and human progress drew criticism from a number of Protestant intellectuals who were concerned with the grim realities of modern culture and the existential angst these realities provoked. These critics focused on the radical nature of Christian faith and the conflict between it and the complacency of modern culture. But they remained liberals in their investment in the symbolic rather than literal truth of biblical language and in their willingness to interpret the meaning of Christian doctrine through the prism of modern psychology and sociology. Unlike fundamentalists who stressed the literal truth of Christ's atonement, resurrection, miracles, and virgin birth, the "realist" critics of liberal optimism worked out of scholarly traditions in biblical criticism and philosophy of religion developed by liberal Protestants.[3]

While Christian realists criticized optimists within the liberal fold, other religious intellectuals schooled in liberal Protestant thought were venturing outside the fold of Christianity altogether, seeking stimulus and direction from psychotherapy and Eastern religions. But here again, the dividing lines between these religious seekers and liberal Protestants were often quite blurry. And even those spiritual seekers who dropped out of liberal Protestantism entirely took with them assumptions about the nature of religion that grew out of liberal Protestant thought. Meanwhile, mainstream religious liberals such as Fosdick and Ditzen were adventurers in their own right, avidly appropriating ideas from Asian religions and psychotherapy and stretching the boundaries of their religious territory to ever wider dimensions. Thus while working to unify the larger culture and pursuing their own aspirations to leadership within that larger culture, liberal Protestants were also investigating and absorbing new forms of religious thought, practice, and experience as a result of their increasing interest in and respect for other traditions. And the more open to other traditions these liberal Protestants were, the more diffuse, plastic, and humanistic their own conceptions of Christianity became.

For all the enthusiasms they pursued and for all their willingness to open up Christian life to new forms of interpretation, mainstream Protestant liberals were not as tender-minded or unprincipled as they were sometimes portrayed. Harry Emerson Fosdick was fundamentally optimistic about modernity and its amenability to Christianity, but he never made Christian living easy or sentimental. In a telephone call he made to a grief-stricken Lowell Ditzen after the Ditzens' sixteen-year old son killed himself on New Year's Eve 1953, Fosdick spoke out from the tough side of liberal Protestantism, offering this bit of consolation: "You and your wife can take this minus and turn it into a plus."[4]

As this message makes clear, Fosdick had little interest in sugar-coated pieties about life or death. His tough advice was pragmatic—Ditzen and his wife, Virginia, must make something positive out of their grief and loss. Echoing the strenuous idealism of the American philosopher Josiah Royce, who also had to cope with a son's suicide,

Fosdick made it clear that the Christian was responsible for working to bring good out of evil. Lowell Ditzen agreed. In a series of essays on overcoming tragedy in a world "where rain falls on the just and unjust alike," he argued "that it's only in this kind of world that character can be nurtured." Admitting that "this makes for a difficult world at times, perhaps even terrifying sometimes," he explained that "the dual possibilities in such a world, and our acceptance of them, create humility and an ability to adjust to changing fortunes." As he went on to say, "We are often forced to make evaluations, to set up goals and standards to pursue, and then dig in to conquer adverse circumstances. Life in this kind of world enables people to do amazing and inspiring things."[5]

This up-by-the-bootstraps emphasis on character building and world improvement was grounded in Reformed Protestant ideas about the activist, energizing, and pragmatic nature of religious life. Developed out of the tradition of liberal Protestant thought, this attitude often found expression in secular, psychological terms that seeped into the larger culture and influenced representatives of other religious traditions. Of course, mawkish expressions of religious piety also flourished in American culture and, in the last decades of the twentieth century, even achieved new prominence through talk shows promoting histrionic self-disclosure and popular rhetorics of victimization. But a pragmatic focus on effect and a relish for personal authenticity continue to persist in many forms of American religious thought. Something like Ditzen's admiration for Christian heroism and Fosdick's tough advice on how to deal with suicide can be traced back to the New England Puritans' commitment to self-assessment and personal transformation, and forward to current interest in various efforts to cut through bad habits, bad karma, and superficial or ineffective forms of religious and spiritual life.

The persistence of this Protestant-based fusion of spiritual idealism and pragmatic concern in American religious thought constitutes one of the two principal themes of this book. The story of its detachment from Protestant ownership since the sixties, its appropriation by a more religiously diversified body of thinkers, and its infusion with new symbolism and fresh vitality constitutes the other principal theme. In other words, this is a book about the endurance of certain Protestant attitudes, ideas, and principles and their profound influence in the shaping of American religious thought. At the same time, it is also a book about the remarkable decline in the authority Protestant people and institutions claim in the larger culture, the success of many external challenges to their hegemony, and their relinquishment, to some extent at least, of the unselfconscious presumption to cultural authority that characterized them in the fifties and early sixties.

The transformation to a post-Protestant culture is the result of a variety of factors working together to loosen the dominance of Protestant institutions over the larger culture while at the same time allowing beliefs and activities rooted in Protestant tradition to interact more freely than ever before with beliefs and attitudes from other traditions. Each of the following chapters focuses on one of the complex factors in this transformative process, describing the historical roots of one key aspect of religious change, its development since the 1960s, its impact on the larger culture, and its accommodation to new forms of religious life.

Chapter 1 addresses the universalizing, evangelical aspect of the Reformed Protestant tradition in America and its role as a major, underlying factor in the recent transformation of American religion. Chapter 2 focuses on the transformation of American Catholicism since the sixties and its role in unleashing American culture from Protestant control. Chapter 3 focuses on the effect of the Vietnam War in dissolving presumptions about the implicit moral authority and cultural leadership of Anglo Protestantism in the United States. Chapter 4 analyzes the role that Buddhism played in new ways of thinking about selfhood that stimulated new developments in Jewish and Christian thought. Chapter 5 examines gender self-consciousness and body awareness as crucial factors in the broad scope of religious change. Chapter 6 examines the impact of the academic study of religion in promoting understanding of religion as a universal phenomenon and advancing appreciation of non-Protestant religions. The conclusion points to some of the reasons that this multifaceted process of religious transformation might be thought of as a new Great Awakening.

A Case in Point

My own life offers a small and partial illustration of how the various forces described in these chapters tend to work together rather than independently. In an encounter with Eastern religions that was far more commonplace than I realized at the time, the transformation of my own religious outlook as a liberal Protestant was triggered by the study of Zen Buddhism. As a junior in high school in 1964, my progressive and somewhat controversial English teacher assigned each student in her class to a long-term independent project. For some reason, Miss Boice chose me to study Zen Buddhism and report back to the class. In the course of this assignment, I read *Zen and the Art of Archery* by the German existentialist Eugen Herrigel and several books by D. T. Suzuki, the influential translator of Asian scriptures and interpreter of Zen Buddhism for Western students. I learned from Herrigel that Zen was a kind of metaphor for an unselfconscious concentration that dissolved the distinction between subject and object. I learned from Suzuki that Buddhism was a dynamic, evolving religion dedicated to the attainment of egoless self-awareness and compassion for others.

I arranged to visit a Zen Buddhist temple. My father insisted on accompanying me to this allegedly exotic and dangerous place, where we attended a service that was so mild and low-key that he fell asleep. Before that, we were introduced to a small congregation that included a few Asian faces and eight or ten Euro-Americans who looked very much like the people in our Reformed church. In fact, as it turned out, there was at least one member of our church who was a Zen practitioner—Mary Todd, whose ashes are buried in the church columbarium not far from those of my father. Mrs. Todd kept a Japanese rock garden, which I was invited to visit. In that tranquil domestic spot, I learned once again that Zen was not as strange as I had first expected.

Looking back on these events, I believe I found in Zen something like the spiritual essence of the Protestant Reformed religion I had grown up with. There certainly was something about Zen that was new and freshly vital, but it was my Protestant orientation to the world that led me to this discovery. My Christian concept of grace was rather abstract and legalistic; Zen provided a way of thinking about grace, and about religious experience in general, that was more concrete than Reformed Protestant theology, and just as stimulating and challenging. Exposure to Zen led me to focus more than I otherwise might have on the idea that life was an experiential quest. In this respect, Zen loosened, altered, and also confirmed my Protestant framework.

In this plastic but persistently Protestant state of mind, I began to look for conceptions of religious experience within the history of Protestant thought that matched the authenticity of Zen existentialism. In my senior thesis as a religion major in college, I wrote about the religious thought of Dietrich Bonhoeffer, the German pastor and theologian who was executed by the Nazis for his role in a plot to kill Hitler. I focused on Bonhoeffer's *Letters and Papers from Prison* and especially on his description of the "Archimedean point" of Christian experience in which the restrictive and exclusivist doctrines of Christian theology fell away in the attainment of a liberating and empowering state of compassionate awareness of self and others. Had I been more aware of how much Zen Buddhism I was reading into Bonhoeffer's Archimedean point, I would not have been so baffled and disappointed to discover that more advanced Bonhoeffer scholars understood the man to be thoroughly moralistic and orthodox. The professional Bonhoefferites did not see his Archimedean point as a breakthrough into something much bigger, as I had argued in my undergraduate thesis. But even as I lost confidence in my interpretation of Bonhoeffer, my study of the man and his thought still felt rewarding. In unwittingly constructing him as a kind of Protestant Zen master, I had become convinced that Protestant theology was a framework that many profound thinkers had utilized in their struggle for happiness, goodness, and truth. Even if I had been wrong about the extent or magnitude of Bonhoeffer's breaking out of the sentimentalism, moralism, and legalism that often constrained Protestant orthodoxy, I thought I would find other Protestant thinkers pursuing similar paths of truth and liberation.

The whirlwind of social unrest surrounding the Vietnam War caught up with me at this point and had a profoundly disorienting affect. Revolution against the Anglo Protestant establishment seemed "right on" and weirdly reminiscent of Protestantism itself. But the irony of the situation left me (and many others) with little ground upon which to stand. Through revisionist interpretations of American history, I imbibed iconoclastic (and overreaching) ideas about Protestants as the real culprits. Their belief in historical progress and their self-confidence about who God was and what he had done and could do were the underlying causes of the war in Vietnam and of many other social problems at home and abroad.

A trip to India deepened my confusion. There among the sadhus, sari-clad women, sculpted temples, green rice fields, beggars, and cardboard shanties, I met an American devotee of Sai Baba who gave me a little packet of dirt blessed by the guru with instructions to rub, sprinkle or eat it whenever and wherever I needed Sai Baba's power. As a deliberate experiment in non-Christian religiosity, I swallowed some. I felt daring but also duplicitous—I had accepted the blessed dirt as if I believed in it. But how much did it actually matter whether or not I believed? This last thought coincided with a feeling of physical queasiness and possible ill heath. What had I really eaten? What was it doing to my body? It also prompted a sense of intellectual uncertainty. On one hand, I thought that my fear of sickness or demonic possession from eating the powder was simply the result of the power of my negative thinking—I had momentarily lost my self-control by allowing the idea of the powder's efficacy to take shape in my mind. On the other hand, what wonderful realms of reality was I shutting myself off from by not being open to this and other forms of belief and practice?

The way I framed this set of questions, and the way I tortured myself thinking about them, had a lot to do with my Protestant upbringing. I had been taught that honesty was a foundational virtue and that intention always mattered. This was tied to the idea that being a Christian was grounded in an internal relationship with God that was intensely subjective and thus closed, at least to some extent, to external view. This investment in religious privacy was in turn linked to the more doctrinally specific idea that the essential meaning of the Eucharist resided in the believer's relationship with God rather than in the elements themselves. And this whole defense of the internal nature of religious authority was carried forward by implicit contrast with Catholicism, and occasionally by explicitly derogatory and stereotypical allegations that Catholics, whom we had righteously risen above, believed that Eucharistic elements exerted a kind of magical power regardless of the receiver's intent or state of mind.

Before going to India and eating Sai Baba's powder, I had met a Carmelite nun a few years older than myself who responded to my expressed curiosity about her life with an invitation to a meal at her monastery. In addition to prompting me to want to unencumber myself from the negative stereotypes about Catholicism that were fundamental to my understanding of Protestantism, this interesting and joyful woman stimulated considerable reflection on my part about the nature of belief. She was open to beliefs that we both found mysterious, in particular the actual presence of Christ in the Eucharist, but she was more than content to live within this mystery. Because she was so bright and articulate, so happy about life, and apparently so well adjusted, I set to wondering how her openness to belief might enable her happiness. This led to ruminations about the existential predicament inherent in the Protestant insistence on the interiority of grace. Our conversations also set me to wondering how intelligence could coincide so smoothly with acceptance of mystery and openness to belief. Perhaps the drive for explanation and intellectual control was more characteristic of Protestant intellectual life than of human intelligence itself.

The fast-growing academic field of religious studies stood at hand, enabling me to pursue the effort to take a broader, more circumspect, and depersonalized look at the question of human belief. In graduate school, after my trip to India in the early 1970s, I charted what seemed at the time to be a fairly straightforward and manageable course of inquiry into the role of religious belief in American history. Convinced that both the political and spiritual turmoils of the times had a strong religious dimension, I set out to find their antecedents and casual conditions in American history. If I could discover these antecedents and conditions, I reasoned, I would have a picture of American religious history that would clarify what was currently happening to American culture (and to me).

This quest led me directly to Perry Miller and his New England Puritans. In hindsight it is not surprising that I found them so quickly or took to them so readily. Miller's own existential quest for intellectual heroes was not so different from my own, and he presented the Puritans as in search of the same kind of intellectual and moral authenticity that had attracted me to Lowell Ditzen, Zen Buddhism, and Dietrich Bonhoeffer. With great enthusiasm, I absorbed all of Miller's value judgments about the Puritans, from his unbounded admiration for Roger Williams and Jonathan Edwards to his disdain for Cotton Mather's pedantry. I was particularly interested in Miller's emphasis on the Puritans' readiness to judge themselves harshly for failing to live up to their own standards of honesty and rectitude. Miller pointed to the sincerity of their remorse, their relentless commitment to truth, and the valor of their internal struggles. He championed the Puritans as originators of American intellectual life.

At the same time I was discovering antecedents of the current transformation of American religious life in the New England Puritans, many of my colleagues in religious studies were calling attention to the exuberant religious pluralism that had always characterized American religious history, and therefore relegating the intellectual tradition of New England Puritanism to the margins. While honoring the new emphasis on religious pluralism that my colleagues have done so well to promote, this book is an attempt to show how the Puritan intellectual tradition contributed to that religious pluralism and to the advancement of religious freedom in the late twentieth century.

As I hope to show, the various forces involved in the recent transformation of American religion are thoroughly intertwined. Intellectual aspects of American religious life that go back to the Puritans have been changed but also rejuvenated. Religious activism, spiritual renewal, criticism of American culture stemming from the Vietnam War era, absorption of Buddhist ideas, new self-consciousness about gender, and the growth of religious studies all reflect this two-way process.

Liberal Protestantism's presumption to cultural authority was discovered, questioned, and dissolved even as the vitality of ideas rooted in that tradition persisted and flourished. Whether they stayed with their original denominations, joined different religious traditions, or developed personalized forms of spirituality independent of any religious group, Americans with backgrounds in liberal Protestantism have all been affected by the same underlying forces of religious and social transformation, as have Americans with backgrounds in more conservative forms of Protestantism or in Catholicism, Judaism, Islam, or other religions. Those with backgrounds outside of liberal Protestantism have become less marginalized with respect to mainstream American culture, while those of us from within liberal Protestantism have undergone a process of becoming at least somewhat decentered. The control over the definition of American culture once exerted by liberal Protestants has been eroded by pressures from both within and without liberal Protestantism. At the same time, the availability of Protestant-based ideas about the authority of individual experience and the utility of religious life have expedited this process.

Like pizza, American religious life has always been an inventive hybrid of old and new ideas. As new religious ideas entered America culture from abroad, they were perceived, and changed, in distinctly

American ways. At the same time, these new ideas altered received interpretations about the religious ideas of the American past. Legacies established by earlier generations persist in the lives and ideas of new generations, underpinning and framing everything new, while at the same time, new generations of interpreters constantly create fresh images of the past.

Complaints About Spirituality

Since the 1960s, changes occurring across the spectrum of religious life have led many Americans to create personalized forms of spirituality that incorporate elements from various traditions and into which new elements can be added at will. Although new religious communities have been established and a number of older religious traditions have been revitalized, some observers take a dim view of this tendency to create personalized forms of spirituality and are concerned about what they see as a loss of religion's power to unify and civilize American culture. These critics complain about a "cafeteria" style of religious life in which individuals feel free to choose whichever beliefs and practices they like without necessarily feeling obligated to join a specific organization or institution, or if they do join, to participate in some activities and adhere to some beliefs without going along with others. Critics lament this lack of commitment and link it to a more general deterioration in the social fabric of American life.

One the most influential critiques of this personalized spirituality has been *Habits of the Heart*, written by Robert Bellah and several coauthors. Notoriously, the book quotes a nurse named Sheila Larson who describes her religious faith as "Sheilaism." Her faith revolves around three things: belief in God, attention to conscience ("just my own little voice"), and compassion—"be gentle with yourself," as she put it, and "take care of each other. I think he [God] would want us to take care of each other." Sheila reported that this faith "has carried me a long way." Nevertheless, Bellah and his coauthors judged her faith to be superficial and narcissistic. Overlooking the social implications of her work as a nurse and the social impact that this kind of personalized religious commitment often carries, the authors shook their heads over the apparent triumph of religious individualism in American culture.

"How did we get from the point," they wondered, "where Anne Hutchinson, a seventeenth-century precursor of Sheila Larson's, could be run out of the Massachusetts Bay Colony to a situation where Anne Hutchinson is close to the norm?"[6]

Sheila Larson may indeed represent a kind of personalized religious faith that can be traced back to the commitment to an internal sense of God displayed by Anne Hutchinson (who was also a nurse). And the enormous popularity of this kind of spirituality today may indeed represent a new level of acceptance for the kind of personalized faith that Hutchinson once exemplified. But Bellah and his coauthors may have been too quick to link this new level of social acceptance for radical religious individualism with the weakening of religion's role as an instrument of civil society.

True, the governors and magistrates of the Massachusetts Bay Colony defended their decision to banish Hutchinson by asserting that her reliance on the authority of her own religious experience was a threat to social order. But questions about the soundness of their judgment have dominated interpretations of the trial at least since the early nineteenth century, as have observations about their hypocrisy in persecuting members of their own society for religious beliefs, as they themselves had sometimes been persecuted in England. The notoriety of the trial in American literature and historiography reflects widespread agreement that the judgment against Hutchinson exemplified the tendency to moralism to which the New England Puritans were only too vulnerable.

The viewpoint expressed by Bellah and his coauthors does represent an important strand of American religious thought. And their antagonism toward Hutchinson and her successors reflected a persistent American controversy about the degree to which social responsibility derives from religious experience. But the real disagreement between Hutchinson and her judges, and perhaps between Sheila Larson and her critics as well, was not about whether religion is or should be socially constructive. All would agree on that. The real disagreement concerns the degree to which individual religious experience should be the arbiter of religious life and the degree to which individual religious experience is the source of religion's genuinely salutary effects.

Even though they disagreed about the *extent* to which religious authority belonged to the individual, both Hutchinson and her seventeenth-century critics agreed that individual religious authority was an important principle. They all understood grace to be a powerful process that transformed individuals into faithful Christians and enabled them to covenant together to establish virtuous families, churches, and communities. As a result of this understanding of how grace worked through individuals to create good societies, they believed that government should flow from the consciences of Christian individuals and not be imposed on them by hostile authorities. Thus government should be moral and just—and not hamper the expression of religious truth. Put more concretely, the government of Massachusetts Bay should contribute to the development of the religious principles that Puritans had not been free to fully express or implement in England. Religious freedom was an important principle for the Puritan leadership in Massachusetts as well as for Anne Hutchinson, although she defined that principle in more individualistic terms while they defined it in terms of their responsibility, as civic leaders, to eradicate threats to what they perceived as religious truth.

The issues raised in the Hutchinson trial have continued to be raised in American religious history. Commitment to the primacy of personal experience and readiness to resist external authority for its own sake have found expression in numerous times and places, including in the enthusiasm for intellectual freedom among writers and social activists of the early twentieth century, who excoriated the Puritans as authoritarian, moralistic, and constantly on the lookout for anyone who might be having fun. It has also nurtured the penchant for religious experimentation expressed in William James's *Varieties of Religious Experience,* Jack Kerouac's *Dharma Bums,* and Annie Dillard's *Pilgrim at Tinker Creek,* to name but three of many titles that might be cited. In the 1960s, emphasis on the authority of the individual to resist the status quo surfaced in protest marches against the military-industrial complex and its war in Vietnam, in which Lyndon Johnson played John Winthrop's role as defender of social order to millions of rebellious and religiously inspired college students.

The Hutchinson trial helped to shape this cultural mentality of fierce personalism. During the trial, asked why she had befriended John Wheelright, a minister officially censored for criticizing other ministers in New England, and why she continued to support him, Hutchinson famously replied, "That's matter of conscience, Sir." In defense of her reliance on conscience, she invoked her experience of the Holy Spirit, claiming that she experienced the Spirit's "immediate revelation" and that she believed it had as much authority as the revelations described in scripture.

The claim about the Holy Spirit speaking directly to her soul marginalized her in the eyes of the governor and magistrates of the Massachusetts Bay Colony. In much of what she said, however, Hutchinson agreed with the teachings of her own minister, John Cotton, whom she and her husband had followed to America from England. Cotton was held in the highest respect by Puritans on both sides of the Atlantic, and his perspective on the Holy Spirit and its validation of personal religious experience was quite similar to Hutchinson's. He stressed the difference between the vital experience of grace and the mere hope of grace, which typically entailed conformity to the outward behavior and intellectual beliefs conventionally associated with grace. In his focus on the need for experiential assurance of grace, he stressed the importance of having a "Seal of the Spirit," an event beyond conversion that gave the soul indissoluble union with God and everlasting life.[7]

Both in the radical way that Hutchinson and Cotton expounded it and in the somewhat more conservative formulations of others, the emphasis on personal religious experience was a distinguishing aspect of Puritan thought. Puritans differed from other Christians of their time in their intense interest in the Holy Spirit and its transformative power in individual life, and in the authority that the Holy Spirit imputed to subjective experience. As the British historian Geoffrey Nuttall observed, the spectrum of Puritan thought, ranging from radical to moderate to conservative, was defined by the degree of emphasis on the authority of subjective experience of the Holy Spirit.[8] All Puritans agreed on the primacy of individual experience, although they disagreed with each other on questions about how spontaneous and independent of scriptural authority it could be and still be authentically Christian. But as a cultural group, it is the Puritans who introduced belief in the primacy of conscience and subjective experience into American religious life. The Holy Spirit represented this belief.

Interestingly, at the radical end of the Puritan spectrum, this emphasis on personal religious experience involved the idea that important aspects of this experience were *impersonal*. Thus Hutchinson believed that she had been "sealed with the Spirit," meaning that any sense of a distinct spiritual identity of her own had been obliterated and that God spoke directly to and through her. Because she believed that the personal identity of the true Christian became swallowed up in the Spirit, she rejected the belief in personal immortality and bodily resurrection to which more conservative Puritans adhered.

Two hundred years later, Ralph Waldo Emerson and his fellow Transcendentalists contributed to the popularization of this kind of religious radicalism and developed it in a much more thoroughgoing way. Inspired by Romantic writers, especially Samuel Taylor Coleridge and Thomas Carlyle, and by the first English translations of Hindu and Buddhist scriptures, the American Transcendentalists came to define God as the flow of consciousness underlying all reality. And they celebrated the religious genius of writers, artists, and philosophers who summoned their attention to this all-pervading but finally impersonal divine. In the Transcendentalist schema, genuine self-reliance was not narcissistic or antisocial. Rather, attunement to oneself and confidence in the authority of one's feelings and intuitions ushered one into a deep kinship with others by virtue of the underlying spiritual intelligence coursing through one and all.

In recent years, this aspiration to connect with the underlying flow of spiritual intelligence or energy has become commonplace. Partly as a result of the popularity of transcendental spirituality in late-twentieth-century American culture, openness to religious experience has advanced in unprecedented ways, melting boundaries between denominations and enabling individuals to incorporate various aspects of different faith traditions into their own personal spirituality. The conception of divine reality as an impersonal flow of spiritual energy works to equalize all religious traditions as well as to validate internal experience as the apotheosis of religious authority.

Critics of this privileging of spirituality over religion argue that the focus on internal experience contributes to the deterioration of civil society by undercutting the sense of moral obligation to society that characterizes traditional biblical religions. But proponents of spirituality often maintain that investment in the authority of internal experience leads to social engagement, much as Emerson argued that self-reliance leads to a sense of kinship with others. At the same time, people on both sides of the issue might agree that there is a trade-off between internally motivated engagement with others and externally motivated obligation. They might also agree that respect for social conformity and acceptance of externally imposed obligations to society have declined as a consequence of the current cultural shift toward a greater investment in the authority of internal experience. And this new freedom from external religious constraint undoubtedly creates new opportunities for greed and social anarchy.[9]

Approaching this debate as an indicator of one of the most important tensions in American religious thought, William A. Clebsch argued that proponents of spirituality have often reacted against what they perceived as a dominant tendency in American culture to define religion in moralistic terms. Beginning with the Puritans, Clebsch argued, proponents of spirituality have celebrated intuitive and esthetic responsiveness to life as something more genuine and profound than superficial appearances of virtue and external acceptance of imposed obligation. Clebsch believed that this reaction against moralism, as well as the prior tendency to it, could be traced to the roots of English Puritanism as a movement aimed at grounding the meaning of virtue in something other than the whims of princes. After the Church of England was established as an entity independent of Rome, Puritans "opposed turning the idea of God's sovereignty into the divine right of Tudor and Stuart monarchs." In an effort to build religious communities based in respect for divine sovereignty, "these forefathers substituted morality" for monarchy, and "the rewards of obeying God's will for the advantage of obeying the King's law." In New England, many Puritans and many of their successors continued down this path rather straightforwardly. Others reacted against the tendencies to hypocrisy and self-righteousness involved in this moralism and struck off on their own. While cherishing the benefits of freedom from monarchy, America's most profound religious thinkers, according to Clebsch, "worked to divert American spirituality from its natural spillover into moralism by translating the religious impulse into being at home in the universe." Thus Jonathan Edwards, Ralph Waldo Emerson, and William James all located the essence of religion in terms of responsiveness to the beauty of life and celebrated this responsiveness as the wellspring of genuine compassion and concern for others.[10]

The distance between Robert Bellah and Sheila Larson is a recent expression of this long-standing tension in American religious thought between moralistic and esthetic definitions of religious virtue. While

Robert Bellah and his fellow moralists weighed the value of religion in terms of its contribution to a humane and civilized social order, the cohort that included Sheila Larson sought attunement to an inner voice that enriched and comforted them. From their perspective, love and compassion for others were the fruit and principal evidence of a sense of spiritual beauty, much as Edwards, Emerson, and James believed. Socially approved behavior not animated by this sense of attunement amounted to conformity and thus to hypocrisy.

The question of how this sense of at-homeness comes to be experienced and developed leads to many other questions. Is it an unexpected event, as Edwards believed, for which no one who receives it is really prepared? Who receives it, when, and why? How much of it can be developed through education, discipline, or faith? How is one to judge which means of developing are best? How is one to judge whether a particular experience is genuine or not?

As these questions begin to suggest, once internal experience comes to the fore as the basis of religious judgment, as it did with increasing force in American culture after the 1960s, religious certainty begins to erode and a certain degree of religious relativism is inevitable. The conviction that religious truth is a fundamentally personal phenomenon can lead to impatience with external authority, as guardians of social order since the time of Anne Hutchinson have feared. It also leads to increasingly diverse forms of religious practice and social engagement and to greater tolerance for religious difference. And once this self-reliance has gone far enough to become culturally embedded, it is difficult, and perhaps even impossible, to turn back, however clearly critics see its dangers and protest its growth.

This emphasis on the authority of internal experience began as a Protestant phenomenon although, to be sure, there are important antecedents predating the Protestant Reformation. In their concentration on the presence of God within the human soul, Christian, Jewish, and Islamic mystics helped lay the groundwork for the Protestant attentiveness to subjective experience that played a central role in defining modern culture. The idea that conscience has priority over external authority has antecedents in Abelard's *Ethics*, the Islamic Qur'an, Augustine's *Confessions*, Paul's letters, Plato's dialogues, and stories about Hebrew prophets who called people to task for not obeying God's will. But the Protestant Reformation and especially its subsequent development within the context of English and American Puritanism led to an unprecedented commitment to the priority of internal experience over external authority that has profoundly shaped American religious life.

In the English context, belief in the authority of individual experience can be traced to John Wycliffe, who was condemned by the Roman Church as a heretic in 1390 for his belief that the presence of Christ in the sacraments was a function of the believer's attitude. Wycliffe's train of thought was taken up by Jan Hus, the fifteenth-century Czech theologian whose ideas influenced Martin Luther and other Continental reformers. Early English Protestants and later English Puritans developed Wycliffe's legacy further by casting Luther's emphasis on salvation by grace through faith in terms of the English legal concept of covenant. In some distinction from Luther, the Puritans believed that the covenant of grace between God and his saints enabled the saints to fulfill God's moral law.[11]

As a corollary of their interest in the Holy Spirit as the connecting link between human subjectivity and divine will, the Puritans attributed new religious authority to the family as the primary school for individual religious development and the principal building block of social order. The "well-ordered household" replaced the monastery as the ideal site for cultivating religious virtue.[12] Puritan insistence on the development of individual experience also found expression in a new understanding of the particular churches as relatively autonomous congregations of individual Christians and their households. Engaged in face-to-face covenants with one another, these individuals and their families came together to hear scripture, receive instruction, and celebrate the Lord's Supper and the baptism of new members to their communities. New England congregations were not subsidiaries of any larger ecclesiastical organization; sister churches and clerical bodies functioned as advisors rather than overseers.

Rooted in the Puritans' insistence on the primacy of personal religious experience, this congregational model of religious organization persisted and grew, outlasting many of the theological doctrines identified with Puritanism and influencing a wide range of religious groups. As James P. Wind and James W. Lewis pointed out in a recent study, "To overlook the congregational character of American religion is thus to overlook much of the source of American religious vitality."

R. Stephen Warner notes that this source of vitality is still increasing today in significance: "In the United States today, we are seeing convergence across religious traditions toward de facto congregationalism, more or less on the model of the reformed Protestant tradition of the congregation as a voluntary gathered community."[13]

This congregational structure of American religion is a by-product of the emphasis on individual experience associated with Protestant thought. And this tendency to congregationalism is by no means limited to churches and other well-defined religious institutions. Indeed, to capture the sweep and vitality of spiritual life in the United States at the beginning of the twenty-first century, it is important to recognize the extent to which voluntary associations that are not churches carry a significant portion of American spiritual life. Americans who join a nature photography expedition to learn how to take pictures of mountain wildflowers, or who find joy and rejuvenation in a modern dance class, or who coach a sixth-grade basketball team because they like to work with kids—many of these Americans are participating in the spiritual life of their culture whether or not they also attend worship services in churches, synagogues, mosques, or temples. The fact that this reality complicates the study of American religion is not a sufficient reason to overlook it. In the transformed world of American religious life, photography expeditions, dance classes, and basketball courts are often places where people find community, spiritual inspiration, and moral development.

Diluting Protestant Principles

To return to the Nativity pageant described at the beginning of this introduction, it may be stretching the term to consider the families gathered at the bottom of the Reformed church's hill on Christmas Eve as a congregation. But they do represent a community. It may also be stretching things to consider them a religious community. But their religious beliefs and experiences do contribute to their involvement in village life and the variety of other communities and organizations to which they belong.

Those who attend the Nativity pageant today are probably no less religious than villagers who attended in the past, and their participation in social activities of various sorts is probably no less shaped and inspired by religious or spiritual experience. But they represent a greater diversity of religious traditions. Moreover, the larger culture in which they participate is no longer as dominated by liberal Protestantism as it was in the fifties and sixties. The authority of the Reformed church in village life is not so much taken for granted as it once was. And the increasing prominence in village life of people from different religious backgrounds has decentered the church's place in the cultural landscape.

Nevertheless, the Reformed church and the Nativity pageant it hosts do contribute importantly to the assortment of religious values that feed the experience of community in this village. Perhaps most important, the church has helped to establish and nurture a general cultural commitment to family and civic life. Both in the drama of the pageant itself and in the composition of the audience, this commitment can be seen as an important legacy of the Puritan devotion to family life as the building block of society. Thus the procession of Mary and Joseph across the church lawn in front of a crowd of families is a way of recognizing the sacredness of the family in American culture and the importance of the family for community life.

Of course, the makeup and dynamics of the American family changed considerably during the second half of the twentieth century. After the Second World War, the image of the patriarchal nuclear family was constantly broadcast as a cultural norm. As the hold of this image of the family on the larger culture has loosened since then, our understanding of what constitutes a family has grown more capacious. In this new context of more expansive and inclusive notions of family, the progress of Mary and Joseph across a church lawn is still a way of recognizing the sacredness of intimate, caring relationships and the importance of families and familylike groups for civic life. Without denying the pain and suffering associated with this process of redefining family life and its moral authority, it is also important to recognize the extraordinary growth and diversification of the family and familylike structures that Americans have come to inhabit.

As part of this celebration of family life, the procession of Mary and Joseph carries vestiges of John and Margaret Winthrop crossing the Atlantic with their famous "Model of Christian Charity," outlining the social responsibilities of a community of religious individuals. Enacted by village fathers and high school seniors representing the families and social organizations of this village, the Nativity pageant highlights this well-ordered community's investment in religious individualism, family life, and social harmony. Thus the pageant reflects some of the most foundational elements of American culture.

It also reenacts the miraculous birth of Jesus and celebrates his redemption of the world. And more than a few of the participants take these particular beliefs very seriously indeed. But at the same time, others who attend the pageant regard the portrayal of these beliefs as quaint and picturesque. For these people, attending the Christmas pageant is like attending *The Nutcracker* or reading "The Night Before Christmas" aloud before going to bed on Christmas Eve. In the pageant itself, beliefs about the meaning of Christ are presented in the most general and culture-affirming way. Specific theological doctrines associated with this meaning lie very much in the background. Protestant Christianity is celebrated in a way that families from a variety of faiths can enjoy and even be inspired by without feeling excluded or offended.

From one perspective, this sinking of religious performance into cultural entertainment might be seen as religion's decline into something more insipid, and thus as evidence of religion's weakening hold on American life. From another perspective, however, this submergence of Christian religiosity into American culture, and its seepage into the land of entertainment, might be said to lend strength and vibrancy to American life. Allegiance to particular religious institutions and specific religious doctrines may indeed have grown weaker. But the power of religious symbols to inspire creativity, affection, intellectual reflection, and social criticism may have increased.

1

The Liberation of Missionary Evangelicalism

Judith Klein called herself Jewish, but she was not observant and she was adamant about the fact that she did not believe in God. This belief did not change over the course of her heroic and ultimately losing battle against breast cancer. Nor did it stand in the way of her deep affection for Anne, whom she had known since high school and with whom she corresponded and visited for thirty years. During the last ten of these years, Anne spent most of her time living as a Catholic sister with poor people in India. Although she was sometimes called a missionary, Anne did not proselytize on behalf of the Catholic Church, nor did she provide any sophisticated technical, medical, or educational services. She simply lived with poor people in a slum, as a poor person herself. This work exposed her to a lot of human suffering, but it also deepened her experience of God and made her feel very alive. Her habit of joining up with people in need spilled over into her friendship with Judith. While in the United States on furlough, she visited Judith before she died and spent some time simply living as Judith lived, sharing ideas and experiences. Both women enjoyed the visit and felt strengthened by it. Half jokingly, Judith referred to Anne as "my missionary."

Jan Sweet is a lay minister of the United Methodist Church in a small university town. Serving as a campus minister to university students is her primary responsibility, which she fulfills by organizing programs that draw students to church and to various community activities. Her church considers this work an important part of its mission, and Jan herself views the work as not just a job, but an outreach to others that is very much part of her own identity as a Christian. While she respects differences in religious beliefs, she views them as relatively unimportant in light of the larger mission of developing personhood, community, and social responsibility to which most, if not all, of the religious groups on campus are committed. Thus she does not consider herself an evangelist in the sense of calling anyone to convert. And she regards those who do proselytize on campus as religious extremists. In this regard, she has been openly critical of the Church of Jesus Christ of Latter-day Saints (LDS, or Mormon Church) because of their active evangelism on campus and also because of their unwillingness to cooperate in programs sponsored by the interfaith campus ministry. In recent months, the Women's Relief Society of the Mormon Church opened their canning factory for members of other churches to use in preparing food for the soup kitchens they sponsor. Jan views this generosity as a hopeful sign of greater interfaith cooperation with LDS in the future.

Bernard Glassman is a Zen Buddhist *roshi*, or teacher, officially recognized as a spiritual descendant by his own teacher, Taizan Maezumi, whose lineage of spiritual authority descends from Dogen Zenji, the thirteenth-century founder of the Soto school of Zen Buddhism in Japan. As part of his teaching mission, Glassman founded the Greystone Bakery in Yonkers, New York, famous for its challah. The bakery also sold specialty dessert foods to Bloomingdale's, Godiva, and Ben & Jerry's. This enterprise employed not only Zen students but also homeless people, who earned a living and developed useful life skills there. Glassman's combination of spirituality, social action, and entrepreneurship has generated some controversy, as did his belief that there is nothing about Zen that prevents one from also being a practicing Catholic or Jew. But Glassman believes that being a lineage holder gives him leeway to make innovations and a mandate to teach Zen in his own way. With regard to his openness to other religions, one of Glassman's best-known students is Robert Kennedy, a Jesuit priest to whom Glassman has transmitted authority. With regard to his own spirituality, Glassman's background as a Jew and his appreciation of Jewish food, and Jewish ideas and practices involving food, contributed to his enthusiasm for the Greystone Bakery and to his appreciation of the Buddhist idea that life is a meal.[1]

Each of these three situations and sets of people illustrates the commitment to both religious pluralism and religious activism that characterizes a good deal of American religious life today. Judith Klein benefited from the friendship and succor of a Catholic missionary who respected her atheism. Jan Sweet pursues her Christian outreach to university students through interfaith cooperation. And Bernard Glassman welcomes Jews and Christians to Zen Buddhism and focuses his spiritual insight as a Zen teacher on business programs designed to help poor people and make the world a better place.

If we think about pluralism and activism abstractly, they might seem to be opposing forces—the more accommodating one is to many religions, the less likely it is that one might be active in the name of one's own. But in fact, by enabling difference and experimentation, on one hand, and consensus and cooperation, on the other, the coinciding forces of pluralism and activist outreach fuel a good deal of religious vitality in the United States today. And when seen in the context of how they work together in people's lives, it becomes clear that these two forces are not just coinciding but actually interdependent. Judith's friend Anne succeeds in befriending and supporting others *because* she does not try to convert them. Jan is enthusiastic about her work as a Methodist lay minister *because* she believes that the moral strength of American society depends on the efforts of many different religious communities. And Bernie encourages his students to integrate Zen practice with social action and entrepreneurship *because* he believes that Zen is a useful way of approaching real-life problems that is relevant to all kinds of people, including to those who also practice Judaism or Catholicism.

Religious pluralism is hardly a new phenomenon in American culture, but never before has it flourished so strongly or pervaded so thoroughly the religious ideas and practices of so many Americans. Of course, religious separatism and exclusivism have not disappeared from the American scene, as Jan Sweet's comments about the Mormon Church suggest. A number of religious minorities—including Orthodox Jews, Amish, some Native American groups, and Mormons—do separate themselves from the larger society in order to maintain their religious purity and community strength. But the economic interdependence of all sectors of American society, our sophisticated information technologies, and our generally increased tolerance and curiosity with respect to religious difference make the separatism these groups seek increasingly difficult to preserve.

Recent enthusiasm for religious inclusivity and interfaith cooperation stems partly from the widespread idea that many religious traditions in the United States share common goals and values. And commitment to active engagement with the world is one of the most visible and unifying of these now commonly recognized goals and values. In fact, increasingly widespread recognition of the need for active engagement in the world may be one of the main reasons that intellectual differences in belief and doctrine have declined in importance.

The activism of contemporary American religious life creates the expectation that religion should be beneficial to society. And this expectation, in turn, encourages the idea that religion should be respected in whatever particular form it happens to take. This expectation also contributes to the general tendency of American religions to play an active role in society, not only through collective ventures of various sorts, but also by defining personal morality in ways that encompass social responsibility.

In important respects, this pervasive endorsement of social responsibility and social activism is an outgrowth of the Protestant evangelical culture that dominated American culture and religious life in the nineteenth and early twentieth centuries. The tradition of Protestant missionary evangelicalism that developed in the United States in the nineteenth century involved a spirit of world engagement and world reform quite different from that of many other religious traditions, and even from that of many other Christian traditions as well. While most religious traditions have been dedicated to the social support of members of their communities, few if any have been as dedicated to reforming the world. The moral athleticism and pragmatic investment in social reform that we associate with Anglo-American Protestantism still flourishes as strongly in American religious life today as it did in the nineteenth century. But now it is carried by a great variety of different religious and ethnic traditions as well as by both secular and interfaith agencies.

The inclusive and pluralistic form of world engagement and activist outreach that characterizes American religious life today would not have been possible if the Protestant missionary evangelism out of which it emerged had not been greatly subdued. The story of this great sub- duing is, to some extent, a story about the collapse of the grandiose and aggressive missionary programs that characterized mainstream American Protestantism from the early nineteenth century through the early decades of the twentieth century. During this long era of mis- sionary zeal, some of those targeted for conversion complained about the disrespect that Protestant missionaries showed for their traditions, and pointing to the conflict between this disrespect and Christian ideas of brotherhood, sisterhood, and community. Inside the American evan- gelical tradition, missionaries themselves often led the way in bringing down the arrogance and militancy of Protestant activism and in forging new conceptions of spiritual outreach that maintained an active en- gagement with the world while at the same time affirming cultural and even religious pluralism.

The slow collapse of old-style Protestant missionary evangelicalism created more space in which other religious were able to develop and interact more freely. Since World War II, this American tradition of world engagement and activist outreach has been buried, reborn, and recast in a new context of religious pluralism and interreligious dem- ocratization. Moved both by the unraveling of liberal Protestant evan- gelicalism and by the coinciding revitalization of their own religions, representatives of these religions lowered the boundaries between their traditions and the larger world. In so doing, they have become more activist both in their commitments to social reform and in their efforts to bring the wisdom of their own traditions to the world.

The Protestant Roots of Liberation Theology

After World War II, Protestant missionary activity was dominated by fundamentalists and other conservatives who directed their main at- tention to preaching Protestant doctrine and soliciting conversions. Many liberal Protestants turned away from evangelicalism to support humanitarian causes or to pursue academic work or careers in public service or foreign policy. But at the same time, some men and women dedicated to education and democratic reform persisted as Protestant missionaries. Their role in the larger history of Christian missions has often been overlooked. And their importance as catalysts of the later transformation of American religion has gone almost completely unnoticed.

In important ways, humanitarian missionaries in the fifties carried forward the "modernist impulse" associated with liberal Protestantism and its tendency to define social problems and gospel values in terms of one another.[2] But many in this group were also critics of liberal Protestantism and its idealism about social progress and tendency to cultural imperialism. They often felt more at home with cultural criticism of neo-orthodox theology and with its call to return to the iconoclasm of the Protestant Reformers. One of the most influential men in this group was the Presbyterian missionary and Princeton Theological Seminary professor M. Richard Shaull. His understanding of the relationship between Christianity and revolution developed in response of the Cold War and in the context of the crisis mentality of neo-orthodox theology. He and the teachers, theologians, and activists associated with him helped to lay the groundwork for what eventually came to be known as liberation theology.

In 1955, a time of social crisis and upheaval in many parts of the world, Shaull wrote "We can no longer think exclusively in terms of rescuing lost pagans from the imminent flames of hell." Having worked as a missionary in Brazil, Shaull was alarmed by the economic and political turmoil in Latin America in the wake of the Second World War and the collapse of colonial rule. He was troubled by the toll in human suffering that both this rule and its collapse exacted and by the inadequate interpretations of Christianity floating around in the midst of this revolutionary situation. University students in Latin American often talked to him about the seeming irrelevance of Christianity to the pressing problems of their societies. "You Protestants seem to be concerned only of about getting people to stop smoking, drinking, and dancing," the students complained. In contrast, as they pointed out, "when the Communists speak to us, they talk about feeding the starving, teaching the illiterate, and putting an end to exploitation and injustice."[3]

"All too often," Shaull maintained, "people cannot see that Christianity makes a real difference, that it has an influence over our whole personality and over all areas of our collective life." Many Protestant missionaries contributed to this underappreciation of Christianity,

Shaull argued, through narrow definitions of personal belief and morality. But Christianity was relevant to every aspect of human life, Shaull believed, because it helped to liberate people from all forms of oppression, including economic and political oppression. He defined the God of Christian faith as one whose purpose in history was to pass judgment against that oppression and to open up "new possibilities of greater freedom, order, and justice." Quoting a 1954 essay entitled "The Transforming Power of the Church" by another American Presbyterian, Paul Lehmann, Shaull argued that just as "the prison-house of fate was shattered by the liberating faith in Providence" for early Christians in the Roman Empire, so Christianity in the twentieth century continued to have power to free people from cruel from destinies imposed upon them.[4]

It wasn't enough, Shaull maintained, to talk about justice and social change as moral imperatives. Idealism was an insufficient response to the situation in which many Latin Americans found themselves. "We should not be surprised that people who know what is happening prefer Communism to such unrealistic talk," Shaull argued, "for Communism understands the problem of power and takes it very seriously."[5]

In his own theology, Shaull drew on Marxist theory and especially on its analysis of capitalism and its language of revolution and liberation. At the same time, he interpreted Marxism as a kind of corrupt and degenerate offshoot of Christianity. What most troubled Shaull about Communism was its lack of any principle of transcendence to counter the otherwise evitable tendency to replace one set of oppressive rulers with another. Criticizing Christians for allowing Communists to be the ones who paid attention to injustice and human suffering, Shaull implied that the Communists simply took over where Protestant missionaries failed, developing the revolutionary response to economic oppression and exploitation that was implicit in the Christian gospel. But while Shaull believed they had some reason to condemn missionary talk for its complicity with or at best irrelevance to this oppression and exploitation, he also believed that Communists completely missed the connection between personal redemption and social change that lay at the heart of the Christian gospel.

The Marxist perversion of Christianity was occurring not only in Latin America, Shaull argued, but in many other parts of the world as well. As evidence of this point, he quoted the Presbyterian Lesslie

Newbigin, one of the first bishops of the ecumenical Church of South India, to the effect that "education for the past 100 years in India has been dominated by the ideas derived from Christianity and often by the figure of Jesus himself." But the ideas about Jesus introduced in India by Protestant missionaries had been only partially and inadequately developed. "Because Christianity puts into men's minds a divine discontent with things as they are," Newbigin argued, "the way is open for the tremendous appeal of Marxism."[6]

Shaull's ideas grew out of the social gospel tradition in American Protestant theology associated with Walter Rauschenbusch, as that tradition was developed and reframed in the context of neo-orthodox theology. While building on many of the ideas and scholarly methods associated with liberal Protestant theology, neo-orthodox thinkers emphasized God's transcendence of every particular culture or social order. They were critical of people who seemed to equate Christianity with middle-class culture. In the United States during the 1930s, a sizable number of liberal Protestants in the social gospel tradition were drawn to socialism and Marxist theory. The subsequent exploitation of Communist theory by Joseph Stalin and Mao Zedong had a chilling effect on liberal theology and helped to stimulate interest in neo-orthodox theology. As a liberal Protestant focused on the shortcomings of Marxist theory but also appreciative of its critical insight, Shaull was particularly influenced by the Swiss Reformed theologian Emil Brunner, who emphasized the perpetually revolutionary nature of divine justice and was one of the leading spokespersons for neo-orthodoxy.

Shaull's theology contributed to the radical Protestant group ISAL (Church and Society in Latin America). According to one commentator, this group functioned as a "trial run" for liberation theology. In the late 1950s and early 1960s, before the 1964 military coup in Brazil, Shaull worked alongside the philosopher of education Paulo Freire, whose Basic Education Movement emphasized a process of "conscientization" that taught peasant children to become conscious of their place in the social order. During the same period, Shaull included Rubem Alves and other Brazilian students in a series of conferences sponsored by the World Council of Churches entitled "Christian Responsibility Toward Areas of Rapid Social Change." Alves later published *A Theology of Human Hope* (1969), which celebrated Freire's pedagogy as an example of the "theology of hope" advanced by the German Lutheran Jürgen Moltmann.[7]

In the fifties and sixties, a number of young priests from Latin America in studied in Europe with the men who played leading roles in the reconstruction of Catholic theology during Vatican II, including Yves Congar, Henri de Lubac, Hans Kung, Johann Baptist Metz, Karl Rahner, and Edward Schillebeeckx. The Latin American priests were impressed by the extraordinary influence of these innovators and inspired by their example to become leaders in transforming the Church in Latin America. But while aspiring to the leadership roles of these men, the Latin American theologians rejected the political liberalism with which many of the leaders of Vatican II were associated. They were especially concerned to distinguish their emphasis on the need for a "radical change in perspective" from the "naive reformism" they associated with the French theologian Jacques Maritain, whose neo-Thomist interpretations of human society had inspired an earlier generation of Christian Democrats in Latin America.[8]

In their development of liberation theology during the 1960s and 1970s, Gustavo Gutiérrez, Juan Luis Segundo, Leonardo Boff, Jon Sobrino, and other Catholic theologians in Latin America built a "theology of liberation" alongside the arguments about justice and social change that Shaull and his Protestant colleagues had begun to construct in the early fifties. At a meeting in Petropolis, Brazil, in 1964, Gustavo Gutiérrez first presented his argument that praxis, the Marxist term for practical experience, should be the focus of Catholic theology. Often identified as the founder of liberation theology, Gutiérrez developed this argument in his own writing over the next few years without reference to the ideas of Protestant missionaries and neo-orthodox theologians in Latin America or elsewhere. In his first book, *A Theology of Liberation*, published in Spanish in 1971 and then in English in 1973, Gutiérrez went further than Shaull by calling for the abolition of capitalism and the establishment of socialism. He emphasized the need for the leadership by the people rather than by a revolutionary elite, the need for an indigenous theology in Latin America, and the need for a thoroughgoing rejection of American and European models.[9]

Meanwhile, Shaull was enthusiastic about the development of liberation theology in Latin America, but he failed to see how deeply its leaders were committed to situating that theology within the context of Catholic symbolism and church structure. Thus in the 1980s, when Shaull praised liberation theology in Latin America by describing it as a kind of second Protestant Reformation, the Catholic liberationists were emphasizing the connections between liberation theology and distinctly Catholic ideas about the centrality of the Eucharist, the need for a papal hierarchy, and the special authority of Mary. "If it was a new reformation," one historian of the movement observed, "it was very different from the one that occurred in the sixteenth century."[10]

In their insistence on defining the movement in distinctly Catholic terms, Latin American liberationists were not simply affirming their loyalty to the Catholic Church and its traditional symbols. They were also defining themselves, and by implication Christianity as well, against the United States. Thus Gutiérrez identified the cause of the problems suffered by the people of Latin America in terms of "the domination exercised by the great capitalist countries, and especially by the most powerful, the United States of America."[11] In defining liberation theology as a resistance movement against American influence, its spokespeople had little reason to explore its antecedents in American missionary thought.

As it developed in Latin America and then later through feminist theology in the United States, liberation theology represented the transformation of ideas about Christianity and social change that were originally developed in the context of American Protestant missionary thought. But these ideas caught on and became widely influential only as liberal Protestants lost control over them and Catholics appropriated and developed them further. Liberation theology emerged as a powerful new incarnation of the social gospel tradition. As Catholics assumed leadership of this tradition, its influence among Protestants only increased, along with their growing respect for Catholicism.

Catholic liberationists in Latin America and the United States have been strongly motivated to look for antecedents to liberation theology within Catholic rather than Protestant thought.[12] From the perspective of those who understand the essence of Christianity in terms of liberation theology, and who want to restructure the Catholic Church in terms of that theology, any recognition of the origins of their theology in American Protestantism can only fuel opposition to it within the Catholic Church. Indeed, members of this opposition have been the first to point to the American aspects of liberation theology. Michael

Novak, one of the most thoughtful American Catholic opponents of liberation theology, attempted to undermine its authenticity as a truly indigenous third-world movement. "The headquarters for liberation theology in the United States, and perhaps in the entire world," Novak claimed in 1979, "are located near the Hudson River at Maryknoll, New York, international center of America's most active missionary order, the Maryknoll Fathers and Sisters." In a related line of attack, the Belgian Jesuit Roger Vekemans attempted to discredit liberation theology by pointing to Richard Shaull as the one who introduced "the liberation theme" into Latin American theology.[13]

Ecumenism

The story of ecumenism is a closely related one. Originally an outgrowth of Protestant missionary envangelicalism, the ecumenical movement expanded enormously after the second Vatican Council as Catholics stepped to the fore as participants and instigators of ecumenical dialogue. Just as liberation theology helped to disseminate the social activism characteristic of Protestant missionary evangelicalism, so the involvement of Catholics in the ecumenical movement advanced the process of interfaith dialogue and cooperation that Protestants had first set in motion.

In its modern form, the ecumenical movement emerged out of desires for strategic cooperation among Protestant missionary boards in the United States, England, Scotland, and western Europe. Interdenominational conferences and cooperative missionary endeavors led by liberal Protestants resulted in the founding of the Federal (later National) Council of Churches in the United States in 1908 and in the founding of the World Council of Churches (WCC) in 1948. These ecumenical organizations carried forward the postmillennial outlook associated with the Reformed Protestant tradition and were deeply influenced by the social gospel and its emphasis on the progressive historical work of building the Kingdom of God on earth.

The antecedents of this modern ecumenical movement can be traced to the seventeenth and eighteenth centuries, when Protestant mission societies based in England, Scotland, and Europe supported missionaries to Native Americans and to "heathens" and Catholics in other lands. European Catholics, especially the Society of Jesus, which was founded in 1540 by the Spanish soldier Ignatius of Loyola, also engaged in significant missionary work in North America and various parts of Asia. But only after the second Vatican Council in the 1960s did Catholics participate officially in the ecumenical movement that derived from Protestant missionary cooperation.

Cooperative Protestant evangelism in North America dated to the seventeenth century, when mission societies based in England, Scotland, and western Europe supported New England missionaries to the American Indians and drew on American help for early missionary endeavors in India and other foreign lands. Cotton Mather corresponded with Danish Pietists involved in missionary work in India, and Jonathan Edwards followed the work of various missionary societies in their efforts to spread the Protestant gospel around the world. In the early nineteenth century, the American Board of Commissioners for Foreign Missions (ABCFM) was founded as an interdenominational organization for Congregationalists, Baptists, and Presbyterians to pool resources and gather personnel for overseas missionary work. In its purpose and organizational structure, the ABCFM was similar to other American evangelical organizations, such as the American Bible Society, which promoted cooperative endeavors among people from evangelical Protestant denominations.

In theory, the ABCFM shared with denominational and interdenominational mission boards in the United States, Britain, and Europe the common goal of spreading Protestant Christianity throughout the world. In fact, however, mission boards representing different countries and denominations often competed with each other for turf and potential converts. To take just one example, in describing a particularly popular mission field in Natal in southeast Africa, one American missionary complained in 1903 that in "a field twenty miles wide and fifty miles long, six mission societies have come in, and between our Umvoti station and Mapunmulo, a distance of twenty-five miles, where our own out-station work joins hands, we find the Wesleyans, Salvation Army, Christian Alliance and Church of Norway, while these and other societies crowd us on all sides." Over and above these competitive enterprises, the missionary went on, "the Church of England regards no other societies, but divides all Natal into districts, with a priest over each division."[14] Concern about the divisiveness of this sort of competition, as well as about the inefficient duplication of effort involved, led to the World Missionary Conference (WMC) in Edinburgh in 1910.

In Edinburgh, Britain's Conservative Party leader and former prime minister, Lord Arthur James Balfour, opened the conference with a ringing endorsement of Protestant outreach around the world and an inspiring forecast of the further accomplishments that interdenominational cooperation might produce. "The Nations in the East are awakening," Balfour announced, and in their awakening, "they are looking for two things: they are looking for enlightenment and for liberty." Proclaiming what his auditors believed to be obvious, Balfour concluded, "Christianity alone of all religions meets these demands in the highest degree." Thus Balfour made it clear that the interdenominational cooperation he had in mind would focus on spreading evangelical Protestantism and assisting people to relinquish other religions. The final address of the conference, by the conference chairman and prominent American Methodist layman John R. Mott, followed through more explicitly on the missionary requirements of this vision. Laying down marching orders that would involve members of every Protestant church around the world in an effort to expand world Christianity, Mott asserted that the missionary agenda of the time "demands from every Christian, and from every congregation, a change in the existing scale of missionary zeal and service."[15]

The vision of world Christianity outlined by Balfour and Mott at Edinburgh involved a mandate to put aside the many doctrinal points that divided Protestant churches from one another. In addition to excluding these differences from official discussion, the "apostles of unity" at Edinburgh promoted a vision of worldwide Christianity based on concepts they believed Christians around the world could agree on and work together to implement. When the WMC met again in Jerusalem in 1928, the effort to define common ground among various Protestant churches revolved around two poles, one emphasizing issues of justice and peace and the other emphasizing the centrality of Jesus Christ and the ultimacy of his message and divine personhood. In the wake of the violence and injustices associated with the First World War and its aftermath, the focus on issues of justice and peace was timely. While not as successful as participants hoped, this expression of strong concern for justice did lead to new initiatives to combat racism in various parts of the world.

This concern for justice was strongly tied to the social gospel tradition and its emphasis on social reform. While those who identified with this tradition were more than happy to carry it forward, some participants in the ecumenical movement balked at the tendency they detected in social gospel rhetoric to define Christianity in secular terms. As part of their insistence on a specifically Christian message, these proponents of a Christ-centered faith focused on the primacy, ultimacy, and uniqueness of both the personhood and message of Jesus Christ. From this Christocentric position, they resisted any movement toward religious syncretism. In doing so, they thwarted (or at least complicated) the effort of many liberal Protestants to find common ground between Christianity and other religions.

Neo-orthodox theologians contributed importantly to this tension in the ecumenical movement by emphasizing Christ's judgment of every effort to domesticate his authority or equate it with any one culture or particular civilization. At one level, neo-orthodox theologians challenged the self-confident idealism about social progress characteristic of liberal Protestantism and turned away from the effort to define Christianity in terms of mutual understanding among the world's religious cultures. But while they criticized liberals and appropriated some of the language of conservative orthodoxy, in their focus on the transcendent power of Jesus Christ neo-orthodox theologians were, at a deeper level, endorsing the liberal movement toward cultural relativism and attempting to free the movement from the old equation between Christianity and Western culture, which they believed encumbered and compromised Christianity. (The complexity of their position contributed to its underappreciation in many accounts of modern American religious history). While responding to new situations of world crisis and to the existentialist mentality so much in vogue among intellectuals, neo-orthodox theologians were also struggling to carry the social gospel tradition forward and to free it from its associations with white, Anglo-American culture. As participants in the ecumenical movement, neo-orthodox theologians played the leading role in creating a space between God and Protestant culture. This space eventually made it possible for representatives of other religions to engage in interfaith dialogue on equal footing.

Beginning in the 1930s, the Dutch missionary Hendrik Kraemer and other neo-orthodox ecumenists emphasized the difference between the transcendent judgment and universality of Christ, on one hand, and the tendency of all churches and religious institutions to become enmeshed in particular cultures and to confuse the value judgments of their own culture with those of Christ, on the other. The growing presence of Christians from Asia and Africa within the ecumenical movement added to the strength and relevance of the neo-orthodox distinction between Christ and culture, as did the ongoing crisis in Europe that challenged earlier assumptions about the interdependence between Christianity and Western culture. The German historian Konrad Raiser described the effect of this crisis on ecumenical theology this way. "The 'Christian world' gave way to a vision which sought to understand the human condition from the perspective of the universal history of salvation." With this shift in perspective, the institutional church declined in importance, while biblical history and eschatology came to the fore. As Raiser put it, "the 'spatial' framework of thought of the earlier paradigm, which was directed to discerning and maintaining 'order,' was replaced by a historical framework."[16]

For many liberal Protestants, neo-orthodox theology marked an important step toward the affirmation of religious pluralism as well as the achievement of an expression of Christian unity that affirmed cultural pluralism. But from the perspective of conservative evangelicals, it seemed overly intellectual, if not perversely obscure, and finally irrelevant. As one historian described this conflict of opinion, "The neo-orthodox movement represented the crowning expression or last paroxysm, according to one's bias, of the long effort to strengthen the idea of Christian finality by purging it of its overtones of cultural finality, to find ways to proclaim the supremacy of 'our God' without proclaiming the supremacy of 'us' ."[17]

From the founding of the World Council of Churches in 1948 through the end of the 1960s, the ecumenical movement grew both in public prominence and in the inclusiveness of its concerns. Issues of peace and justice functioned as organizing principles, and churches themselves were identified as arenas for peace and justice work, along with universities, revolutionary movements, and urban centers. According to the "Renewal in Mission" report issued by the Fourth Assembly of the WCC at Uppsala, Sweden, in 1968, the aim of all missionary work was to "place the church alongside the poor, the defenseless, the abused, and forgotten, the bored" and to encourage "Christians to enter the concerns of others [and] to accept their issues and their structures as vehicles of involvement."[18]

ENTER CATHOLICISM

In addition to marking the high point of neo-orthodox involvement in ecumenism, the sixties were also a "golden age of maximal ecumenical openness" exemplified by the "ecumenical breakthrough" of Catholic involvement. Prior to the 1960s, Catholic teaching emphasized disengagement from the modern world. And Catholics were only marginally involved in the ecumenical movement. In 1920, the Swedish Lutheran bishop Nathan Söderblom had urged the WMC to issue an invitation to Catholics. When the WMC finally extended the invitation some ten years later, Pius XI made it clear that Catholics should not accept. Although Catholics did attend meetings run by the WCC on an unofficial basis, it was not until 1961 that John XXIII sent his church's first official observers to the WCC. At the Third and Fourth Assemblies of the WCC in New Delhi and Uppsala, Catholic observers stimulated by the transformation of their own church made significant contributions.

In the early 1960s, John XXIII asserted his role as an ecumenical leader by convening the second Vatican Council as an ecumenical gathering of Catholic delegates from around the world and by inviting Orthodox and Protestant churches to send observers. In their commitment to opening the Catholic Church's mission to the world, John and the council he assembled were equally committed to the idea that, in the words of one historian, "Christ had provided only one structural center for his Church." John referred to himself as "the Pastor of all Christians," and in the first message he delivered after his election as pope in 1958, he affirmed the conviction of five predecessors that "there shall be one fold and one shepherd."[19]

This assertion of Catholic leadership established a competing as well as cooperating center of ecumenical effort alongside the WCC. Furthermore, it marked a significant development in institutional support for ecumenism and a significant shift toward linking ecumenism with ecclesiastical structures. After decades of downplaying both the role of religious institutions in the ecumenical vision of world Christianity and the many doctrinal differences among various churches, the ecumenical movement suddenly, and somewhat surprisingly, had a Church. As a result of discussions at Vatican II, the ecumenical movement had a renewed understanding of the nature and importance of the Church as the people of God. As far as the leaders of Vatican II were concerned, this more inclusive understanding of the Church was still tied to the institutional structure and magisterium of the Holy Roman Church. But in their vision of renewal, the Church was now defined as much by the laity as by the priesthood. And it would be deliberately and strategically oriented toward the needs and sufferings of people as well as to the performance of ritual.

While calling for a renewal of the Roman Catholic Church and its ecumenical mission to the world, the second Vatican Council also stressed the need for dialogue with people of other faiths. Without relinquishing commitment to either the ultimacy of Christ or the superiority of the Roman Catholic Church as the world's preeminent divinely appointed religious institution, the council nevertheless stressed the need for better understanding of other religions and for increased respect for the grace and love of God represented in those religions. In an effort to balance belief in the universal need for Christian salvation under the authority of the Roman Catholic Church with the call for greater understanding, respect, and dialogue with people of other faiths, the council argued that salvation might include those "who through no fault of their own do not know the gospel of Christ or His Church, yet sincerely seek God and, moved by grace, strive by their deeds to do His will as it is known to them through the dictates of conscience."[20]

In the view of Karl Rahner and other theologians committed to this new emphasis on interfaith dialogue, the Catholic Church recognized people who, without knowing it, experienced the "hidden Christ" in other religions and areas of life. Although unable to participate in the sacraments that united people with Christ, many Hindus, Buddhists, and Muslims had encountered the mystery and power of God, these theologians believed, and their religious experiences should be respected. Prompted at least partly by this Catholic form of "inclusive

Christocentrism," the World Council of Churches established its first program for dialogue with people of other faiths in 1971.[21]

While venturing into non-Christian territory in this new way, Protestant, Catholic, and Orthodox ecumenists were also struggling to forge a common religious language that, as Christians, they could all use. Along with principles of justice and peace and commitment to active engagement in the world in their behalf, language associated with the term *spirituality* emerged as a means of representing the common ground of religious experience and feeling that Christians from all three traditions might share. Like the language of justice and peace, the language of spirituality served as means of avoiding more controversial topics of dogma, creed, and ecclesiastical authority. At the same time, the language of spirituality also functioned as an alternative path to Christian unity for those who resisted the move toward secularity they found in many expressions of ecumenical commitment to justice and peace. As Konrad Raiser observed with regard to this important tension within the ecumenical movement after 1960, "[S]pirituality became the key word of the efforts for 'spiritual renewal' and for 'spiritual ecumenism' in contradistinction to the various forms of 'social ecumenism.' "[22]

SPIRITUALITY UNLEASHED

In the context of American culture, the term spirituality took on a life of its own. While it came into common parlance through the ecumenical movement of the 1960s and 1970s and through the emphasis on the renewal of Christian spirituality associated with Vatican II, American usage of the term quickly expanded to include personal experiences and attitudes associated with a variety of different religious traditions. American Protestant, Catholic, and Orthodox participants in the WCC and other ecumenical forums resisted syncretistic interpretations of spirituality that sought to blend aspects of Christianity with features of other traditions. But many other Americans had no such qualms. Indeed, in 1975, when the WCC declared its formal opposition to any "conscious or unconscious attempts to create a new religion composed of elements taken from different religions," many Americans were already engaged in the process of creating highly personalized religions of their own, or highly personalized interpretations of their old religions.[23] And by the 1980s, many had adopted *spirituality* as a term preferable to *religion* to characterize their mystical experiences and personal outlooks on reality. Far from excluding non-Christian religions in the development of these new forms of spirituality, Americans were inspired by Hinduism, Buddhism, Native American religions, and various forms of "paganism," and drew freely from these alternative traditions.

Critics feared that this trend toward spiritual eclecticism encouraged religious relativism and undermined loyalty to established traditions. There was no denying the increased emphasis on personal experience associated with the term spirituality, especially in the context of the eclecticism of American culture. But while American aficionados of spirituality gave pride of place to internal reality and authority, they also wanted to contribute to the betterment of the world. In this regard, the spirituality people carried forward the progressive impulse of the American Protestant missionary movement while leaving behind at least some of its ties to Protestant institutions. As a result, the vitality of American religious life in the late twentieth century, in which innumerable groups participated, including many Christian churches, was at least partly a result of the spirituality movement and its emphasis on personal engagement.

In their enthusiasm for spirituality, many Americans overrode or simply overlooked the opposition to syncretism expressed in the 1970s and 1980s by Protestant, Catholic, and Orthodox participants in the ecumenical movement. But if they went further in their openness to other religions, the spirituality people were nevertheless indebted to the ecumenical movement for its pioneering of interfaith dialogue and for the emphasis on the primacy of religious experience implicit in its rediscovery of the language of Christian spirituality. No less important, the commitment to justice and peace that played such a central role in the development of the ecumenical movement in the twentieth century shaped American expectations of what all forms of religious faith might have in common. In this respect, the general friendliness and openness to religious life in the United States in the late twentieth century was an important legacy of the ecumenical movement and its commitment to missionary outreach in the world.

The History of American Benevolence

The close relationship that often existed between concern for social justice and enthusiasm for spirituality in the late twentieth century can be understood through the prism of neo-orthodox theology and its restimulation of a set of religious ideas that go back to the Puritans. While neo-orthodoxy in the United States is most often connected with Reinhold Niebuhr and Paul Tillich, the Lutheran thrust of their theologies worked to resist the connection between grace and moral outreach emphasized in the Anglo Protestant tradition. H. Richard Niebuhr, on the other hand, delved more deeply into the Puritan tradition through his study of Jonathan Edwards and his analysis of the "responsive self." Writings by Sydney E. Ahlstrom, William A. Clebsch, Harvey Cox, William Hamilton, Perry Miller, and others pushed in similar directions, linking up the expressive side of the American Puritan tradition with the impulse to social welfare and reform.

In tracing the religious impulse to social reform backward in time, no concept figures more prominently than that of benevolence. For eighteenth-and early-nineteenth-century Protestant evangelicals who strove to reinvigorate the spirit of New England Puritanism, benevolence was the quintessential element of Christian life. Grace transformed people's lives, these reformers believed, not only bringing genuine happiness to each recipient, but also motivating every Christian to reach out to others. Thus many nineteenth-century evangelicals believed that people truly devoted to Christ actually embodied his activist love, outreaching devotion, and transforming grace in their own lives.

This emphasis on evangelical outreach was deeply rooted in Christian tradition—selfless commitment to others was hardly an American invention. And yet American evangelicalism does have a distinctive history and a set of characteristics that grows out of allegiance to the Puritan concept of the covenant of grace between God and each Christian. In this agreement, God's grace enabled the individual to have faith and to act in accordance with God's will. Puritans believed that individuals might not know whether they actually participated in the covenant of grace. Overconfidence on this point was a sure sign of pride, which counted against the likelihood of sanctity. But the Puritans *were* confident that those who had entered the covenant of grace were able to live in the world in a way that carried out God's will. Again, they could never be entirely sure they were God's chosen people, and this uncertainty about their actual relationship to God involved considerable anxiety. But they were strongly motivated by the hope of grace and by the desire to be part of God's historical work. If apparent efforts to be on God's side were not sufficient proofs of grace in themselves, lack of such efforts indicated lack of grace. If in the wilderness of the New World Puritans could establish a Christian society that would be a light to the world and a model for others to follow, their success would help confirm their own chosenness and sanctity.

In the eighteenth century, some Protestants speculated that the religious revivals known collectively as the Great Awakening might be signs that the millennium was dawning in America and that a universal Protestant society would be constructed in the years ahead. No less important for the history of American evangelicalism, Jonathan Edwards celebrated the nature of genuine benevolence, which he defined as love to God and others not motivated by self-love, and argued that it was an essential expression of Christian life. According to Edwards, no one was able to truly love God or his creatures unless the radically transforming power of grace intervened to liberate him or her from the imprisoning circle of self-love. Once so liberated, the individual behaved with the same spirit of benevolence with which he or she had been transformed.[24]

Edwards's disciple Samuel Hopkins emphasized the necessity of every Christian's active participation in this work of disinterested benevolence and promoted missionary service as the primary vehicle for that work. Like Edwards, Hopkins believed that historical events were contributing to the building of a universal Protestant society; advancing the spread of Protestant Christianity was the most important work anyone could do. And Hopkins went even further than Edwards in promoting organized missionary work and in urging Americans to commit themselves to God through this work.[25]

With regard to the question of how individuals actually came to be responsible to other persons and motivated to undertake the larger process of social change ordained by God, evangelicals differed with one another on certain points and changed their minds over time. Before the Civil War, the vast majority of American missionaries and their supporters accepted the idea endorsed by John Calvin and Jonathan Edwards that God predestined some people for salvation and others for damnation. In this view, human dependence on God was especially emphasized. Christian love toward others was the manifestation of divine grace working within the self and could never be truly manifest in anyone who lacked this grace, however much they seemed to have or want it. When Methodists began to assert a strong presence in foreign missions in the second half of the nineteenth century, their emphasis on the role of free will in the process of salvation, and their more straightforward encouragement of the human effort to love others, had an impact on the development of Protestant Christianity at home and abroad. But this difference between Edwardsean Calvinists and free-will Methodists did not diminish the underlying agreement among American evangelicals that, in their innermost being, people moved by the experience of grace or the hope of it could not help but want to pass on to others something of what they had been given. Nor did it diminish their underlying agreement that evangelical Protestants were the people helping God to bring earth and humanity toward the kingdom of God.

Throughout the nineteenth century, enthusiasm for foreign missions caught fire among young people eager to carry forward this idealism about God's plan for the world and to express the virtue of benevolence that was so closely identified with their own hope of salvation. Linking their own worth as Christians to their contribution to the building of God's kingdom on earth, these energetic Americans envisioned themselves and their converts launching the conquest of Islam from Persia, overturning "Satan's seat" in India, drawing the African descendants of Ham into the fold of Christendom, and separating ill-gotten children of the Church of Rome from their whorish mothers in every land. The underlying concern about not being qualified to lead the way in earthly service to God, which persisted as part of the Puritan heritage of American evangelicals, helped fuel their eagerness to prove their love of God. Motivated by the effort to master anxiety about their own unworthiness as well as by their investment in an idealistic picture of the role of divine providence in history, missionaries often measured benevolence more in terms of their own heroic acts of self-sacrifice than in terms of what the people they served said they needed or wanted.

Idealism about the providential course of human history was so strong and deeply rooted in missionaries that the equation between benevolence and wiping out other religions was not questioned until the last decades of the century. At the same time, however, the concept of benevolence as genuine love for others operated as an equalizing and democratizing force among American missionaries and also among the people they intended to serve. For both groups, the concept of benevolence forced attention to people's lives, both to the social conditions of the people that missionaries hoped to serve and to the actual impact that Christianity made. The discovery that missionary effort could have ambiguous results, and in some respects could even be harmful, caused religious liberals to distinguish commitment to God's work in the world from disrespect for religions other than Protestant Christianity. As part of this process, recognition of cultural relativism emerged as an expression of belief in the transcendent sovereignty of God.

REPUBLICAN IDEALISM

After the War of Independence and the ratification of the United States Constitution in the late eighteenth century, the concept of missionary benevolence as the quintessential expression of Christian virtue coincided with idealism about republican government in the United States and its enabling of enlightened citizenship. Millennialist expectation about the coming of God's kingdom and Enlightenment optimism about the triumph of reason became intertwined in the minds of many Americans during the nineteenth century. These Americans often expressed their hopes for their new nation with imagery that suggested it would become both a New Jerusalem and a new Greece or Rome.[26]

Through this double-streamed process of idealization, many Americans came to imbue the system of republican government established in their own nation with a kind of sacred status that transcended the inevitable power struggles and corruptions of ordinary politics. Thus American evangelicals believed that as the kingdom of God came into being around the world, the system of government that would characterize it would be a republican one, like that of the United States. At the same time, evangelicals tended to hold themselves aloft from ordinary politics, which they regarded as beneath their higher enterprise of carrying forward God's work of redemption. Thanks to the underlying fusion of Protestant and classical idealism, missionaries were able to connect the concept of republican government with the divine work of redemption even while acknowledging that, at the mundane or profane level, ordinary politics went on in the United States as well as elsewhere. As one historian put it, Americans tended to insist on "a mental separation of the spiritual and the political realms combined with a conviction of the superlative excellence, if not the universal relevance, of the historic constitution and values of the[ir] nation."[27]

This aura of sacredness surrounding republican government was easier to maintain in the century and a half before the United States became a world power. In contrast to Russia, France, Germany, the Netherlands, and especially Britain, whose empires were fueled and maintained by the strength of their political and military outreach, the United States in the nineteenth century was incapable of exercising much political or military power in Asia, Africa, or the Near East. Because of the relative weakness of American political and military strength before the mid-twentieth century, American missionaries found it easier than their British counterparts to maintain a naive and rather primitive form of political idealism. Because of their innocence with respect to colonial politics in Asia, Africa, and the Near East, American missionaries could celebrate their system of government as an ideal system for everyone while imagining themselves to be apolitical.

Although it did encourage many nineteenth-century American evangelicals to be culturally imperialistic in their attempt at benevolent outreach to people of other lands, this idealism about republican government also contributed to the construction of an international framework in which a more broad-based commitment to human rights could develop. The religious idealism that allowed American evangelicals to think of themselves as apolitical also supported people of other cultures who wanted to incorporate American ideals of self-government into their own religious and cultural contexts. This privileging of American-style self-government has also been challenged in recent years, but it remains one of the most powerful and persistent legacies of American Protestant missionary activism.

THE PRAGMATISM OF AMERICAN BENEVOLENCE

For all its idealism, the cultural tradition of American benevolent outreach rooted in evangelical Protestantism is also famously (or notoriously) pragmatic. A characteristic focus on results has linked American outreach with the realities and problems of everyday life and oriented American idealism in a strongly this-world direction. Even when the goal of evangelical outreach shifted away from social reform toward a more exclusive emphasis on salvation and eternal life in heaven, Americans were preoccupied with head counts of converts and thus measured their results in this-world terms. While such an outcome-oriented approach commanded respect for its emphasis on the resolution of problems, it also attracted criticism as superficial, simplistic, anti-intellectual, and even antireligious. In this regard, a Japanese Christian described Americans as "the least religious among all civilized peoples." While "mankind goes down to America to learn how to live the earthly life," Kanzo Uchimura wrote in 1926, "to live the heavenly life, they go to some other people." Somewhat more positively, another observer commented that Americans tended to view "theology, evangelism, and church life in terms of addressing problems and finding solutions." American missionary work could thus be distinguished from other forms of Christianity by its "vigorous expansionism, readiness of invention; a willingness to make the fullest use of contemporary technology, finance, organization, and business methods."[28]

This pragmatic orientation stemmed partly from the influence of Calvinist theology and its power to make people feel that history had providential meaning and direction and that their own lives should be animated by a sense of purposiveness. As another historian put it, "Calvinism has injected a spirit of vitality and drive into every area in which Calvinists have been disposed to enter. They have exhibited unceasing endeavor whether they were subdividing a continent, overthrowing a monarchy, or managing a business, or again reforming the evils of the very order which they helped to create."[29]

As we have seen, the pragmatic orientation of American evangelicalism was also rooted in the English Protestant understanding of moral action as an inevitable outcome and visible sign of grace. This concept of moral action as the fruit of grace developed in new ways in the entrepreneurial culture of nineteenth-century America. In the early decades of the century, when the missionary movement first caught fire as a popular religious movement in New England, American society was in the midst of a shift from localized, self-sufficient farm and village economies to a national, consumer-oriented market economy characterized by more specialized forms of labor, broader flows of goods within and across regions, and transactions that were more rationalized and impersonal. On one hand, missionaries strove to retain the religious consensus, moral virtues, and face-to-face solidarity of the earlier world out of which they came. On the other hand, they were enthusiastic about new labor-saving devices and improvements in transportation and communication, and they were as zestful, hardheaded, and entrepreneurial in accomplishing their goals for missionary outreach as any businessman was about building railways or manufacturing shoes.

The strongly activist character of American evangelicalism was fueled not only by the process of industrialization in which nineteenth-century missionaries were caught up, but also by the relatively unfettered idealism of American evangelicalism. With their tremendous openness to social mobility and their impatience with intellectual privilege and obfuscation, Americans were relatively free of both the burden of British empire and the British preoccupation with class. While resembling British evangelicals of the same period in their theological and practical orientation, American evangelicals were more straightforward and unhampered in their outreach to others. Of course, most of the people missionary evangelicals reached out to already had religions of their own. This fact, in combination with the religious arrogance that so often offended people of other nations, meant that the actual number of "heathens" and "infidels" converted by Americans was usually disappointing. But however small the number of full conversions, the impact of American missionary ideas about social progress was considerable, as was the Reformed Protestant commitment to personal and social responsibility underlying those ideas.[30]

THE DENOUEMENT OF ORGANIZED MISSIONARY PROGRESSIVISM

American evangelicals believed they had a biblical mandate for missionary outreach that explained and legitimated their compulsion to reach out to others and change the world. In their reading of the Bible, missionary work was central to the unfolding history of God's plan of redemption. Finding a mandate for missionary work in biblical passages about the future coming of God's kingdom on earth, American evangelicals pointed to the last two verses of the Book of Matthew as evidence of the firm link between Christian discipleship and missionary work. In delivering the "Great Commission," as Protestant evangelicals came to call it, the resurrected Jesus met his eleven remaining disciples on a mountain in Galilee and commanded them to "go and make disciples of all nations, baptizing them in the name of the Father and of the Son and of the Holy Spirit, and teaching them to obey everything I have commanded you."

Throughout the nineteenth century, American Protestant missionary work comprised three kinds of effort—to convert heathens and infidels by proclaiming the Protestant gospel, extend humanitarian relief from hunger and disease, and institute educational and social reforms designed to nurture the development of Protestant principles in unconverted or recently converted individuals and their societies. In many cases, these forms of outreach were closely intertwined. Missionaries prepared people for conversion by promoting literacy, social change, and self-government. And they promoted these things by teaching people to read the Bible. Missionaries who emphasized education and strategic social reform often found themselves engaged in humanitarian emergency efforts, like famine relief. And missionaries who focused on preaching and conversion often found that the people they baptized were dependent on them for food and work. While all missionaries agreed that promoting Christianity was essential to their work, serious debates occurred over the question of whether funds should be allocated to anything beyond preaching and publishing aimed solely at evangelization. As a result of their face-to-face encounters with native peoples and societies, missionaries were often the first to argue, in many cases against administrators of mission boards who supported them back home, that education and social reform were important aspects of missionary work. Not only were they necessary in preparing the way for conversion, as most early-nineteenth-century missionaries believed, but they were inherently worthy and inherently Christian forms of outreach, as some later missionaries argued.

Evangelicals who took a stricter view of missionary work argued that missionary funds should be devoted primarily if not exclusively to disseminating the gospel. In most cases during the nineteenth century, these stricter evangelicals were not opposed to social reform along Protestant lines. They simply believed that social reform would inevitably follow as the result of conversion and hence was not an appropriate target of missionary funds. Despite the vehemence with which each side advanced its argument, however, for most of the nineteenth century both sides agreed that the conversion of individuals and the reform of society finally went hand in hand. This underlying consensus enabled individuals with different priorities to work together in the same missionary agencies and to see themselves as part of a broad-based and ultimately united effort to Christianize the world.[31]

This underlying consensus began to come apart in the last quarter of the nineteenth century. Controversies about how to read the Bible and, more specifically, about what it said about the day of judgment and second coming of Christ, and what that implied for missionary work, forced open a split in evangelical Protestant culture. Until the late nineteenth century, the vast majority of American missionaries and their supporters understood the kingdom of God as the goal toward which history was progressing. This understanding of the millennium was clearly outlined in Jonathan Edwards's popular *History of the Work of Redemption*, which portrayed the kingdom of God as a building constructed during the course of history. In the picture Edwards painted, a grand and harmonious social edifice was being built out of the lives and work of God's people. As Edwards explained, "First the workmen are sent forth, then the materials are gathered, the ground is fitted, and the foundation laid, then the superstructure is erected, one part after another, till at length the top-stone is laid, and all is finished." This plan of redemption had been in place since creation and was being systematically constructed "from the fall of man," Edwards explained, "to the end of the world." The kings and prophets of the Old Testament were essential to this work, as of course was Jesus Christ. "We are told," wrote Edwards, citing Ephesians 2:20, that "the church of the Redeemer is built on the foundation of the prophets and apostles, the Redeemer himself being the chief cornerstone." The superstructure of the work was the historical Church, which Edwards believed was hastening on to "a time of great light and *knowledge*," thanks to its purification by Protestants. When this edifice neared completion at the end of the millennium, Edwards predicted, Christ would come again and his restored presence as the "top-stone" would crown the work and "all the world [will] be united in one amiable society."[32]

This progressive concept of history was called into question in the late nineteenth century by readers who found a very different picture of history in the Book of Revelation. In a famous interchange in 1879 that was later recalled as a turning point in the history of American missions, the British biblicist George Muller challenged the American Presbyterian Arthur Tappan Pierson about his understanding of how Jesus would return to earth. As Pierson told the story, Muller convinced him to rethink the idea that Jesus would return to earth after "a thousand year period of prosperity brought in by human effort and benevolent Christian civilization." When Muller responded to his optimist claims about world progress by saying, "My beloved brother . . . not one of them is based upon the word of God," Pierson claimed that he was forced to abandon them.[33]

Muller, John Nelson Darby, and other premillennialists interpreted the monsters, catastrophes, and warfare described in the Book of Revelation to mean that the second coming of Christ would be preceded by cataclysmic disaster and not, as the progressives hoped, by a thousand years of culminating enlightenment and world harmony. Of course, this preoccupation with disaster was not simply a result of studious attention to biblical texts. Anxieties about social disorder and lack of Christian faith beset many evangelicals and fed the tendency to view history in premillennial terms. And as a result of these anxieties and the rising popularity of premillennialist ideas, a new emphasis on the evils of the present age and the immanence of world disaster provided a new kind of impetus for missionary work. Time was short, and those who would be gathered up to sit on God's right hand needed to be converted now. Abandoning the progressive hope of a Christian world order, premillennialists swelled the ranks of older missionary societies and established new societies dedicated solely to proclaiming the gospel. In the context of this shift in missionary outlook, the slogan that became popular at the turn of the twentieth century, "Evangelize the world in this generation," was more of an apocalyptic watchword than an expression of confident hope that the people of all nations would soon become civilized Protestants, as it has sometimes been interpreted.

Meanwhile, many liberal Protestants disregarded these premillennial ideas and held on to their commitment to world progress. Exposure to the "higher criticism" of the Bible flowing out of German universities enabled these liberals to ignore or resist the efforts of fundamentalists such as Pierson, Muller, and Darby to read biblical prophecy as a coded blueprint of history. As German scholars identified different strands of authorship within the Bible—some older, some more recent, and each with its own religious outlook—this critical reading of texts made the Bible into a collection of relatively disparate parts and challenged earlier assumptions that it was wholly and seamlessly authoritative. This challenge outraged some and disheartened others. But at the same time, more than a few evangelicals who embraced progressive views of history were ready to step along with the new criticism and even found themselves energized by it. Thus while premillennialists worked to defend their belief that the Bible must be a divine and homogeneously inspired autograph and were eager to criticize the overconfidence of evangelicals who read their own optimism about the future into it, progressives responded to new developments in biblical criticism in a way that inspired rather than undercut further outreach.

New developments in biblical criticism encouraged liberals to be bolder in interpreting the Bible in terms of their own commitments and new ideas. Of course, earlier readers had also interpreted the Bible through the lens of their own situations and worldviews, but new theories about the Bible's multiple authorship and uneven religious quality enabled readers to take their liberty more self-consciously. In this new situation, liberal interpreters of the Bible such as Baptist pastor and theologian Walter Rauschenbusch went beyond earlier images of the progressive construction of history to a depiction of the kingdom of God that focused even more on social reform and justice in this world. Concerned by the plight of the urban poor and especially by the impact of industrialization on the millions of immigrants squeezing together in New York and other American cities, Rauschenbusch very deliberately removed the kingdom of God from its supernatural associations and made it the earthly goal to which every Christian should strive. In his culminating work *A Theology for the Social Gospel* (1917), Rauschenbusch defined genuine spiritual life as prophetic anticipation of a just and humane society and as brotherhood and solidarity with people in need.[34]

At the same time that Rauschenbusch moved toward recasting

Christianity in terms of a prophetic vision of ethical commitment to brotherhood and social reform, he also worked to drive a wedge between the prophetic mentality that he identified with this ethical commitment and Protestant institutions and middle-class culture. Thus Rauschenbusch began to separate the essence of spiritual life from the dogmas, rites, and organizational structure of Protestant churches as well as from some of its conventional associations with middle-class respectability. In this regard, he anticipated the arguments of neo-orthodoxy.

Social gospel ideas had revolutionary implications for understanding the nature and purpose of missionary work. But they were also expressions of a line of thought missionaries themselves were pursuing and that in fact was a logical if not inevitable result of the kind of missionary work that concerned itself with the social conditions in which people lived. Thus Rauschenbusch's prophet of ethical revaluation was preceded in 1893 by A. J. Gordon's concept of the missionary-as-prophet who "translates the example of Christ in to the dialect of daily life, into the universal speech of pain and poverty and suffering for the sake of others."[35]

Rauschenbusch's missionary sister, Emma Rauschenbusch Clough, was like her brother in wanting to define Christianity as a basis for social change. In her work with Telegu women in India, she went much further than her brother in trying to disentangle Christian ethics from Western culture. While Walter's understanding of the brotherhood of man and the fatherhood of God was grounded in unexamined assumptions about the superior values of Victorian family culture, Emma's exposure to Telegu culture led her toward the new science of ethnology as a means of understanding this non-Western culture and conveying its strengths to a Western-audience. With a greater degree of cultural relativism that her brother, although still not fully rid (and perhaps not fully consciousness) of her own paternalism, Emma hoped that Protestant missionaries might lead the way in bringing about the revitalization of Telegu culture.[36]

While fundamentalist and other conservative missionaries and their supporters were focusing on apocalyptic interpretations of the kingdom of God and striving to get the message of repentance and salvation out to as many people as possible before it was too late, more liberal missionaries such as Emma Rauschenbusch Clough were laying the groundwork to challenge the legitimacy of the very ideas of missionary evangelization and conversion. The full, frontal attack on these ideas, when it finally came about in the context of the Vietnam War, was quite dramatic. But the unraveling of progressive concepts of missionary outreach that led up to it was a long time in coming. And in the process of this unraveling, numerous strands of religious thought and feeling that had been balled together as part of the intertwining of American evangelicalism and historical progressivism began developing independently or in new combinations with one another.

The Laymen's Report *Re-Thinking Missions*, published in 1932, represented an important step in this process. Funded by the liberal Baptist John D. Rockefeller Jr, the report was based on a survey of American Protestant missionary work in India, Burma, Japan, and China conducted by a commission whose members were drawn from the major Protestant denominations. Harvard professor William Ernest Hocking, a leading voice among liberal Protestants, chaired the commission and took primary responsibility for writing the report. In a kind of culminating expression of liberal theology, the report endorsed educational and other humanitarian efforts not only as genuine expressions of Christian love but also as legitimate forms of Christian mission in and of themselves. On top of that, the Hocking Commission raised concerns about the process of explicit evangelization that was often invoked to justify education and social reform. Finally, the report argued that missionary work should contribute not to religious conflict or competition but to better understanding of different religions around the world and to greater cooperation among people from different religious backgrounds.[37]

For more than a century, missionary work had served as one of the principal arenas in which American investment in education, women's and children's rights, and other forms of humanitarian social reform developed. To be sure, missionary commitment to these issues was always accompanied, justified, or compromised by commitment to conversion. When Hocking and other liberals not only made conversion optional, but even suggested that explicit evangelization could obstruct the interreligious cooperation and world understanding necessary for historical progress, liberal investment in missions became difficult to maintain. Hocking himself eventually came to question the whole concept of Christian missions. Other liberal Protestants who viewed

Christian love in terms of humanitarian outreach and the advancement of world understanding also became convinced that explicit evangelization conflicted with these goals. In response to the shock and outrage that this challenge generated among the many conservatives in their ranks, Protestant denominations and mission boards reacted to the Laymen's Report with varying degrees of hostility and criticism.

The Laymen's Report marked both a culminating moment and the beginning of the end of liberal influence in American Protestant missionary work. How could anyone be more liberal in terms of respecting other religions and affirming religious pluralism without relinquishing the whole concept of Christian missions? After the publication of the Rockefeller-funded report, conservatives stepped into this breach and to a large extent assumed leadership of American missionary work. But the liberal Protestant commitment to humanitarian outreach and social reform did not disappear or even diminish. The liberals simply stepped out of the evangelical confines of missionary work and into new philanthropic agencies funded by the Rockefeller, Ford, and Carnegie Foundations, or into academic research, or into development programs funded by the United States government. In many respects, the impact of these endeavors has been even greater than that of American missionary boards. The "green revolution" sponsored by the Rockefeller Foundation in Mexico and India, the cultural interchange programs sponsored by the Ford Foundation in China, and the Marshall Plan, Peace Corps, and numerous U.S. Agency for International Development programs sponsored by the United States government all had roots in the liberal side of the American Protestant tradition of missionary outreach. As the historian of American religion Grant Wacker wrote, "One could argue that broad public support for humanitarian programs such as the Marshall Plan, the Peace Corps, and world famine relief marked not the demise but the consummation of the liberal search for a mandate that would respond to the deepest impulses of Christian faith while respecting the integrity of other cultures"[38]

The academic field of religious studies also emerged out of liberal Protestantism and, to a significant extent, out of the realization on the part of Protestant missionaries that effective effort on behalf of non-Western peoples required some understanding of their religions and cultures. Some of the first scholarly studies of non-Western cultures were produced by missionaries. In this context, Emma Rauschenbusch

Clough's *Sewing Sandals: Tales of a Telegu Pariah Tribe* might be mentioned, as might the earlier *Zulu-land; or, Life Among the Zulu-Kafirs of Natal and Zululand, South Africa* (1864), by Lewis Grout, who published articles in *American Orientalist* and served as a member of the advisory council on African ethnology at the World's Columbian Exposition in 1893.

In the late nineteenth and early twentieth centuries, groundbreaking studies in comparative religions were published by scholars who were not missionaries themselves but shared with many of them the belief that other religions foreshadowed, or participated in a partial way, in the true and ultimate religion of Christianity. F. Max Muller of Oxford University, whose studies of the sacred texts of the Orient provided some of the foundational scholarship for the academic study of religion, delivered a paper at the World's Columbian Exposition in which he argued that "there was a purpose in the ancient religions and philosophies of the world." This purpose could be grasped in terms of "the perfect realization of the Divine Thought or Logos of mankind in Christ."[39]

As Wacker observed, "Whatever the exact connections, it is indisputable that classical Protestant liberalism provided the institutional and cultural matrix within which world religion scholarship was born and grew to maturity, both in North America and in Europe."[40] But at the same time, as Western scholarship about religion developed, scholars from other traditions participated in increasing numbers. In this process, the cultural matrix of liberal Protestantism out of which religious studies emerged grew increasingly faint and outmoded.

WHAT HAPPENED TO PROTESTANT EVANGELICALISM?

Erosion of belief in a fundamental connection between American culture and Protestant evangelicalism did not mean, of course, that Protestant evangelicalism disappeared. Indeed, in absolute numbers, there were more American evangelicals working as missionaries around the world at the end of the twentieth century than there were in 1920, when many hoped to "evangelize the world in this generation." In the mid-1980s, thirty-nine thousand American Protestant evangelicals were working as career missionaries and thirty thousand had short-term appointments, whereas in the 1920s, fourteen hundred missionaries represented American Protestantism. But in the late twentieth century, the great majority of American evangelical missionaries came from conservative evangelical missionary agencies unaffiliated with the mainstream denominations and mission boards that represented American evangelicism in the nineteenth century. While these evangelicals have made considerable strides toward the establishment of a global Christian fundamentalism based in conservative American religious thought, they have tended to see themselves, and Protestant evangelicalism as a whole, as disjoined from the main currents of American culture, of which they disapprove. Earlier American Protestant missionaries, while not identifying with everything about American culture and often resisting the exploitive treatment of native populations sanctioned by colonial governments, did not distinguish American culture and Protestant evangelicalism so firmly or self-consciously.[41]

In the late twentieth century, many Protestant evangelicals prided themselves on maintaining a countercultural relationship to American society. At the same time, important aspects of the old evangelicalism continue to define the underlying cultural framework in which new religious developments in American culture occurred. Put somewhat negatively, the collapse of mainstream Protestant evangelicalism and the decline of its hegemony in American culture created a vacuum in the leadership of American social outreach that many different religious and secular groups stepped in to fill. Stated more positively, the vitality and pluralism of American social outreach today is rooted in American Protestant evangelical and missionary history and, to some extent at least, represents the fruition of that history.

2

The Catholicity of American Spirituality

The brutal torture and fatal beating of Matthew Shepard in the fall of 1998 was a traumatic event for the people of Laramie and especially for students and faculty at the University of Wyoming, where Matthew was a political science major who openly acknowledged his gay identity. On Wednesday, October 7, another student out on his mountain bike discovered Matthew tied to a fence outside of town, covered in blood. Eighteen hours after he had been left for dead, Matthew was alive only because the cold temperature slowed his metabolism and blood flow. He died early Monday morning after being moved from the community hospital in Laramie to a trauma center in Ft. Collins, Colorado, seventy miles away.

Matthew clung to life over the weekend, when alumni from various parts of the region gathered in Laramie for homecoming at the University of Wyoming. Students and faculty obtained a permit for a hastily organized demonstration of solidarity with Matthew to coincide with the homecoming parade on Saturday morning. As the horror of what had happened to Matthew, and what it meant for the community, continued to sink in, word spread that Father Roger Schmit would lead a vigil for Matthew outside the Newman Center that night.

Roger Schmit is a Benedictine monk admired for his learning and for his kindness and commitment to students. As a part-time instructor in the religious studies program and also the Roman Catholic chaplain on campus, he represented both the academic identity of a state university and its concern for student welfare. While Father Roger's identification with a particular religious tradition and his special responsibilities to catholic students were well known, many non-Catholics also admired him. At one level, this high degree of universal recognition reflected the man's excellence as a person and a professional. At another, equally important level, it reflected the spiritual authority that many Americans today attribute to Catholic monks and, underlying that, the increasingly central and influential role of Catholic spirituality within American culture.

While there are more differences than similarities between the vigil for Matthew Shepard and the Nativity pageant described in the introduction to this book, in both cases a quasi-religious gathering on a church lawn brought a community together and contributed to its strength. In the past, the honor of providing the sacred space for such community-building events almost always belonged to churches in the Reformed Protestant tradition. In 1998, in the community where Matthew Shepard was beaten, the Catholic Newman Center stepped quickly and easily into the role of providing the symbolic space in which the larger community could find itself.

The vigil that Father Roger conducted for Matthew Shepard drew Catholics and non-Catholics alike, and no distinctions were made between them. It was a public vigil open to the whole community, whatever the religious identities of its members. At the same time, the tenor of the vigil was deeply consonant with Catholic theology. Concentrating on the need to "be with" Matthew in his suffering, Father Roger was the first to publicly suggest a connection between Matthew and Christ. Implicitly drawing on Catholic ideas about the real presence of Christ in the world and the mystical union between Christ and believers, Father Roger encouraged participants to acknowledge both the actual reality and the cosmic significance of Matthew's suffering and to identify with it. Journalists from out of town picked up on the connection between Matthew and Christ but tended to express it less mystically and more politically, referring to Matthew's being beaten and tied to a fence as a "crucifixion" for being gay. (Following those stories, a false rumor circulated that Matthew had literally been crucified by his assailants.)

Acknowledging the role that Matthew's homosexuality played in the attack, Father Roger encouraged participants at the vigil to look into their own hearts for any lack of love they might feel for their gay brothers and sisters. While not apolitical, this admonition reflected the mystical idea that sinners are all alike in their estrangement from God. It also recognized a painful truth about the community that had come together that night. During the vigil at the Newman Center, individuals felt that they were part of a larger whole and, by gathering together for prayer and reflection, sensed the reality of this corporate entity. By experiencing the community as a living reality in this way, they realized that they themselves were, at some level, responsible for Matthew's suffering.

Catholic theology played an understated but central role in an event that brought a community together in response to a gruesome and tragic event. The Catholic chaplain's personal capacity for religious leadership certainly contributed to the meaningfulness of the event. But in an even more fundamental way, the incarnational mysticism of Catholic theology provided the context out of which his leadership emerged. An instinctively Catholic sensitivity to the need for ritual led to the creation of a vigil that brought Catholics and non-Catholics together as part of a collective whole. Without any discrimination against non-Catholics or explicit appeals to Catholic theology, Roger Schmit drew implicitly on the incarnational mysticism of American Catholic thought in order to bring the community together in solidarity with the suffering of Matthew Shepard.

Ritual occupies a central place in Catholic theology as the acknowledged vehicle of divine power, personal transformation, and religious insight. According to Catholic teaching, the living presence and mystical body of Christ is present in the sacraments, and especially in the Eucharist, which celebrates the crucified body and blood of Christ. In partial contrast to Reformed Protestant understanding of the Eucharist as an opportunity to celebrate the grace within each believer's heart that enables faith in Christ, Catholic doctrine emphasizes the ongoing, objective reality of the crucified body of Christ in the Eucharistic elements themselves as well as within each confirmed believer's soul. Catholics are expected not only to believe in the objective reality of the divine presence, but to identify and participate in it, to be cleansed and transformed by it, to be reconciled with Christ and, through atonement, receive eternal life.

According to Catholic teaching, the mystical body of Christ is present in the Church as well as in the sacraments. As a result of the second Vatican Council and its emphasis on the Church as the people of God, this identification of the Church with the body of Christ has taken on new meaning. While earlier forms of mystical devotion focused more narrowly on such things as the sacred heart within the actual Eucharistic elements, later devotions broadened the meaning of this living presence of Christ to include the people of God. In its narrow sense, "people of God" refers to individuals who are baptized, forgiven, confirmed, and certified by the Church as eligible to participate in the Eucharist. But in a broader sense that resonates with many American Catholics today, "people of God" has a more universal and ecumenical reach. In this broader sense, the people of God are the human community that is bound together, in a mystical way, as a corporate whole. In this broader interpretation, the living presence of Christ can be seen in the face of a starving child, whether or not that child is Catholic. It was also be revealed in the bloodied body of Matthew Shepard, who was baptized, confirmed, and buried in the Episcopal Church.

In the vigil for Matthew held at the Newman Center in Laramie, Wyoming, the sacrament of the Eucharist was not performed. Technically speaking, the vigil was a secular event that did not include performance of any sacred ritual. There was no wafer elevated as a sacred Host and no chalice containing wine that was transformed into sacred blood. And yet the ideas, images, and experiences associated with the sacrament were very much in play during the vigil, and the whole event had a Catholic, sacramental feel. Matthew Shepard, dying in a hospital room seventy miles away, his body both objectively real and imagined by those praying for him or simply thinking about him, functioned to some extent as Christ functioned in the sacrament of the Eucharist. And the people gathered at the vigil, many of them connected to Matthew by virtue of their membership in the nonsectarian, state university where he was a student, functioned as the people of God, drawn together in atonement for and through a young man's suffering.

American Interpretations of Catholic Spirituality

The American Catholic sensibility expressed in this event was not simply a product of official Roman Catholic teaching. In some important respects, it was also a product of American Protestant culture and its hospitality to Catholicism. Historically, American Protestants may be better known for hostility to Catholicism. However, the effectiveness of Roger Schmit and other American Catholics as public religious figures is partly a result of a history of positive expectations of Catholicism on the part of Americans with backgrounds in Protestantism. Beginning in the nineteenth century, quite a few Protestants have been attracted to the beauty and spiritual realism of Catholic ritual and to its power to create community and overcome the isolation associated with American individualism. And some of those Protestants converts have played important roles in shaping the character of American Catholic spirituality.

In the nineteenth century, New England Transcendentalists were among the most influential of these Catholic converts and fellow travelers. In 1835, William Henry Channing considered conversion to Catholicism because he thought its emphasis on the organic unity of the human race offered an antidote to the narrow and highly rationalistic individualism of his own Unitarian background. Julia Channing, William's wife, continued on in this way of thinking and almost converted in 1849. Several people who lived at the Transcendentalist commune of Brook Farm became deeply involved in Catholicism, including George Leach, Charles Newcombe, and most notably Isaac Hecker, who went on to become a Redemptorist priest and founder of the Paulist order. Some residents of Brook Farm attended mass in a village church, and at least one owned a crucifix and experimented with Catholic devotions. Sophia Ripley, who founded Brook Farm along with her husband, George, professed her commitment to Catholicism in 1846 and went on to compose and translate Catholic devotional literature. She was drawn especially to devotions focused on the Blessed Mother, whom she cherished as an ideal type of her own spiritual development as a woman in a society dominated by men.[1]

Orestes A. Brownson was the first Transcendentalist to actually become a Catholic, and his understanding of Catholicism attracted others to the faith. Pointing to the Catholic "doctrine of life" as the inspiration for his own conversion, Brownson explained that while man can "be" alone, he "lives" only in Christ. Protestant churches relied on preaching about Christ, he asserted, but the Catholic Church offered the "concrete existence" of Christ through its rituals. Brownson believed that only by actual participation in the living presence of Christ offered through the sacraments of the Catholic Church could Americans overcome alienation from Christ and isolation from one another.[2]

Brownson believed further that the communal solidarity offered through the sacraments of the Catholic Church was precisely what was needed if Americans were to carry forward their mission to build God's kingdom on earth. Unlike nineteenth-century Catholic intellectuals in Europe who looked to the past for inspiration and resisted any identification between Catholicism and historical progress, Brownson saw the Catholic Church of the future as the realization of Protestant post-millennial dreams.

The religious liberty Americans enjoyed was strongly advantageous to the building of God's kingdom, Brownson argued, because it enabled them to enter freely and vigorously into the rituals that created the experience of communal solidarity. In countries where Catholicism was the established church, Brownson believed, formalistic procedures and authoritarian worldviews encouraged passivity in believers and undermined the spiritually energizing effects of the sacraments. In the United States, by contrast, Catholics were able to recover the original vitality of the Church because of the personal religious liberty they enjoyed and because the Church in the United States was free of the state and its unholy preoccupations. As Brownson wrote in 1860, the Catholic Church in the United States was "thrown back on its naked rights and resources, as the spiritual kingdom of God on earth."[3]

Like Ralph Waldo Emerson, Henry David Thoreau, and other participants in the Transcendentalist movement, Brownson was preoccupied by the need for a spiritual understanding of human life and history. Like these Transcendentalists, his thinking was deeply influenced by Protestant theology, and especially by its emphasis on the individual human soul and the soul's close relationship to what Transcendentalists called the divine Spirit. As was the case with other Transcendentalists, Brownson's understanding of this relationship combined the emphasis on the sacredness of individual conscience that stemmed from New England Puritanism with the Romantic idealism that emerged in nineteenth-century German philosophy and in British poets and literary theorists influenced by German idealism. Equating religious inspiration with intuition, Brownson and other Transcendentalists complained that the orthodox Protestants of their day were too rationalistic and overly preoccupied with narrow and conventional readings of the Bible. In their view, the Bible was best understood as a book of inspired poetry that required a similar quality of poetic inspiration in its readers in order to be understood.

Like other Catholics of their day, those who converted from Transcendentalism affirmed the spiritual realism of Catholic metaphysics and the transformative power of Catholic ritual. But Transcendentalist converts differed from many other Catholics of their day in their mysticism, which the Church did not encourage, and in their interest in both the process of spiritual development and the organic connection between each individual and the larger human community. These converts conceptualized Catholicism as an antidote for the rationalism of the various forms of Protestantism with which they were acquainted. And they were extremely receptive to the beauty of the Catholic liturgy and to the sensuality of Catholic art and the grandeur of Catholic architecture. Catholicism served as a means of carrying forward the esthetic and mystical side of New England Puritanism as well as a means of developing the religious implications of the Transcendental fondness for Romantic idealism. In their appreciation of the esthetic quality of Catholicism, the Transcendentalist converts were reaffirming Jonathan Edwards's conviction that true religion was grounded in responsiveness to the beauty of being. And in their appreciation of Catholic mysticism, they were reaffirming an even more basic Protestant and Puritan commitment to the inspiration and transformative power of the Holy Spirit.

Sixteenth century Protestant Reformers revived long-neglected doctrines about the Holy Spirit in the context of their interest in the transformative power of grace in the individual soul, personal conscience, and comprehension of scripture. Interest in the Holy Spirit intensified in England during the seventeenth century as Puritan theologians tried to define the nature of religious experience and personal faith. Puritans voiced their preoccupation with the nature of subjective experience and the extent of its authority in the form of questions about how the Holy Spirit acted and what the Christian knew about it. Thus in their emphasis on the Spirit and its power to transform the individual, the New England Transcendentalists were reaffirming a commitment to the experience of grace that was part of their own religious heritage in Reformed Protestantism and New England Puritanism.

Radical Puritans believed that the Holy Spirit inspired Christians directly and that the individual was aware of that direct inspiration. Conservatives believed that Christians knew the Spirit only through experiencing the inspired truth of biblical texts. On questions of the Spirit's indwelling, the meaning of fellowship in the Spirit, the value of lay prophecy, and the merits of prescribed versus spontaneous prayer, radicals emphasized the authority of individual experience, while conservatives emphasized conformity to social order and rationality.[4]

Like her spiritual heirs among the American Transcendentalists, Anne Hutchinson also expressed a radical understanding of the Spirit's power in her life. Hutchinson also foreshadowed the Transcendentalist understanding of the difference between personal religious experience and personal autonomy. Perhaps influenced by English Familists, who were moved by the teachings of the Dutch mystic Hendrik Niclaes to establish "families" of Christians devoted to mystical illumination, Hutchinson believed that the soul of each saint dissolved in the Spirit of God at the moment of election and that the saint's body, like all bodies, was annihilated at death. As a result of this understanding of the mystical power of grace, she denied personal immortality and the bodily resurrection of the saints.[5]

In the eighteenth century, a similar interest in the interior, personal agency of the Spirit and its synthetic, universalizing power attracted Jonathan Edwards, who wrote about the mystical infusion of grace in the individual soul in a way that was reminiscent not only of Anne Hutchinson but of Thomas Aquinas as well. Like Aquinas and also Augustine, he understood original sin as estrangement from God and viewed the human race as an organic whole, sunk in darkness, and in desperate need of the supernatural light of grace. While Edwards had little respect for the institution of the Roman Church, he studied the Church fathers and was committed to the building of a universal form of Christianity, equating this with the kingdom of God, which included those fathers as foundational stones. He pictured this universal Christianity as a huge building, like a church of cosmic proportions. In Edwards's vision, this building was being constructed over the course of history. The lives of people filled with God's Spirit constituted the building material.[6]

A century later, under the influence of the Romantic movement in German philosophy and British literature, the American Transcendentalists reaffirmed and reformulated Edwards's vision of the beauty of being. Their appreciation of Catholic worship resonated with his emphasis on awareness of divine beauty as the essence of holiness. And their appreciation of the Catholic Church as a universal institution took shape in a cultural context deeply influenced by Edwards's vision of the history of God's redemption as a cosmic church. Most important, Catholicism offered Transcendentalists a way of combining investment in personal interiority with a commitment to synthetic universalism that carried forward New England's theological investment in the underlying correspondence between the soul and God, and between the enlightenment of the individual soul and the progress of society.

HECKER'S THEOLOGY OF THE SPIRIT

No one played a more influential role than Isaac Hecker in Transcendentalism's shaping of American Catholic thought. Born in 1819 and raised in New York City, Hecker acquired strong commitments to personal holiness and evangelical outreach from his Methodist mother. Partly as a result of meeting Orestes Brownson, Hecker became a Transcendentalist, and in 1843 he took up residence at Brook Farm. Brownson served as Hecker's spiritual mentor as he moved through Transcendentalism into the Catholic Church, which he joined in 1844. As a Redemptorist priest and later as the founding father of the Paulist order, Hecker was enthusiastic about combining the religious principles of the Catholic Church with the democratic spirit and futuristic outlook of the American people. He developed a theology of the Holy Spirit that reflected not only his commitment to the Catholic Church as the culminating expression of religious life, but also his background as a Methodist, a Transcendentalist, and an heir to the English Puritan tradition.

Hecker defined his views on the Holy Spirit partly in response to the work of the Catholic archbishop of Westminster, Henry Edward Manning, an Anglican convert, whose writings were the principal European source of ideas about the Holy Spirit in the nineteenth century.

Like Hecker, Manning argued for the centrality of the Holy Spirit in religious life and its power to infuse the believer with divine life. And like Hecker, Manning believed that the Catholic Church was the living embodiment of the Holy Spirit and the true conduit of its power and authority in individual lives. But Manning focused on the Spirit's role in establishing the religious authority of the Church and its priestly hierarchy. While Hecker agreed with Manning that the saving grace of the Spirit occurred only through the Church and its sacraments, he was much more concerned with the indwelling of the spirit in the soul of every believer. He was far more interested than Manning in the Spirit's power in the lives of lay people and, by implication, in the democratization of religious authority.

Hecker also differed from the vast majority of European priests of his time in his enthusiasm for the separation of church and state. As an American raised in a society with a lot of religious activity but without an established church, Hecker never equated religious freedom with loss of religious life. And as an American Catholic in a society dominated by Protestants, he appreciated the protection that religious freedom conferred on religious minorities. Most important, Hecker's commitment to religious freedom underlay his understanding of the centrality of the Holy Spirit in religious life. His earlier religious experience, first as a Methodist and then as a Transcendentalist, led to his later interest as a Catholic in the spiritual development of each individual and to his persistent belief that this development required an informed mind and an active will. Against the passive subservience to authority that he associated with many of the Catholic devotions of his day, he held up the activity of the Holy Spirit as the inspirational force within each soul and, through the lives of inspired individuals, the force behind true social progress, ultimately leading to the redemption of human society.[7]

Hecker's theology of the Holy Spirit strongly influenced the next generation of American Catholic leaders. Those who followed Hecker's line of thought about the Holy Spirit included John Joseph Keane, Augustine Hewitt, John Ireland, and James Cardinal Gibbons. Keane was Hecker's foremost intellectual heir and founding rector of the Catholic University of America. Hewitt was Hecker's successor as rector of the Paulist Fathers. Ireland was the archbishop of St. Paul who called for a crusade to bring the Church into the modern age. And

Gibbons's intervention while in Rome to receive his cardinal's hat in 1887 persuaded the Vatican to lift its ban against the Knights of Labor. Each of these influential men carried forward Hecker's emphasis on the spiritual life of the laity and his belief in the progressive development of society.

At the World's Parliament of Religions held during the Columbian Exposition in Chicago in 1893, Keane, Hewitt, Ireland, Gibbons, and fourteen other progressive Catholic leaders participated in discussions about religion's role in leading human society toward the Kingdom of God. Addressing delegates representing Hinduism, Buddhism, Zoroastrianism, Shintoism, Taoism, and Theosophy as well as Judaism, Islam, Orthodox Christianity, and numerous forms of Protestantism, Keane urged everyone to pray for world religious unity. In his reflections immediately after the parliament, Hewitt spoke for the Catholic delegation about the leading role the Catholic Church was destined to play in the process of religious unification in the United States. "Our great republic must find its vital force and strength in morality," he wrote. "The only sufficient basis of morality is in religion, the only possible religion for America is Christianity, and," he continued, "the only pure and perfect embodiment of Christianity is the Catholic Church."[8]

Despite their expression of firm belief in the authority of the Catholic Church and its providential destiny as the redeemer of all humanity, the Catholic delegates to the parliament were strongly criticized in Europe, and the Vatican consigned the whole business to "unholy memory." The parliament had been orchestrated by American Protestants, the Vatican pointed out, one of whom had been so impertinent as to propose that the pope issue an infallible declaration of his fallibility. No less problematic, the parliament had afforded Hindus, Buddhists, and representatives of a variety of other religions the opportunity to set their religious traditions on an equal footing with the Catholic Church. While Keane maintained that presentations by Hindus and Buddhists at the parliament "only served to show more clearly that the Christian religion contains the fulness of all that is good and true in all," the exchange of religious ideas at the parliament opened the door to discussions in which even Christians themselves might be convinced otherwise. Even as Keane expressed his confidence that a comparison of world religions would demonstrate the supremacy of Christianity, his personal secretary was quoted as claiming that the Hindu exponent Vivekananda was "beyond question the most popular and influential man in the Parliament." In 1895, in response to these intolerable developments, Pope Leo XIII sent official word through his apostolic delegates that Catholic priests in the United States were forbidden to participate in any more "promiscuous conventions." The following year, Keane was fired from his position as rector of Catholic University.[9]

In their vision of world progress, Hecker's followers challenged the view of most nineteenth-century European church leaders that fidelity to the Church meant animosity to modernism and its celebration of human progress. Although these progressive American Catholic were firmly committed to the Catholic Church as the living embodiment of the Spirit of God, their affirmation of social progress, emphasis on lay inspiration, and commitment to religious freedom placed them outside the mainstream of nineteenth-century Catholic thought. In the last decades of the century, as the Church moved in the direction of even greater centralization, Romanization, uniformity of devotion, and dependence on priestly authority, it also moved toward greater detachment from public life and the concerns of modern society. As this defensive, antimodern posture solidified, the devotion to the Holy Spirit associated with Hecker and his followers came to be distinguished from true Catholic teaching and condemned as "Americanism." In his 1899 encyclical *Testem Benevolentiae*, Leo XIII defined Americanism in terms of its failure to emphasize the central role of obedience to authority in Catholic teaching. In its discussion of devotion to the Holy Ghost, the encyclical emphasized the need to rely on the authority of a spiritual director. It also denied that the gifts of the Spirit were increasing in modern times and rejected the idea that modern culture could produce any form of social progress.[10]

In the years between the condemnation of Americanism and the second Vatican Council in the early 1960s, Hecker and his followers fell under a shadow of disreputability. Most twentieth-century Catholic theologians in Europe overlooked the theology of the Holy Spirit developed by Hecker and Keane, tainted as it was by association with papal condemnation and with the supposedly naive and excessively individualistic nature of American religious thought. At the second Vatican Council, the pragmatic approach to the modern world that characterized the Americanist tradition remained in the background on some issues raised at the council, as did some delegates to the council from the United States. Many of the changes in Church policy launched during the second Vatican Council were proposed and defended by European Catholics whose thinking was influenced by German phenomenology and French existentialism. However, on the important issue of separation of church and state, the Americans played a central role. In the estimation of one historian, the council's endorsement of this separation "was not only the most controversial of all" the issues discussed by the council, "but perhaps the most significant as well."[11]

In his important essay on the historical development of Americanism, R. Scott Appleby showed that acceptance of the separation of church and state was one thing that most twentieth-century Catholics in the United States agreed on. In response to the Vatican's condemnation of Americanism as a species of modernism, American Catholic leaders worked effectively to show that the Americanist commitment to separation of church and state had nothing to do with the materialism and atheism associated with modernism and that, in fact, religious freedom enabled American Catholics to express and develop their loyalty to the Church. In the context of American Catholic discussions about religious freedom and separation of church and state during the 1950s, a second important development occurred. The American Jesuit John Courtney Murray emphasized the relevance of Catholic ideas about natural law for American public life. Some aspects of Catholic teaching were addressed specifically and exclusively to Church members, but others had much to contribute to the strength and development of American civic life. In conceptualizing Catholic teaching in this way, Murray argued that separation of church and state not only protected Catholic religious freedom, but also created an opportunity for Catholic ideas of natural law to help shape a larger culture in which Catholics were a religious minority.[12]

Murray was the principal author of the Vatican Council document on church and state. New York's Cardinal Spellman and a number of American bishops at the council strongly supported it and lobbied successfully for its passage. But the document was controversial because it challenged the Church's right to rule the world as the only true church. This claim, which the Church had asserted for centuries, required rejection of other religions as well as assertion of claims to authority in political matters and rights to protection by the state. While the American proponents of separation of church and state at the council affirmed the ultimate truth of the Catholic Church and equated its spiritual authority with the reign of God, they argued that the vitality of the Church and its authority in people's lives was strongest when people entered and participated in the Church through free consent. In the spirit of Isaac Hecker, they linked religious freedom to both lay leadership and ecumenical dialogue. While some council members believed that lay leadership and ecumenical dialogue could be supported without endorsing the separation of church and state, from the Americans' democratically minded perspective, religious freedom was the essential prerequisite.

Dispute persists over the exact meaning and appropriate application of many of the documents produced by the second Vatican Council. Liberals cite the progressive spirit of the Council and endeavor to carry it forward, while others assert, with some reason, that the spirit of the Council was far more conservative than some of its liberal interpreters claim. This debate over the meaning and implications of Vatican II has been especially intense in the United States, where progressive interpretations of Catholicism have played a significant role and where countervailing beliefs in the need to instill greater obedience to authority are nevertheless also robust.[13]

On the progressive side of the ledger, the vast majority of practicing American Catholics embraced the reforms initiated by the second Vatican Council. Many individuals and groups within this majority carried forward the spirit of those reforms into new forms of liturgical, theological, and social expression. New or revised forms of meditation, prayer, and spiritual development became popular among Catholics across the country, along with new ideas about the nature and presence of God and new forms of social engagement and religious activism. Measured in terms of intellectual creativity and active participation in religious life, progressive Catholicism flourished in the United States in the late twentieth century with an exuberance and openness to experiment that may be unprecedented in the history of the Church.

This openness coincided with the growing affluence, education, and status of Catholics within American society. In the nineteenth century, Protestant evangelicals often stigmatized Catholics as backward and ignorant. While poor immigrants from Catholic countries poured into American cities, Protestants used the public school system, print media, and various forms of public policy to equate Protestant and American values and to instill them in newcomers. Meanwhile, American Catholics developed their own vast network of churches, schools, hospitals, charitable organizations, devotional programs, and religious orders and communities. This thriving and heterogeneous network of Catholic institutions comprised a variety of competing forces. Concerns for ethnic preservation vied with devotion to the centralizing power of Rome. Respect for the authority of Rome contended with enthusiasm for American democracy. Eagerness to be accepted by other Americans conflicted with efforts to develop a strong Catholic counterculture. And coming full circle, the desire for a unified counterculture coincided with allegiance to Rome but competed with the desire for ethnic preservation as well as with enthusiasm for American democracy and eagerness to be accepted by other Americans.

As these coinciding forces developed, the network of Catholic institutions burgeoned and Catholic people became increasingly well established in American society. The Catholic Church grew to become the largest denomination in the United States, and the per capita wealth, education, and professional status of American Catholics eventually surpassed that of American Protestants. The inauguration of John F. Kennedy as president of the United States in 1960 marked the transition of Catholics from the margins to the mainstream of American culture. It also coincided with the beginning of the second Vatican Council and the council's opening of the Church to the modern world.

Underlying affinities between the reforms initiated in the second Vatican Council and the Americanist approach to Catholicism contributed to a new flourishing of progressive Catholicism. Vatican II rejuvenated the same tendencies to freedom of religious expression, lay leadership, and ecumenical dialogue that defined this earlier, Americanist branch of Catholicism. The European theologians at the second Vatican Council who called for Church renewal certainly did not intend to revitalize Americanism. But the extraordinary takeoff of Catholic religious reform and renewal in the United States since the 1960s cannot be explained without reference to the underlying affinity between the council's most important reforms and the ideas planted in American Catholicism by Isaac Hecker and the Americanist followers of the Holy Spirit.

DEMOCRATIZATION OF RELIGIOUS AUTHORITY

Some of the most important and far-reaching forms of renewal endorsed by the second Vatican Council were those associated with the development of lay leadership. In an effort to address problems of alienation and passivity among Catholic lay people, the Council focused on the Church's domination by clerics as one source of those problems. To diminish the religious gulf that separated clergy from other Catholics, the Council encouraged all Catholics to think of the Church as the people of God. It was no longer sufficient to conceptualize the Church as a priestly hierarchy, as the source of authoritative religious teaching, or as the sacred place where Christ was present in the sacraments. While these aspects of the Church remained important, the reformers at the second Vatican Council argued that the Church's identity as the people of God was no less important and that alienation and passivity among the laity were the price the Church paid for its neglect.

The importance of the laity for the life of the Church also came to the fore in the council's emphasis on the Church's responsibility to care for the world. And this emphasis on the Church's pastoral role coincided with efforts to develop the Church's mission to promote social justice. John XXIII drew attention to the gap between rich and poor in modern societies and committed the Church to work for more just and humane social conditions. John's concern for social justice was rooted in the Church's long-standing criticism of modern society, and especially in Leo XIII's encyclical letter *Rerun Novarum* (1891), which attacked industrial capitalism as a brutal system that encouraged employers to calculate wages without taking account of workers' needs. Leo's appeal for more humane treatment of the poor had been essentially paternalistic and reflected nostalgia for an idealized medieval world in which the Church played a central role in maintaining a stable and hierarchical social order. John's encyclicals on social justice were more positively influenced by democratic philosophy. They also advanced his primary aim of bringing the Church into a less hostile and more open relationship with modern society.

The council's emphasis on the Church's pastoral outreach to the modern world dovetailed with older ideas of identification with the poor as a means of purifying oneself of worldly ambition and emulating Christ. Such ideas had long been associated with the Benedictines, Franciscans, and other religious orders dedicated to poverty and, more recently in the United States, with lay groups such as the Catholic Workers, who found Christ among the poor and lived with them as a means of serving him. In the new context of the second Vatican Council's emphasis on lay leadership in the Church's pastoral mission to the world, the older idea of identifying with the poor as a means of spiritual purification and identification with Christ gained new meaning and drew new adherents. Partly influenced by ideas associated with liberation theology, an increasing number of proponents of devotion to the poor began to connect the suffering and injustice experienced by people around the world with the suffering of Christ. This expanded and updated vision of the mystical embodiment of Christ in the world required the Church and its members to become more actively engaged in the world. And this concern for the Church's greater activism in the world coincided with the council's emphasis on the need for a more activist laity and also with the Church's effort to combat the alienation and passivity caused by earlier preoccupations with ritualism and obedience to priestly authority. In response to the call for an activist Church, new cooperative efforts sprang up between priests and lay people that better utilized the talents of the latter and encouraged their leadership as representatives of the Church.

In the United States, the development of lay leadership also coincided with a precipitous decline in clerical vocations. Between 1965 and 1998, enrollments in seminaries specializing in education and training for the priesthood declined 60 percent. Between 1990 and 1998 the number of priests in the United States deceased from 58,621 to 47,582. At the same time, the number of Catholics in the United States increased from 49.6 million to 61.5 million. This precipitous decline in the percentage of priests in the Catholic population may have reflected the lessening of priestly status brought on by the Church's postcouncil emphasis on the importance of lay people. An even more significant cause was the turmoil and confusion, initially brought on by Vatican II, about the nature of the Church and its sacraments, mission, and priesthood. As conservative Catholics often pointed out, enrollments were higher in seminaries that emphasized traditional conceptions of the Church.

Among progressive Catholics, the shortage of priests, together with commitment to the democratization of the Church and to greater justice inside its walls, led to efforts to expand the priesthood to include women and married men. Although in the 1990s Pope John Paul II forbade women's ordination even as a topic of discussion, polls showed that the majority of American Catholics were positively disposed to the idea of ordaining women and married men. They saw this reform as a good solution to the problems posed by the shortage of priests. Among proponents of such change, the Chicago-based Call to Action lobbied American bishops on the issue of ordination, while the Cleveland-based FutureChurch focused on increasing grassroots acceptance of a more open priesthood. Christine Schenk, the director of FutureChurch, spoke for many American Catholics in expressing her belief that "[t]he Eucharist is at the core of everything we are about as a Catholic community. We think the gender or marital status of the presider is not nearly as important as having Mass available."[14]

In many cases, this pragmatic appeal to the need for more priests as a reason for women's ordination worked to reframe, in less politically charged terms, the idea that the Church owed women reparation for its unequal treatment of them. Appeals to the need for more priests both affirmed and softened the belief that love of Christ demanded greater justice toward women within the Church. And the mysticism of Americanist Catholic theology supported this pragmatic argument. Because the Spirit was construed either as without gender or as implicitly female, women could more easily express a spiritual authority that made the rule against women's ordination seem odd and antiquated.

AMERICAN INTERPRETATIONS OF IGNATIAN SPIRITUALITY

In their emphasis on the oneness of humanity and the incarnational presence of Christ and his Spirit in the world, various forms of Catholic spirituality offered criticism of the problems of American society and promoted alternative ways of living. As one of the most influential of these, Ignatian spirituality developed as a means of countering the perceived hedonism of American society while at the same time promoting a progressive approach to a variety of Church matters, such as the ban against the ordination of women. This commitment to progress within the Church supported an underlying belief in society's profound need for the truths provided by a reformed Catholicism. In the eyes of the missionaries of Ignatian spirituality, Catholicism had a central role to play in the transformation and redemption of American culture.

Founded in the early-sixteenth century by the Spanish soldier Ignatius Loyola, the Society of Jesus has a long history as both a missionary order and a brotherhood of scholars and educators. In both aspects, Jesuits have been famous for adapting their view of Christianity to many different cultural situations. In the United States, the Jesuit order is associated with some of the most elite and progressive institutions in Catholic education. In many Jesuit schools, innovative programs in service learning have been developed since the sixties that encourage both Catholic and non-Catholic students to bring the missionary principles of Ignatian spirituality to bear on the problems of American culture. Without relinquishing the mystical sense of identification with the poor generally associated with Catholic monastic traditions, these courses interest students in social policies that do not make poverty inevitable and in strategic efforts to help break its cycle. Seen in the context of American religious life, such courses represent a merger of long-standing pragmatic elements in Ignatian spirituality and American Protestant culture.

The service-learning course developed at one Jesuit university, and described in an ethnographic study undertaken in 1996–97, provides a good example of how these new programs of spiritual formation blended a mystical view of service to the poor with a realistic assessment of social injustice and a pragmatic approach to social change. Designed to help students establish personal relationships with the "losers" in society, the course led students to discover the limitations of old-fashioned but still prevalent American beliefs about poverty. Through volunteer service in the community, religious readings, class discussion, and the guidance of their instructors, students found that poverty was not simply the result of lack of self-determination. They also found that respect for the dignity of people who suffered in poverty demanded more than ensuring them a supply of economic entitlements. Instructors encouraged students to love the people they tried to serve and to interpret this love as agape, the love manifest in Jesus Christ. As the reality that drew people together in life, students learned, agape was the most appropriate basis for conceptualizing justice.

Students originated the course during the sixties as a way of putting their concern for social justice into action and as an alternative both to the violence advocated by Marxist groups such as Students for a Democratic Society and to the cloistered piety of more traditional religious clubs. Over time, it became clear that the original hoped-for outcome of transforming the neighborhoods around the university was not being realized, but that the students involved in the course were themselves being transformed. During the eighties and nineties, the course was reorganized to incorporate a wider variety of political opinion and to produce, more deliberately than in the past, transformational religious experiences in students who enrolled. As it developed, the course shifted away from leftist ideology to center on a form of Christian identification with human suffering that involved realistic social analysis as well as encouragement of compassion and mystical feelings of love. As one student observed, "The course brings everyone together—liberal, conservative, and not religious. It gives us a common bond even though we're very different. A lot of us are religious," he went on to explain, "and a lot of us have become more religious because of the program. It brought me closer to God, and to realizing the importance of God in my life. It also changed my understanding of God. I used to think God was a person up there. Now I think of God as a presence within myself and others. I think of God as agape."

Although the course was originally founded out of desire to transform American society, it evolved into a course that succeeded in transforming college students. As one student who had taken the course explained, "You get into this course thinking you're going to help others, but you barely touch their lives. Meanwhile, your life has been changed." Seeing how "stuck" the women were at the shelter where she worked, and how many huge problems they had to cope with, prompted this student to acknowledge how much she had. "Before taking this course," she explained, "you believe that people could change and improve their lives if they really wanted to. You think about yourself as on an equal plane with others. But then you realize that you happen to have been born at a different level, and the shoe could be on the other foot. It makes you ask, why am I really here?"[15]

This student's awareness of the privileged character of her own life, and of the underlying humanity she shared with less fortunate people could be described as an Americanist version of the experience of self-transcendence advanced by the German Jesuit Karl Rahner to explain Catholic religious life in existential terms. Rahner recast the ideas of the medieval theologian Thomas Aquinas in philosophical terms derived from German transcendental phenomenology and French existentialism, arguing that the self's capacity to recognize its own finitude involved an experience of self-transcendence that implied the existence, mystery, and power of God. In the context of the pragmatic orientation of American culture, this concept of self-transcendence merged with an activist agenda of social reform. Partly as a result of the influence of Catholic liberation theology and partly as a result of an underlying American tendency to think about religion strategically and in terms of its effects, Rahner's concept of self-transcendence came to be interpreted as a means to social responsibility.

This Ignatian approach to social responsibility has some kinship to the mystical personalism of Dorothy Day and the Catholic Worker movement. But as we will see in Chapter 3, Day's mysticism was more absolutist and literalistic than that of most Jesuits—she never ventured down the path of making the presence of Christ a metaphor for feelings of love and respect for the poor, as many Jesuits did. And her attitude toward social policy was less pragmatic than that promoted in Jesuit service learning—she was more concerned with doing penance for social injustice than with developing realistic policies to change it. The modified, postsixties form of Catholic personalism represented in the Jesuit service learning reflect the mainstreaming of Catholic spirituality in the United States and its adaptation to American culture as well as its attention to the international conversation about Catholic theology.

The Jesuit's turn toward existential and transcendental philosophy marked an important development in their long-standing mission of *cura personalis*. In the context of Jesuit education in the United States, *cura personalis*, often translated as "helping souls," came to be interpreted in terms of attention to the individual person and in terms of friendship and mentoring in the course of a person's journey through life. Increasing numbers of non-Catholics in the United States were seeking Jesuit educations, and Catholic populations were no longer living mostly in ethnic, urban communities, outsiders to mainstream American culture. As part of the mainstreams of American culture, Catholics were increasingly shaped by the individualism and preoccupation with personal journeying that characterized American middle-class culture.

While coming into dialogue with psychologisms associated with American individualism, the long-standing Jesuit mission of *cura personalis* was also recast in terms of concerns about social justice that had roots in the social gospel tradition of American Protestantism as well as in the later development of that tradition in Latin American Catholicism and liberation theology. After Vatican II, as Jesuits became leading spokesmen for liberation theology, they also became leading spokesmen for linking the mission of Christian universities to service to the poor. As Ignacio Ellacuría, a Jesuit murdered for his activism by government agents in El Salvador in 1989, explained in a 1982 commencement address at the Jesuit-run University of Santa Clara in California, "The poor embody Christ in a special way, they mirror for us his message of revelation, salvation, and conversion." Ellacuría argued that embodying a preferential option for the poor within a Christian university "does not mean that the university should abdicate its mission of academic excellence—excellence needed to solve complex social problems." But the Christian university "should be present intellectually where it is needed to provide science for those who have no science; to provide skills for the unskilled; to be a voice for those who have no voice; to give intellectual support for those who do not posses the academic qualifications to promote and legitimate their rights."

As they developed in the context of American higher education, Jesuit concerns for social justice and for helping souls along in their spiritual journeys were conceptualized in highly inclusive terms. Ignatian spirituality attracted at least as many women as men, and non-Catholics often found it compelling as well. As one non-Jesuit spokesperson put it, the university "is not about Jesuits as a particular group of men, but about the vision of Ignatius, which Jesus shared, along with many other people, not only Catholics, but Protestants, Jews and probably others outside the Judeo-Christian tradition." As evidence of this general enthusiasm for the religious inclusivity of Ignatian spiritually several students with backgrounds in Hinduism participated in the service learning course described above and found it congenial to their own religious beliefs. These students embraced the Ignatian motto of "men and women for others" as a guide for developing spirituality within the context of American Hinduism, which they viewed as having important areas of overlap with American Catholicism.

The vitality of Ignatian and other forms of Catholic spirituality represented a challenge to Protestantism's historical role as the moral arbiter and cultural unifier of American society. Through various programs of spiritual formation and spiritual development in schools, colleges, universities, local parishes, and retreat centers across the nation, Catholics in the nineties renewed and reinvented their commitments both to their devotional lives and to public and community service. More was going on here than simply the revitalization of a subculture with minority status in American society. While those who participated in Catholic forms of spirituality were heterogeneous with respect to age, sex, ethnic background, and political allegiance, they shared experiences of the oneness of humanity and the incarnational presence of Christ and his Spirit in the world. They also shared a belief in the rightful place of spirituality at the center of society.

This belief in the central and unifying role of spirituality in American life was partly a reflection of its associations with the Catholic Church. While degrees of loyalty to the current pontiff and obedience to his directives varied considerably among American Catholics, the image of an ideal Church, uniting and transforming society, persisted. But at the same time, this commitment to an ideal Church coexisted with commitment to individual religious freedom as an important aspect of spirituality and thus represented a significant departure from the commitment to the union of Church and state that characterized official Catholic teaching until the second Vatican Council. With respect to this belief in the importance of religious freedom, and its connection to an emphasis on the authority of individual religious experience and the need for it to be available to everyone, American Catholic spirituality at the end of the twentieth century had as much affinity to American Transcendentalism—and to Puritan ideas about the Holy Spirit, the work of the Spirit in human history, and the invisible Church constructed out of the lives of Christian people—as it did to traditional, precouncil Catholic teaching. Thus the vitality of Catholic spirituality in the United States reflected not only the loss of Protestantism's hegemonic role in American culture, but also the reemergence of ideas once associated with both the mystical and social reform aspects of American Protestant thought.

AMERICAN INTERPRETATIONS
OF CISTERCIAN SPIRITUALITY

Visiting the Trappist monastery of Gethsemani in Bardstown, Kentucky, nine months before the bombing of Pearl Harbor, Thomas Merton was awestruck by the beautiful simplicity of the monks and by the power of the mass they celebrated. In its disclosure of the presence of God, the Trappist mass brought Merton to a "tremendous truth"—the church at Gethsemani was "the real capital of the country in which we are living. This is the center of all the vitality that is in America. This is the cause and reason why the nation is holding together." He went on to explain the monks' role in the world: "These men, hidden in the anonymity of their choir and their white cowls, are doing for that land what no army, no congress, no president could ever do as such: they are winning for it the grace and the protection and the friendship of God."[16]

Like others whose mysticism helped to shape the distinctive contours of American Catholic thought, Thomas Merton was a convert. Drawn to the Catholic Church by the mysticism of its sacraments, Merton found spiritual satisfaction through his experience of the real presence of God in the mass. Like the Transcendentalists of an earlier generation, Merton looked to Catholicism as a means of entering the realm of the Spirit, which he understood to be the realm of essential spiritual reality undergirding the material world. At his first communion on November 16, 1938, Merton completely invested himself in the idea that this event would fully unite him with God. Upon receiving the Eucharist, he felt that "Heaven was entirely mine—that Heaven in which sharing makes no division or diminution." He had "entered into the everlasting movement of that gravitation which is the very life and spirit of God." He found himself "incorporated into this immense and tremendous gravitational movement which is love, which is the Holy Spirit."[17]

Like other American Catholics, Merton often described the power of God in the world in terms of the movement of the Holy Spirit, and he defined the Spirit in terms of love. And like the college students at the Jesuit university described above who also learned to think of God in terms of agape, Merton believed that this love could be realized through identification with the poor. Before joining the Trappists, he lived and worked with lay Catholics at Friendship House in New York's Harlem. These Catholic Workers were drawn to the people of Harlem not only out of compassion for the misery suffered there, but also (and perhaps even more important) because they found God in the midst of that human misery. Merton agreed that the sufferings of the poor were an integral part of a larger human drama. More affluent Americans participated in the same humanity, Merton believed, and were responsible for these sufferings.

Merton's identification with the poor as a means of religious experience and spiritual development might be compared with current expressions of Ignatian spirituality, as might his respect for dedicated lay people. But at the same time, the balance of Merton's spirituality, like that of the Trappist order he joined, was more completely defined in terms of contemplation than Ignatian spirituality, in which contemplation is also central but continually directed toward activism in the world. Trappists belong to the Cistercian Order of the Strict Observance, distinguished from the Common Observance by its commitment to ritual uniformity and monastic austerity. Founded at the end of the eleventh century, the Cistercian order originated within the Benedictine order as a reform movement dedicated to poverty, separation from the world, and the renewal of monastic life. Apart from Merton, the best-known figure in the Cistercian line is the twelfth century mystical writer Bernard de Clairvaux, who is famous for his descriptions of the mystical union between Christ and believer. In calling believers to participate in this union, Bernard recommended poverty and selflessness as means of distancing one's soul from what was not God.

Merton followed Bernard in emphasizing the ecstasy of union with God and also in successfully engaging a wide audience in his celebration of mystical experience. As more than one observer has pointed out, Merton's influence on subsequent generations of Trappist monks has been enormous. His autobiography, *The Seven Storey Mountain*, functioned as a canonical text for many individuals drawn to the Trappists as exemplars of Christian spirituality.[18] Merton's account of the mystical power of the Catholic sacraments, his criticism of the materialism of American culture, and his subsequent exploration of analogues to Catholic mysticism in other religious traditions came to define Catholic spirituality for many lay Catholics in America, and many non-Catholics as well. A wide range of religious seekers, including

Baptist seminary students and Episcopal bishops, visited Merton at his monastery in Kentucky. The black activist Eldridge Cleaver read "Brother Merton" in prison. After his unexpected death in 1968, Merton's fame increased even more and contributed significantly to the success of the Trappists as recording artists with several popular CDs of religious chants to their credit. Ironically, but in distinctively American fashion, the man who left worldly life to contemplate God in monastic silence became a celebrity.

As a poet, Merton expressed a combination of world-weariness and spirituality that appealed to intellectuals torn between alienation from the violence and materialism of American culture and enthusiasm for mysticism and religious experimentation. For example, in *The Geography of Lograire,* an epic poem written near the end of his life, he compared the airplanes being fueled at O'Hare Airport with "big slow fish" surrounded by armored insects. Once aloft, he looked down on the city below, naming it "Sewage Town." This image of disdain and detachment from the world led to an invocation of the Hindu god Shiva, whose cosmic dance mastered both creative and destructive forces. Shiva, in turn, led to images of Eucharistic sacrifice represented by the wheat, rice, and corn fields tilled by Christians, Buddhists, and Native Americans, by the exploitation of their labor, and by the destruction of life ongoing in Vietnam. As a "dance of Shivashapes," the sacrificial "hosts" of that destruction, like the divine Trinity itself, were at once many and one: Christian bread, Buddhist rice, maize from the Americas. "I am one same burned Indian," Merton declared. "All is my Vietnam charred."[19]

In this and other poems written near the end of his life, Merton gathered Hindu, Buddhist, and Native American mythologies together within the framework of Christian mythology and Catholic monasticism. At the same time, he loosened the connection between monastic mysticism and the Catholic Church and set it free for anyone to use as a base for uniting the mystical and mythological aspects of various religious traditions in various forms of personal spirituality. Relying on the long tradition of Cistercian, Benedictine, and Pauline mysticism as a kind of metaphysical anchor, Merton drew on psychological studies of comparative mythology by C. G. Jung and Joseph Campbell to find echoes and cross-cultural variants of the same mystical insights in Hindu, Buddhist, and Native American religions.

The psychological turn in religious thinking stimulated new forms of ecumenical dialogue that had far-reaching effects on a variety of religions. A fair number of Hindus, Buddhist, Jews, and Protestants came to understand their relationships to one another differently as a result of dialogues among representatives of different religions in which Catholics play an important role. Leading representatives of these religions responded thirstily to the Catholic emphasis on spirituality, as well as to the Catholic sense of the corporate unity of humankind, epitomized by the presence of Christ in the Eucharist and recast in the light of psychological theory about the universal characteristics of human spirituality and the importance of spiritual journeys.

The Syncretism of Catholic Spirituality

Just as Merton was not the only Catholic engaged in this kind of psychological approach to religion during the sixties, neither was he the first one to syncretize Christianity with other religions. In India, China, and North America, Jesuits missionaries were well known for their ability to incorporate indigenous religious ideas and practices into Catholicism. Thus in south India in the seventeenth century, Roberto di Nobli adopted the dress and diet of a Brahman and the lifestyle of a native religious teacher and used the Hindu Upanishads as a basis for his lessons in Christianity. Matteo Ricci acted similarly among Confucians in sixteenth-century China. And among the Huron in seventeenth-century North America, Jesuit missionaries accepted the indigenous belief that dreams were messages from the spirit world and encouraged natives to dream about Mary and Jesus.

Beginning in the 1960s, Catholics led the way in exploring commonalities between Catholic spirituality and Eastern mysticism. In India, both Protestant and Catholic missionaries lived in ashrams that combined Hindu and Christian practice. But while Protestants were inspired in their endeavors by the social-resistance ashrams of Gandhi and Tagore, Catholics were more interested in traditional Hindu ashrams devoted to mystical contemplation. By the 1960s, joint Catholic-Hindu ashrams were flourishing on the cutting edge of Catholic ecumenism. As one admirer wrote in 1965, "These places of daring spiritual experiments and of single-eyed concentration on the interior life" have produced "countless souls, whose spiritual yearning has driven them insatiably to plunge into the interior mystery and to seek the ineffable Presence." Among the foremost of these contemplative pioneers was Sebastian Kappen, whose work focused on the "search for a Hindu form of Christian expression and practice." Shortly before his death in Bangalore in 1993, he drew on Hindu conceptions to describe his Catholic belief that "[t]he Divine pulsates in that primal telluric desire (eros, *kama*, in Sanskrit) that makes the sun rise and shine and set."[20]

Catholics have also been in the vanguard of efforts to incorporate Buddhist insight into Christian experience and practice. Since the 1960s, Catholics have often led the way in initiating ecumenical dialogues aimed at stimulating new forms of Christian practice and discovering common ground between Christian and Buddhist insights into the ultimate nature of reality. The Irish Jesuit William Johnston coined the phrase "Christian Zen" to describe the religious breakthrough that he hoped would result from these endeavors. In 1981 he predicted "a revolution in Christian spirituality" based on the realization "that one can pray not just with the mind but also with the body and the breathing." And he claimed that this realization was creating "a great leap forward in consciousness that will dominate the religious experience of the future."[21]

Beginning in the sixties, the constructive role of Catholic spirituality in ecumenical dialogue was clearly manifest in the conversation between Christianity and Buddhism initiated in Dharamsala in 1968 by Thomas Merton and Tenzin Gyatso, the fourteenth Dalai Lama. Inspired by Merton's pioneering work, exchange programs developed that contributed to the fast-growing interest in Buddhism among American Catholics as well to the Dalai Lama's interest in Christian monasticism. Beginning in 1981, the Monastic Hospitality Program brought Tibetan and Zen Buddhist monastics to Christian monasteries in North America, and Christian monastics from North America to Tibetan and Zen Buddhist monasteries in Asia. At the Parliament of the World's Religions in 1993, the Monastic Interreligious Dialogue Board, made up of monks and nuns in the Benedictine, Cistercian, and Trappist traditions, hosted an interfaith dialogue session with the Dalai Lama and other Buddhist leaders. As a follow-up to that meeting, "a weeklong, indepth intermonastic encounter on the spiritual life" was held in July 1996 at Gethsemani, Merton's home abbey in Kentucky. A religious gathering with strong international connections but in which most participants were citizens of the United States, the Gethsemani Encounter marked an important moment in the transformation of American religious thought.

In the opening dialogue, "Ultimate Reality and Spirituality," the Catholic lay theologian and professor of religious studies Donald W. Mitchell defined Catholic spirituality in a way that reflected its hospitality to mysticism in other faiths as well as its recent turn toward depth psychology. Admitting that Christian spirituality might be seen by outsiders in terms of efforts on the part of believers to relate to "an external, separate supermundane deity," Mitchell argued that if one examined the religious experiences of insiders, the nature of God as Spirit comes to the fore. Mitchell's emphasis on the Spirit would have appealed to Isaac Hecker and other Transcendentalists attracted to Catholicism as an expression of the divine presence within the human soul. It also reflected the more recent emphasis on human consciousness as the context of religious life. "For us," Mitchell explained, "the term 'spirit' does not denote a subtle form of matter, as in some Asian traditions, but refers to the very pure and clear essence of consciousness." And he speculated that this was "something similar to the 'mind of clear light' as understood in the Tibetan traditions."[22]

The interchange between Catholic spirituality and Asian traditions was a two-way process involving both absorption and recasting of Asian traditions within Catholicism. The development of the Maharishi Mahesh Yogi's Transcendental Meditation (TM) exemplified this two-way process. As Gene R. Thursby pointed out, while American Protestant churches were incorporating the simplified form of psychoanalysis known as transactional analysis (TA) into their adult programs, Catholics were incorporating the simplified Hinduism of TM. And this incorporation had a significant impact on the development of American Catholic spirituality in the 1960s and 1970s. In conjunction with the mandates for spiritual renewal and lay development that issued from the second Vatican Council, "TM stimulated Catholic leaders to adapt their own traditions of spiritual formation, previously restricted mainly to religious orders, and make them available to the laity." Thursby cited the success of the Centering Prayer movement developed by the Trappist Basil Pennington as a result, at least in part, of the appeal and influence of TM.[23]

As various forms of Catholic spirituality expanded beyond their monastic settings and absorbed Asian influences, the influence of Catholic spirituality on various forms of American Protestantism also grew. Thus Catholic spirituality served as an important vehicle for the dissemination of Asian ideas within American Protestant churches. Through a process of liturgical renewal that swept through many American churches after the sixties, Protestant and Catholic spiritualities drew closer together, and new developments in Catholic spirituality influenced American Protestants as well as Catholics. New forms of congregational participation, performing art, and scriptural interpretation were part of this widespread movement of liturgical renewal. At the center of this movement was the Catholic *Lectionary for Mass*, published in 1969 and revised in 1993. Presbyterians, Lutherans, Episcopalians, and Methodists adopted these liturgical manuals and commentaries based on them. Because many different religious groups came to use the same lectionary, pastors from various Christian churches began to meet to discuss common biblical texts and other readings.[24]

This lowering of denominational boundaries was part of the greatest liturgical reform movement in Christianity since the Protestant Reformation in the sixteenth century. And Catholic renewal, Catholic spirituality, and Catholic ecumenism stood at its center. Not only in liturgical reform, but in the larger transformation of religious life in the United States since the 1960s, Catholic spirituality functioned for many Americans as a kind of matrix of a larger whole. The current resurgence of spirituality in the United States developed in a culture strongly shaped by Protestant thought. At the same time, American Catholic leadership galvanized this resurgence. The central place that Catholic spiritualities occupied in mediating ideas and practices from Asian traditions marked the eclipse of Protestant hegemony in American culture and the emergence of a post-Protestant form of American religious thought and cultural renewal.

3

Vietnam and the Ethics of Disenchantment

"To live outside the Law you must be honest" Drunken aggressive beer bottles'll never redeem anybody—But clear conscious song can . . . NOT for bummer ego put-down but instead for egoless enunciation of exact phrasings so everyone can hear intelligence—which is only your own heart Dear.

How far has he gone? All the way from scared solitude inner prophetics—building on that mind-honesty strangeness—to open-hearted personal historical confession. As "Coffee for the Road" 's Semitic mode, "Sara" is profound ancient tune revealing family paradigm . . . Who woulda thought he'd say it, so everybody'd finally know him, same soul crying vulnerable caught in a body we all are?—enough Person revealed to make Whitman's whole nation weep. And behind it all the vast lone space of No God, or God, mindful conscious compassion, lifetime awareness, we're here in America at last, redeemed.

Allen Ginsberg on Bob Dylan[1]

The German founder of sociology, Max Weber, understood the success of Puritanism in terms of its demystification of economic and political life. More-traditional religions embraced economic and political life as processes grounded in sacred realities, such as the gods of sun and rain or the divine right of kings. In the early modern era, Weber argued, Protestants (and Puritans especially) succeeded economically because of the extent to which they conceptualized and managed profits in de-sacralized, rational terms. As Weber understood it, Puritans freed much of their world from the mists of religious enchantment not because they were irreligious, but because they shifted the locus of religion to the inner life, and especially the conscience, of the individual. This shift entailed a change of focus from ritual procedures that enabled people to feel they could manage, placate, or at least resonate with the sacred powers governing their material worlds to an internalized focus on ethical judgment.

This focus on ethical judgment required analysis of how the world was organized, and it opened the way for criticism of that organization and its social effects. As Weber pointed out, such analysis often led individuals to situate themselves in moral opposition to the dominant structures of society. "The more a religion of salvation has been systematized and internalized in the direction of an ethic based on an inner religious state," Weber wrote, "the greater becomes its tension with and opposition to the world." Moreover, Weber continued, "priesthoods have always (in the interests of traditionalism) protected patriarchalism against impersonal relationships of dependence, whereas prophetic religion on the contrary breaks through patriarchal social structures."[2]

Without entering into fine points of scholarly controversy about early modern Protestantism or the full adequacy of Weber's understanding of it, we can utilize his contrast between priestly and prophetic types to understand both the religious outrage that burst forth with revolutionary intensity in American society in the 1960s and the strong opposition, fear, and hatred with which it was met. In other words, Weber's analysis of the difference between priestly and prophetic types is useful not only for understanding the Protestant Reformation in the sixteenth century and the success of Puritanism in the seventeenth, but also for understanding the explosion of moral protest and countercultural experimentation in the United States at the end of the sixties.

In the earlier instance, the difference between prophetic and priestly types reflected a fundamental split between Protestants and Catholics. In the 1960s, elements of this Protestant-Catholic difference could still be detected. But it was vastly complicated by the fact that many Prot-

estants had come to invest religious authority in the patriarchal structures and traditions of American culture. As a result, they did not
display that prophetic edge associated with other forms of Protestantism, at least with respect to their attitudes toward American society.
This cultural situation was also complicated by a rapidly increasing
infusion of Catholic sensibilities into mainstream American culture and
by the long tradition of Catholic ambivalence toward American society.
On one hand, Catholics wanted to be recognized as full-fledged Americans and made great efforts to demonstrate their patriotism. On the
other hand, Catholics felt that their religion existed in some tension
with the materialistic values of American society. They could be ethi-
cally critical of the impersonal structures of American society while at
the same time being invested in the priesthood and patriarchy of their
own religious subculture.

In the context of the Vietnam War, this complex mixture of religious
sensibilities became explosive. With respect to American involvement
in Vietnam, there were Protestants as well as Catholics who behaved
like priestly types, expressing religious loyalty to the powers governing
their material world and extending that loyalty to support of the United
States and its involvement in Vietnam. The prophetic types who expressed moral outrage at the United States and attacked its involvement
in Vietnam also came from both Protestant and Catholic churches.
And in many cases, Jews joined hands with Protestant and Catholic
prophetic types and often led the way in developing ethical reasoning
against the war.

Many of the Americans opposed to the war in Vietnam were economically and educationally privileged. And many of them were young
and self-centered. They had been educated, and were still in the process
of being educated, to internalize the religious beliefs they had grown
up with. To a large extent, this internalization proceeded in the direction of an ethic of integrity and fair play based on an inner state of
authenticity and good conscience. An outrageous contrast existed in
their minds between the ethical values they had internalized and what
seemed to them to be the mindless destruction of life going on in
Vietnam. But because they were young and self-centered, they did not
comprehend, at least at first, how privileged and potentially subversive
their education in ethical reasoning had been. They mistakenly assumed that their commitment to this reasoning, which necessarily en-

tailed willingness to stand in moral opposition to society, was what everyone meant when they referred to truth.

Thinking along these lines, David Obst, the young Jewish antiwar activist who helped Seymour M. Hersh break the My Lai story, believed that publication of the story would end the war. Like other Americans whose worldview was organized in terms of prophetic-type ethical reasoning, Obst thought that once people had sufficient evidence of what was really going on in Vietnam, they would see the double talk and disinformation put out by Washington for what it was, withdraw their support for the war, and make it impossible for the politicians in Washington to do anything but put an end to it. The simple rehearsal of facts outlined by Hersh in the breaking story published in *The Washington Post* on November 13, 1969, was all that would be required.

About eighty people were taken quietly from their homes and herded together in the center of the village. A few hollered out, "No VC. No VC." Calley left Meadlo and a few others the responsibility of guarding the group. "You know what I want you to do with them," he told Meadlo. He came back ten minutes later. "Haven't you got rid of them yet? I want them dead. Waste them." Meadlo followed orders. He stood ten feet away from them and then he and Calley began shooting them. There are seventeen M16 bullets in a clip of ammunition. Calley and Meadlo each used close to four or five clips each. Women were huddled against their children, vainly trying to save them. Some continued to chant, "No VC." Others simply said, "No, No, No." . . . A lot of women had thrown themselves on top of the children to protect them, and the children were alive at first. Then the children who were old enough to walk got up and Calley began to shoot the children.[3]

Hersh's report of the deliberate and cold-blooded massacre of Vietnamese women and children at My Lai was an important turning point, not in the war itself, which continued on, but in the unfolding of American religious attitudes toward the war. In some respects, the My Lai story was also an important element of the larger tear in the social fabric of American culture that occurred in the late sixties in the context of the Vietnam War. Two very different religious worldviews pulled apart, one rooted in the internalization of religious principles in the direction of prophetic forms of ethical reasoning and the other rooted in the more traditional religious concern to preserve the stability of the material world and enhance its benefits through religious commitment to its underlying and ultimately sacred authority.

For opponents of the war, the My Lai incident was clear evidence of the moral bankruptcy of American military involvement in Vietnam. It was hard for them to imagine how anyone who had learned about what happened in My Lai could continue to support the war in good conscience. When graphic images of the My Lai victims taken by the combat photographer Ron Haeberle appeared in *Life* magazine, including one of several persons huddled together and crying out just before they were shot, many opponents of the war could hardly contain themselves.[4]

But not all Americans viewed the war with such receptivity to the disjuncture between internalized ethical principles and external social structures. Many people simply would not tolerate the idea that the cause for which young Americans were risking or losing their lives was unworthy. And many of these people supported the war because, at some fundamental and ultimately religious level, America was true and good and right, whatever it did. It was their world, and they were loyal to it and to the sacred authority underlying it. In this respect, supporters of the war were like traditional religious people in many parts of the world, intent on managing their relationships with the powers governing their material worlds, and religiously invested in those powers and in their underlying sacredness.

As Max Weber might have predicted, the prophetic types focused on the system of impersonal, bureaucratic forces at work in keeping America in Vietnam, which they often described as a machinelike military-industrial complex impervious to human feeling and ethical judgment. Meanwhile, as Weber also would have predicted, the priestly types worked to personify and humanize American military, political, and economic forces. They attacked critics of American policy in Vietnam for betraying the young Americans fighting there. And in an effort to defend a traditional worldview in which combat on behalf of these forces was noble and valiant and loyalty to those forces was expressed in highly personalized terms, they even defended William Calley. Alabama governor George Wallace said he was proud to meet the lieutenant and sorry that he had been subjected to a military trial. "They ought to spend the time trying folks who are trying to destroy this country," Wallace said, "instead of trying those who are serving their country." A lot of people agreed. Many Americans spoke up for Calley as a way of declaring their religious love for America and defending the sacred authority of its traditions. Richard Nixon's mail at the White House ran a hundred to one in support of the lieutenant, who sold his life story to Viking Press for $100,000. And American patriots bought nearly 250,000 copies of the audio record of "Battle Hymn of Lieutenant Calley," set to the tune of Julia Ward Howe's famous evangelical hymn about the glory of fighting for the cause of Christ. "My name is William Calley, I'm a soldier of this land," the first verse went. "I've vowed to do my duty and to gain the upper hand. But they've made me out a villain," the stanza went on. "They have stamped me with a brand. As we go marching on."[5]

In many important respects, the prophetic, countercultural perspective on America won out and the traditional, priestly worldview that George Wallace tried to defend began to crumble. Cynicism became widespread, especially toward the structures and leaders of the United States government. And some of the people who came to feel most alienated from that government were conservatives, such as George Wallace, who blamed the antiwar activists of the sixties and seventies for destroying the traditional religious fabric of American society. With regard to the shambles into which they perceived America to have fallen, conservatives became right-wing countercultural critics who emulated the ethical outrage, although not the same ethical values, as the antiwar protesters in the sixties and seventies. Across the spectrum of religious and political identification, belief in the sacred authority of the forces governing the world came under intense questioning and broke down.

In some ways, this breakdown of belief in the sacred canopy of American culture was unprecedented. A torrent of countercultural protest, expression, and experiment erupted and dominated music, art, fashion, academic life, and various forms of spiritual expression for some time to come. Ironically, the countercultural resistance to tradition and desire for alternative forms of expression was so powerful that it acquired some of the authority of the traditional worldview it sought to replace. Meanwhile, the traditional worldview, now deposed from its position of relatively unquestioned authority, acquired new status as a sacred myth of how America used to be, before the dark ages of cultural relativism and rampant hedonism that began in the sixties.

In other ways, however, the breakdown of traditional religious belief had strong precedents and antecedents in American history. The cultural critics of the sixties and seventies were part of the biggest and best-educated middle-class generation that America—and the world— had ever seen. And the writers and teachers who educated this generation laid the groundwork for the process of disenchantment that their readers and students went through. Henry David Thoreau's *Walden,* highly popular as a high school and college text for decades after World War II, made a carefully reasoned, ethical case for civil disobedience. Walt Whitman's *Leaves of Grass* called for the dissolution of conventional boundaries of race, class, and religion. Nathaniel Hawthorne's *The Scarlet Letter* made many young people in high school and college think twice about social sanctions against sex outside of marriage. And Arthur Miller's *The Crucible* encouraged a lot of American people to think that the authority figures presiding over American society could be dangerously unfair and harmful, not only by virtue of the material forces at their command, but also by virtue of the sacrality invested in them.

The teaching of internalized ethical analysis could be traced back to the Puritans, and especially to Puritans who stood up against the equation of cultural and religious values that other Puritans were trying to establish. One of the most celebrated examples of commitment to conscience was Roger Williams, of whom Perry Miller wrote in 1953 that "possibly no figure out of the American past today enjoys a greater prestige." Interestingly, in his widely used edition of William's writings, Miller sought to correct the impression that the founder of Rhode Island was in any way less pious or intensely committed to religious life than other Puritans in seventeenth-century New England. In fact, Miller argued, Williams's deep internalization of Christian and Puritan principles led him to call for complete religious freedom and to resist any government interference in religious life as well as any confusion between obedience to Caesar and obedience to Christ. In his discussion of this internalization of religious principle in the direction of ethics, Miller praised Williams as "the symbolic embodiment of that heroism which resists all those who, under whatever slogan, would force the conscience to things it cannot abide."[6]

Miller's celebration of the heroism of conscience epitomized by Roger Williams dovetailed with Weber's idea of the "prophetic type" as well as with the more general critique of social conformity that pervaded American education in the fifties, sixties, and seventies. Among theologians and religious types, "prophetic" criticism of conventional religion proved to be one of the most attractive aspects of neo-orthodox theology. The theologian Paul Tillich, who enjoyed immense popularity among American intellectuals in this era, emphasized the importance of "Jewish prophetism" within Protestant thought and defined the "Protestant principle" as an iconoclastic rejection of the external forms of religion. H. Richard Niebuhr, whose influence during the same decades was also significant, although not as pervasive as Tillich's, followed Weber's concept of the prophetic type more closely. In building on Weber's understanding of the prophetic type and using it to analyze various expressions of Protestant Christianity in American religious history, Niebuhr distinguished between forms of Christianity that invoked Christ in order to legitimate cultural norms and those that understood Christ as the ultimate, universal figure who transcended and passed judgment on the limited and self-serving values of every particular culture.[7] Niebuhr's emphasis on the need for ethical tension between Christ and culture had a profound impact on theological instruction in divinity schools across the United States as well as on coursework in the philosophy of religion in departments and programs of religious studies at many colleges and universities. And this appreciation of the need for ethical tension between ultimate values and cultural ones stoked the fires of countercultural protest ignited by the Vietnam War.

Personalism

Along with a willingness to stand up against society for the sake of conscience, a coinciding emphasis on personality also played a significant role in the dramatic events of the sixties. Insofar as the person was regarded as the context in which conscience and moral reasoning developed, efforts to understand the human personality and nurture its development reinforced the emphasis on conscience and moral reasoning widespread among educators and intellectuals in the fifties, sixties, and seventies. But many of these educators and intellectuals also considered the human personality and its development to be ends in themselves—the essence, goal, and achievement of civilized society as well as means to its creation. While at one level this attribution of ultimate value to personality reinforced commitment to ethical reasoning, it also personalized both the process and the outcome of ethical-reasoning in a way that made right ethical judgments hard to pin down. Of course, the complex relationship between personal expression and ethical reasoning was nothing new. As the very image of the prophet and its association with legendary biblical characters such as Jeremiah suggests, personalities strong-willed enough to internalize religious principles to the end of passing moral judgment on their societies often rendered both the process and the outcome of ethical reasoning in highly personalized form. As a result, prophetic types have not always been rationally consistent or law-abiding. In fact, in the process of expressing a vision or conveying a higher truth, prophetic types have often been mercurial and outrageously unconventional.

While prophetic types may always have tended to recast the meaning of moral truth in terms of their own personalities, never before had the phenomenon of personality been so cherished, celebrated, or democratically dispersed. In the fifties and early sixties, when many prophetic types were growing up, the whole culture seemed committed to the expression and development of the personalities of both children and adults. Benjamin Spock's permissive advice to let babies eat when they were hungry, rather than by preordained schedule, was widely followed, and many mothers took to heart his confidence-building encouragement to rely on their own common sense in handling almost any situation. Artistic expression of all kinds flourished, not only in schools and studios for professional artists, but also in elementary schools, churches, clubs, and adult classes. Psychoanalysis, psychotherapy, and human psychology boomed. And psychological thinking entered American religious life in full force. From the hottest and most sophisticated forms of theology to the most basic forms of pastoral care and counseling, the deliberate, self-conscious concern expressed for the individual personality and its needs was unprecedented. All of this attention to personality, and all of this enshrining of personality as an end in itself, helped to create a bumper crop of prophetic types, not only swelling the marketplace of ethical analysis against social conformity, but also personalizing and thereby relativizing moral truth to an extent never seen before.

In some cases, this unprecedented investment in personality was not as fully balanced with the process of ethical analysis as advocates of the centrality of human personality assumed it would be. For example, David Obst invested his own personality in the breaking of the My Lai story and the end of the war he expected it to bring in a way that coincided with an overreaching desire for fame. While this investment contributed to his tireless effort to overcome various obstacles to the story's exposure, it also may have interfered with his ability to think through the implications of the story more thoroughly. In his eagerness to expose what happened at My Lai, Obst did not take sufficient account of the fact that Calley had disobeyed the rules of military engagement he was sworn to follow. Nor did he really absorb and acknowledge the fact that once the story broke, Calley was arrested and brought to trial. Even if some of Calley's superiors had tried to cover up the incident, and even if many conservative Americans leapt to his defense, there was still a difference between what Calley did and officially sanctioned combat behavior. And even if Obst was right that the absence of any moral reason to invade Vietnam led directly to the breakdown in moral discipline exemplified by Calley, it was still something of a logical leap to equate the war effort with Calley's actions and to conclude that exposure of the story would end the war. Obst took all these leaps without hesitation because he completely gave himself over to the story, because he equated his own feelings of outrage against the war with moral truth, and because that equation was also an opportunity to build his own reputation and express himself on a national stage. A blurb by Taylor Branch on the jacket cover of Obst's memoir of the sixties and seventies alluded to this opportunistic participation in historic events: "Doubtless the most compelling book about David Obst yet written in this century."

MARTIN LUTHER KING JR.'S PERSONALISM

A more religiously significant instance of the interplay between ethical reasoning and investment in personality occurred in the mid-fifties in the mind of the man who was to become, in the following decade, one of the greatest prophetic activists the world had ever seen. As much as anyone else, Martin Luther King Jr. contributed to the transformation of American religion that began to crest in the sixties. And as well as anyone, he exemplified the prophetic type that emerged powerfully in the sixties as a complex expression of both ethical reasoning and ultimate commitment to personality.

As King himself told the story, the most prophetic moment of his life occurred in Montgomery, Alabama, in the early hours of January 28, 1956. He had received a disturbing phone call around midnight that kept him awake, and he was sitting alone afterward at his kitchen table while his wife and baby daughter slept. "Nigger, we are tired of you and your mess," King recalled the voice on the telephone saying, presumably in reference to the ongoing boycott of city buses that he had helped organize. "And if you aren't out of town in three days," the caller had threatened, "we're going to blow your brains out and blow up your house." As King sat brooding on this threat, an internal call from Jesus transformed his life. "It seemed at that moment," King remembered, "that I could hear an inner voice saying to me, 'Martin Luther, stand up for righteousness. Stand up for justice. Stand up for truth. And lo I will be with you, even until the end of the world.'" As he later recalled, "I heard the voice of Jesus saying still to fight on. He promised never to leave me, never to leave me alone. No never alone. No never alone. He promised never to leave me, never to leave me alone." In the months and years ahead, King looked back on this "kitchen conversion" as the pivotal moment of his life and often invoked it as a claim to public religious authority as well as a source of internal strength and purpose.[8]

Six months earlier, King had been awarded a Ph.D. in theology from Boston University, partly on the basis of a dissertation, written during his first year as pastor of Dexter Avenue Baptist Church, that compared conceptions of God in the writings of Paul Tillich and Henry Nelson Wieman. As Theodore Pappas discovered more than thirty years later, King plagiarized large portions of the dissertation from a previous dissertation on Tillich written at Boston University by Jack Boozer. While no one can know exactly how King fell into this dishonesty or rationalized it to himself, it is easy to imagine that he believed he had more important work than to research an original academic thesis. As one man who had been a classmate and friend at Boston University suggested after the story broke, "It was possible that the press of his work caused him to be careless."[9]

If King had immersed himself more fully in the work of an original thesis, he would have been less involved in religious and political life in Montgomery and history might well have passed him by. History might also have passed him by if he had forgone or postponed the dissertation in order to concentrate exclusively on religious and political life in Montgomery in 1955. As a young man who had grown up in the shadow of a father strongly identified with one part of the black community in Montgomery, the degree gave him an independent stature that enabled him to command respect from a wide cross section of that community. His stature and broad appeal among blacks in Montgomery was an important stepping-stone to his prominence as a national leader. A Ph.D. in theology from a prestigious white institution enhanced King's status and enabled him to assume a position of public leadership that would have been more difficult, if not impossible, to attain without the degree.

However much (or little) guilt King felt about it, the decision to plagiarize the dissertation was part of a larger network of decisions and opportunities that led to the religious call from Jesus that he experienced in January 1956. Over the course of the preceding year, King had already embarked on a powerful trajectory of public leadership. And the ethical message that launched this trajectory was one of commitment to the higher truth of the sacredness and dignity of every person. This commitment entailed resistance to the fear and hatred that prevented respect for persons and, if need be, resistance to laws that enshrined disrespect and perpetuated that fear and hatred. As well as justifying civil disobedience, this commitment to the higher law of personhood created a framework in which plagiarism might be excused. Whether or not he was concerned enough about the plagiarism to hope that a momentous historical role would ultimately justify his dishonesty, it is certain that when King heard Jesus say to him, "Stand up for justice. Stand up for truth," he understood Jesus to be referring to something larger and ultimately far more important than the originality of an academic thesis.

While King may have viewed his dissertation more as a way of getting his ticket stamped than anything else, other aspects of intellectual life at Boston University seem to have had a profound impact on his thinking. In fact, King's immersion in the personalist tradition of the School of Theology at Boston University contributed significantly to the message of his public leadership and to his highly self-conscious embodiment of it. As King himself declared in his 1958 book *Stride Toward Freedom*, personalism was his "basic philosophic position." And his teachers at Boston University agreed that his life and work exemplified the approach to social ethics that they taught. As Walter G. Muelder wrote in 1977, personalism "influenced his role in the civil rights struggle, the method of non-violence, and the extension of the struggle to issues of peace and economics."[10]

Emphasis on the ultimate importance of personal choice was a constant theme during King's years in graduate school. As Peter A. Bertocci, one of King's professors, explained this emphasis, making decisions about what one "ought" to do in a particular situation was the essence of what it meant to be human. The "irreducible existence of oughting," as Bertocci put it, was always constituted in the context of the alternatives of a given situation. People chose X over Y because X was better than Y. In other words, at the most fundamental level, the important process of ethical decision making was not really about intellectual adherence to some independent theory or set of rules about truth. It was about making choices, in real and specific situations, between one option and another.[11] Given this fundamental human reality, Bertocci and his colleagues believed, the clearer, larger, and more comprehensive the view a person had of a situation and its alternatives, the better the choices that person would make. Thus an important part of King's personalist education at Boston University involved training in situation ethics—the conceptualization of moral reasoning in terms of situations that centered on persons choosing higher goods over lower ones, and lesser evils over greater ones.

Boston University's investment in the personalist school of thought began in 1876, when Borden Parker Bowne took up a teaching post as professor of philosophy after graduate studies at New York University and then at universities in Paris, Halle, and Göttingen where various forms of philosophical idealism were taught. In a series of influential books, Bowne argued that personhood was the core of religious life and that the indivisible unity of the person mirrored the indivisible unity of God. By focusing on personhood as ultimate reality, he argued, men and women could escape the oppressive authoritarianism associated with more supernatural interpretations of Christianity. Focusing on personhood would enable them to strengthen their active commitments to religious and ethical life and bring those commitments into a modern, scientific age.

After Bowne's retirement in 1910, a cadre of philosophers and theologians at Boston University carried forward his commitment to personalism by spelling out its implications for social ethics. Through the work of these scholars, Boston University became the most prestigious and influential Methodist university in the northern United States. The School of Theology attracted thousands of ministerial students over the years as well as a significant number of graduate students, many of them with bachelor's degrees from Ohio Wesleyan, Millsaps, Baker University, Nebraska Wesleyan, DePauw, and other Methodist-affiliated schools, seeking to prepare for academic careers in church-related colleges.

Although King was a Baptist and not a Methodist, he was drawn to Boston University because it was the philosophical and theological center of the personalist approach to social ethics that he had learned to admire as a divinity student at Crozer Theological Seminary in Chester, Pennsylvania. At Crozer, he was torn between the idealism of the social gospel movement, with its emphasis on the kingdom of God as a world of social justice that all Christians should work to bring about, and Reinhold Niebuhr's critique of the naivete involved in thinking that social institutions could ever be cleansed of corruption or injustice.[12] The personalist approach to social ethics offered a way out of the problem with the social gospel that Niebuhr identified. As Niebuhr himself believed, persons were capable of love, while social institutions were not. It was unrealistic to suppose that government or industry would ever exemplify Christian ideals. Nevertheless, individuals did have real influence on those institutions and could redirect specific policies carried out by those institutions toward more humane ends. This modified, personalistic approach to social justice suited King and became the focus of his graduate study at Boston University from 1952 to 1955.

In working his way through the ideas expressed by Rauschenbusch, Niebuhr, and the Boston personalists, King constructed a form of Christian theology that not only worked for him, but represented the combined efforts of several generations of American Protestant thinkers. More compellingly than anyone else of his time, King synthesized the insights and spiritual characteristics of different denominational traditions. He joined the neo-orthodox critique of moral perfection advanced by the Lutheran Reinhold Niebuhr to the social gospel tradition of the Baptist Walter Rauschenbusch by focusing on the interplay between personality and society characteristic of Methodist personalism. He pulled these intellectual and religious traditions together in the context of his own African-American Baptist tradition, which emphasized the real and immediate need for both personal and social salvation. While other American Protestants were working across denominational boundaries to create new forms of ecumenical cooperation, King brought this ecumenism into the public square in the form of a mighty demonstration of personhood.

King went to Boston University intending to study with Edgar S. Brightman, whose understanding of the "personality principle" was often identified with personalism in the forties and fifties. Focusing on the human personality as the "seat of value," Brightman emphasized the freedom of the individual to rise above the norms and injustices of society by idealizing something better. Brightman believed that the human personality incorporated a social principle that enabled people to recognized their interdependence and work together despite their differences. Through a dialectical process of balancing ends and means and accepting the fact of evil yet striving to overcome it, Brightman believed that the human personality could undergo a developmental process in which it became more and more like Christ, the ultimate exemplar of rational love and unifier of all humanity.

In the fall of 1952, soon after King enrolled in his two-semester course on Hegel, Brightman fell ill, withdrew from teaching, and died soon thereafter. Responsibility for the Hegel course shifted to Peter Bertocci. And responsibility for directing King's dissertation devolved on L. Harold DeWolf, who had supervised Jack Boozer's dissertation, and who also undertook the task of formalizing Brightman's moral laws. In his representation of these laws, DeWolf added a principle of community in order to emphasize "that individuals are not only affected by and are in turn obligated to other individuals, but are also in reciprocal relations with the communities of which they are members and also frequently with other communities." Brightman's emphasis on personality as the seat of value, DeWolf's emphasis on personality as a potent factor in the development of community life, and Bertocci's emphasis on the necessity of choosing between alternatives in the process of ethical decision making all contributed to the sense of moral resolve that King came to experience and to embody.

The underlying connection between self and community was an aspect of personalism in which another of King's professors at Boston University, Walter G. Muelder, was especially interested. Muelder stressed the essential creativity of personality, its unpredictability, and its freedom from any determinative scheme of history. According to Muelder, "In all historical wholes pulsates creative personality. Persons interact with a physical environment and with impersonal, unconscious forces such as Marx identified in the economic order, but personality is the bearer of common spirit and the key to the temporal development of meaning and value."[13] In the case of Martin King, the personality that crystallized as a result of an inner, transformative call from Jesus became the bearer of a process of communal and ultimately national transformation.

As David Halberstam's book on the young people involved in the civil rights movement showed, King was not the only one whose personal identification with Jesus enabled heroic acts of self-sacrifice that changed America. In the context of the highly personalized idealism of their religious faith, the young people who inspired the civil rights movement claimed respect for themselves, each other, and their communities, and stood up against forces of racism and oppression that in other times and places had seemed insurmountable. King stood out among these young people and came to embody and also overshadow their heroism, at least partly because of his advanced education in theology and his consequent ability to unify several different strands of Protestant thought.[14]

DOROTHY DAY'S PERSONALISM

In his book on personalism as the defining and galvanizing element of postwar radicalism, James T. Farrell argued that the 1960s really began on June 15, 1955, when Dorothy Day and twenty-seven friends gathered in New York City to protest the annual nationwide civil defense drill known as Operation Alert. In violation of the New York State Defense

Emergency Act of 1951, which required citizens to participate in civil defense drills, Day and her colleagues from the Catholic Worker movement, along with other activists representing the Fellowship of Reconciliation and the War Resisters League, were arrested for noncooperation. Over the next six years, the number of protesters at the annual civil defense drills multiplied. In 1960, a thousand protesters sang the civil rights anthem "We Shall Overcome" as police ordered them to comply with the law and participate in the drill. In 1961, the last year of the drill, a crowd of two thousand gathered for the protest rally in City Hall Park. "After that," Farrell wrote, "there were the Sixties."[15]

Day's civil disobedience was rooted in a form of personalism that was similar to King's in certain important respects. Like King and the Boston personalists with whom he studied, Day attributed ultimate value to persons and believed that resistance to governmental laws was justified if those laws violated the higher law of respect for the dignity and sanctity of persons. But her background and early adult life were very different from King's. And the concepts and experiences associated with her form of personalism were at once more radical and more conservative than his. While King's personalism was essentially a modified form of social and religious liberalism, Day's personalism was more radical in its alienation from democratic individualism and liberal currents of religious thought and more conservative in its loyalty to traditional forms of religious authority and supernatural belief.

Raised by parents from Protestant backgrounds but without much church commitment, Day often found loneliness coinciding with her own religious introspections. An idealist at heart, as a young woman she participated in leftist organizations of various kinds, including the Communist Party. But dissatisfaction with the intellectual abstractness of leftist, secular philosophies, a strong desire to identify more completely with the lives and sufferings of the poor, and intense feelings brought about by the birth of her daughter Tamar led Day into the Catholic Church. The mysticism of the Church relieved what she referred to as her "long loneliness" and enabled her to define her life in terms of a religious vocation of commitment to the poor and in terms of the sanctity of human life.

Through her fellow worker Peter Maurin, a former De La Salle brother who had worked to establish rest homes for the poor in Paris before emigrating to the United States, Day encountered a form of personalism rooted in the French Catholic idealism of Emmanuel Mounier and in the Russian Orthodoxy of Nicolas Berdyaev. These thinkers emphasized the antagonism between modern industrial society and the mystical idealism of the Catholic Church, arguing that capitalist society treated persons like cogs in a machine rather than as ends in themselves deserving of moral respect and a living wage. Like Dorothy Day and the Catholic Workers inspired by her example, the French personalists sided with the poor against the impersonal and depersonalizing forces of modern society. And they were willing, even eager, to sacrifice themselves by standing up against these forces. But they were not social reformers in the same sense as Martin Luther King Jr. and other American Protestant civil rights activists. Day was not striving to obtain voting rights and other forms of social enfranchisement. She was not an advocate of democratic individualism, as King was, attempting to make a modern democracy live up to its own principles by extending civil rights to a disenfranchised sector of society. King was a religious visionary, but a religious and political pragmatist as well. He was trying to create a more politically just society, and he understood how religious values and religious idealism could help bring that about. He was not a mystic, or a utopian, or an opponent of what he regarded as the fundamental democratic principles of American society. He did not love poverty, as Day did, or seek spiritual sanctity, as Day did, by identifying with poverty.

A shrewd and effective politician, King utilized civil disobedience as a means to the end of overturning Jim Crow laws and attaining voting rights for blacks. He utilized religious principles and religious rhetoric in much the same way, as highly effective means for attaining quite specific and realistic political ends. As an ethicist, he invested persons with ultimate value. But he translated the implications of that investment into concrete, political terms. And he was a pragmatist in his ethical relativism, willing to plagiarize a dissertation not because plagiarism was good, but because it enabled him to devote himself more completely to a higher cause.

As a religious man, King experienced Jesus, and the voice of Jesus, in a very concrete, personal way. In his response to Jesus's call to stand up for truth and justice in the midst of formidable and terrifying opposition, King held nothing of himself back. He showed great heroism, even to the point of continuing to speak out in public knowing that numerous enemies were planning his assassination. But this personal identification with Jesus carried him through to death in a way that was completely pragmatic. King was able to surmount his fear of death because he knew that the personhood for which he fought would be diminished if he backed down or ran away. And like other pragmatists, he believed that human beings created their futures through imagination and will and that the means by which the future came about was the stuff out of which the future was made. In the context of this understanding of the interdependence of means and ends, he went on toward his goals with the prospect of death around and before him.

Dorothy Day was much more of an absolutist. With respect to politics, she conceptualized her antiwar activism as a protest against all forms of war, as a witness to the peace represented by Christ, and as penance for especially atrocious military violence, such as the bombing of Hiroshima, that had occurred in the past. With respect to ethics, Day was like King in her strong commitment to nonviolence, in her attribution of ultimate value to persons, and in her emphasis on the organic connection that existed among persons and between persons and society. But Day's commitment to nonviolence was not a strategy for facilitating social change involving the use of public pressure to force specific changes, as King's was. Day was a more radical witness to the principle of nonviolence, a principle to which she was committed regardless of its strategic benefits or deficits. And rather than being an ethical relativist willing to think about choosing the lesser of two evils or between one good and another, higher one, Day conceptualized her choices more starkly and less pragmatically. For example, the abortion she had as a young woman was never something she could excuse in pragmatic terms, as King may have excused his plagiarism. Rather, it was "the taste of hell in her mouth" that only the birth of her daughter Tamar "cleansed from her soul."[16] This tendency to absolutize ethical choice and invest in moral absolution reflected religious beliefs and experiences rather different from King's. While King emulated the courage and self-sacrifice of Jesus in the process of trying to bring about political change, Day witnessed to divine atonement and mystical union with Christ by protesting against violence and committing herself to solidarity with the poor.

Day was much more of a radical religious figure than King. She was a political activist but not a politician. Religious experience and commitment justified and compelled her activism, but political considerations did not shape her religious experience or define her religious commitment. In these respects, her activism in the fifties and early sixties was more of a harbinger of the religious radicalism in the late sixties and seventies than was King's liberal pragmatism. But the commitment to personalism they shared represented the larger context in which converging, competing, and to some extent conflicting religious agendas were played out. This complexity needs to be taken into account in order to understand the personalist ethos of the sixties and the confusion, creativity, and wild challenges to conventional religious wisdom that it produced.

Sacramental Resistance and Confusion

In May 1968, the Josephite priest Philip Berrigan and his brother Daniel, a Jesuit priest, along with seven other radical priests and nuns, broke into government offices in Catonsville, Maryland, seized draft records, and destroyed them with homemade napalm, the chemical sprayed by U.S. bombers in raids over Vietnam. In similar break-ins at other draft board offices, the Berrigans and other Catholic war resisters poured lamb's blood or red paint over official records. In the early eighties, after Daniel Berrigan was arrested for breaking into a General Electric plant and vandalizing two nuclear warheads, he pointed to Dorothy Day as the inspiration for his activity. "Without Dorothy," he said during the trial, "the resistance we offered would have been simply unthinkable."[17]

In the late sixties and early seventies, dramatic acts of resistance by the Catonsville Nine and other groups of priests and nuns inspired a wave of student antiwar activity at Catholic colleges and universities and led to a significant increase in the number of Catholics petitioning to avoid the draft as conscientious objectors. At Notre Dame during this time, more than a few students burned their draft cards during masses on campus.

There was a theatrical, ritualistic, and sacramental element to these acts of resistance that derived from the Catholic sensibilities of those who performed them. Like parodies of the mass, the burning of draft cards and the spilling of blood and napalm on draft records linked the sacrificial presence of Christ with suffering and death in Vietnam.

These acts were highly provocative because of their religious dimension, but if their political meaning was clear, their exact religious meaning was not. These acts of ritualized resistance were invested with strong allusions to the sacrificial presence of Christ. The blood of the Lamb was being spilled in Vietnam, as it was everywhere people were suffering and dying. But the Catholic war resisters were not celebrating suffering and death in Vietnam in the same way as they celebrated the redemptive power of Christ's presence in the Eucharist. In protesting the carnage in Vietnam in these parodies of the mass, the resisters were, in part, affirming the mystical unity of Christ. But at the same time, they were breaking through that unity and its affirmation of the unity of the Church and its people in a spirit of personal, political, and prophetic outrage.

More than the spilling of blood was involved in these and other parodies of Catholic ritual and iconography. In interesting (and to some people horrifying) ways, the whole phenomenon of Catholic sacramentalism was split open and spilled out into the larger culture in the late sixties and early seventies. For Catholics, the meanings and expressions of sacramentalism were expanding as a result of the new spiritual openness and revitalization associated with Vatican II. This expansiveness and openness to innovation coincided with the increasingly influential roles that Catholics were playing as leaders in American society and as definers of the American culture. As Catholic assimilation to American culture accelerated, partly as a result of the mainstreaming and middle-classing of Catholics within American society and partly as a result of the openness to other religious traditions encouraged by Vatican II, Catholic sensibilities increasingly affected Protestants and Jews. In the volatile context of the Vietnam War, the sacramentalized forms of resistance that characterized Catholic reactions to the war had an impact on those belonging to other religions, as did the Catholic habit of deep ambivalence toward American culture.

Some of the most creative (and horrifying) expressions of this volatile mix occurred in celluloid form. Because of its visual plasticity, film proved to be a medium particularly amenable to the splintering and spilling over of sacramental visions of reality. Among the films whose parody of the Catholic sacramentalism was as startling and as ambiguous as pouring lamb's blood on draft records, *The Godfather* surely tops the list. Based on a 1969 novel about the Sicilian American mafia

by Mario Puzo, Francis Ford Coppola's first two *Godfather* films, re-
leased in 1972 and 1974, respectively, have been described as together
representing "the most significant American film since *Citizen Kane.*"
In ushering in a film era of operatic violence and religious irony, *The
Godfather* exemplified important aspects of the extraordinary transformation of American religion and its role in American culture.

One of the most provocative episodes in the 1972 film involves back-
and-forth cutting between scenes of a Catholic baptism and a series of
Mafia assassinations. Michael Corleone's establishment of his own authority as the new don of the Corleone family coincides with a church
ceremony in which he becomes godfather to his sister's baby. While
Michael (Al Pacino) is in church becoming his niece's godfather, his
men are assassinating other dons and their accomplices to ensure Michael's supremacy as a Mafia godfather. Images of the detailed formality
of the priest's preparation for the baptism are interspersed with scenes
of Corleone henchmen preparing themselves, dressing carefully and
loading their gleaming weapons. Scenes of the priest's sprinkling holy
water onto the baby's head are juxtaposed with images of surprise at-
tacks and violent, unanticipated death. Michael's somber, ritual renunciation of Satan during the baptismal ceremony coincides with more
scenes of elegantly choreographed and gory death. As Paul Giles wrote
in an insightful analysis of the film, "In *The Godfather,* big business,
crime, and theology are represented as cognate, with each system ironizing and destabilizing the others."

This ironizing style, Giles went on to explain, involved a kind of
duplicity that, in a twisted way, resonated with Catholic theology itself:
"Michael's duplicity, our sense of him facing two ways at once, is a
(blasphemous) counterpart to that philosophical irony endemic to the
Catholic tradition." This philosophical irony involved the idea that the
spiritual nature of the material world could be radically transformed
without any loss of its visceral and palpable reality. In the film, what
it means to be a godfather has coinciding religious, familial, criminal,
and business meanings that all revolve around the reality, mystery, and
esthetic spectacle of life and death. The material aspects of this process
are always elevated by spiritual analogues even as the spiritual aspects
of the process are being pulled down and out through material analogues. To paraphrase William F. Lynch, "matter is always attending
its putative transubstantiation into spirit." In the case of *The Godfather,*

this transubstantiation was not only putative but cinematic. And this cinematic transubstantiation was controlled not by the Church, but by the reckless genius of artistic originality.[18]

One did not have to convert to Catholicism to become acquainted with, and affected by, its spectacular, mystical sensuality. An infusion of Catholic sacramentalism transformed American culture through a variety of dislocated forms, from the spilling of blood on draft records to the interplay of violent crime, big business, and ritual atonement in *The Godfather*. Many Americans, including a sizeable number baptized in the Catholic Church, did not understand either the connections or the disconnections between these cultural outgrowths of Catholic sacramentalism and its traditional religious expression in the Eucharist. Consequently, Americans of various religious stripes absorbed these new permutations of Catholic sacramentalism without really knowing what had hit them. And not surprisingly, this process did not result in an influx of conversions to Catholicism but in a more diffuse attunement to sacramentalism wherever it could be found or invented.

In 1959, while contrasting what he perceived to be the more straightforward this-world emphasis of American Protestantism with the double vision and mysticism of Catholicism, the Jewish-born Norman Mailer declared the former to be "square" while the latter was "hip." In 1960, Mailer joined Dorothy Day and other radical Catholics to protest the nationwide civil defense drill, and in 1961 his name was listed as a supporting contributor to *The Catholic Worker*, along with that of other New Left writers, including Gary Snyder, Robert Duncan, Allen Ginsberg, and William Burroughs. This group's unorthodox appropriation of sacramental experience and application of it to a politics of protest against American society led the cultural critic Theodore Roszak to characterize their activism as "the politics of the Loony Left."[19] In the work of these and other writers and activists, the sacramentalism that traditional Catholics linked to their Church became a free-floating affair independent of Catholicism and even of Christianity itself.

In his 1968 book *Armies of the Night*, Mailer described an especially creative demonstration of this free-floating sacramentalism. In Washington, D.C, in 1967, the antiwar activist and hippie leader Abbie Hoffman circulated a petition to levitate and exorcise the Pentagon. As

Hoffman told the newspapers, once the Pentagon was three hundred feet off the ground, it would "turn orange and vibrate until all evil emissions had fled," and through the magical cleansing that resulted, the Vietnam War would come to an end. Mailer described this half-serious, countercultural parody of a protest demonstration this way.

> Now while the Indian triangle and the cymbal sounded, while a trumpet offered a mournful subterranean wail . . . so did a solemn voice speak something approximate to this: "In the name of the am-ulets of touching, seeing, groping, hearing and loving, we call upon the powers of the cosmos to protect our ceremonies in the name of Zeus, in the name of Anubis, god of the dead . . . in the name of the lives of the soldiers in Vietnam who were killed because of a bad karma, in the name of sea-born Aphrodite, in the name of Magna Mater, in the name of Dionysus, Zagreus, Jesus, Yahweh, the un-nameable, the quintessent finality of the Zoroastrian fire, in the name of Hermes, in the name of the Beak of Sok, in the name of the scarab, in the name, in the name, in the name of the Tyrone Power Pound Cake Society in the Sky . . . in the name of the flowing living universe . . . we call upon the spirit . . . to raise the Pentagon from its destiny and preserve it."[20]

Mailer connected this wild call to the divine principles of several different religions and pseudoreligions with a sudden, hard turn toward religious radicalism taken by hippies in their explorations with LSD. Until the exorcism of the Pentagon, Mailer reported, only "the blandest reports from the religious explorers of LSD" had surfaced. For several years, "vague Tibetan lama goody-goodness auras of religiosity" were "the only publicly announced or even rumored fruit from all trips back from the buried Atlantis of LSD." But "now suddenly an entire gen-eration of acid-heads seemed to have said goodbye to easy visions of heaven, no, now the witches were here, and rights of exorcism, and black terrors of the night." In their countercultural, psychedelic travels, these hippies had come back to the Vietnam War through the under-side of Christianity and its medieval past. "The hippies had gone from Tibet to Christ to the Middle Ages, now they were Revolutionary Alchemists," and from Mailer's perspective "that was all right." After all, "he was a Left Conservative himself." And thus with some enjoyment, he joined in the chanting, "Out, demons, out! Out, demons, out!"[21]

LSD was not always a prerequisite for the witchcraft and revolutionary alchemy. While Mailer associated witchcraft with bad acid trips and "black terrors of the night," some religious folk took a more benign view of the old arts and extraecclesiastic forms of sacramentalism. The feminist philosopher Mary Daly was among the most influential of these radical religious innovators. Stimulated by the dislocation of sacramentalism in the sixties, she became a practitioner of the redemptive art of witchcraft in the seventies.

In the early sixties, when there were no doctoral programs in Catholic theology in the United States that admitted women, Daly pursued graduate studies in theology and philosophy at the University of Fribourg, Switzerland, where the state prohibited the exclusion of women. While completing her doctoral work in medieval philosophy at Fribourg in 1965, she also began a book on the status of women in the Catholic Church. Her vision of the book crystallized during a month in Rome in the fall of 1965 when she attended a session of the second Vatican Council. As she recalled the experience ten years later, the visual impact of one event in particular stimulated a thought process that shaped her critique of the Catholic Church and eventually led to her renunciation of Christianity altogether.

Having borrowed a journalist's ID that enabled her to observe the spectacle of a pontifical mass from seats reserved for the press high up in St. Peter's Basilica, she recalled "a multitude of cardinals and bishops—old men in crimson dresses." She also recalled the presence of "a few Catholic women, mostly nuns in long black dresses with heads veiled," in a separate section reserved for "auditors." "The contrast between the arrogant bearing and colorful attire of the 'princes of the church' and the humble, self-deprecating manner and somber clothing of the very few women was appalling," Daly wrote in 1975. "Watching the veiled nuns shuffle to the altar rail to receive Holy Communion from the hands of a priest was like observing a string of lowly ants at some bizarre picnic. In retrospect," she added parenthetically, "it seems to have been an ant-poisonous picnic." In interviews after this plenary session, Daly remembered, the women "repeatedly expressed their gratitude for the privilege of being present" and seemed not to fully comprehend the extent to which the whole performance constructed their inferiority as women. Daly herself "did not grasp the full meaning of the scene at once," but its visual impact persisted. "Its multileveled message burned its way deep into my consciousness. No Fellini movie," she concluded with telling insight into the ironizing dislocation of sacramentalism that occurred in the sixties and seventies and its disjointed, cinematic quality, "could have outdone this unintended self-satire of Catholicism."[22]

In 1968, Daly published *The Church and the Second Sex* while teaching as a junior faculty member in the philosophy department at Boston College, a Catholic university affiliated with the Jesuit order. She was denied tenure at Boston College in 1969, but the administration reversed its decision and awarded her tenure and promotion after students organized a large demonstration on campus in her support, obtained more than two thousand signatures on a petition submitted to the administration on her behalf, and sponsored a seven-hour teach-in on academic freedom in which she and several professors who had been fired from other universities participated. Witches from the Boston area arrived on campus and put a hex on the university. The night following that ritual, protesters covered the administration building in red graffiti. "The campus became a circus grounds," Daly recalled, and "my case was receiving national, international, supernatural publicity."

It was "a transforming process" in which Daly herself became a religious and political icon. Her intuitions, insights, and free associations attained a kind of pseudorevelatory status. While her influence was significant, her own celebration of herself and her increasingly ribald and unfettered mockery of Christianity had the effect of destabilizing and personalizing her own and her followers' concepts of revelation, prophecy, and sacrament. In the 1970s, she denounced Christian belief in the fatherhood of God and its unjust and harmful implications for women. By the 1980s she was arguing that, as part of its misogynist agenda, Christianity had usurped the authentic and inherent power of women's natural sacramentality and replaced it with an authoritarian, repressive, and woman-hating institution called the Church. She described the dresses of priests, bishops, cardinals, and popes as expressions of transvestism that hinted at the true origins of sacramentalism in women's nature and at the appropriation of women's nature-based sacramental power by otherwise impotent and essentially unnatural male priests.[23]

Countercultural Efforts to Reenchant the World

Revolutionary reversals and revisions gained strong footholds in American religious and cultural life during the late sixties. A disjointed, dislocated sacramentalism spilled into the larger culture from Catholicism, coinciding with the internalization of religion in the direction of ethical analysis associated with prophetic types in Protestantism and Judaism. Neither one of these sources of religious counterculturalism was predictable or manageable. Taken together, as they were in many minds, the two constituted a powerfully volatile and transformative mix.

One area of cultural understanding in which reversal and revision made especially strong headway had to do with popular perceptions of Native American peoples and their relationship to the government and people of the United States. "Once," as Tom Engelhardt recalled in *The End of Victory Culture*, "any moviegoer knew that out there somewhere, behind those rocks or up in those trees, down that valley or on the ledges above that mountain pass, *they* waited patiently for the moment when their ambush would be sprung and the whites would fall like leaves." As "the canvas-covered wagons of civilization rolled forward," cunning and bloodthirsty Indians waited to descend upon the pioneers. Indians were essential to the plot, as was a harrowing and violent encounter between Indians and whites and the inevitable triumph of Euro-American civilization. After all, asked Engelhardt, "[w]ith good cover and better technology, what choice did the whites have but to mow down the enemy, wipe them out?"[24]

These cinematic expectations were rooted in historical reality, and especially in the history of violence between whites and Indians in the western territories of the United States in the nineteenth century. After the Indian tribes of the eastern woodlands had been subjugated and either pushed or forcibly removed west, western tribes were moved further west, antagonized in various ways, and eventually pressed onto relatively small land reserves in order to minimize their interference with white settlers. Dime novels and traveling Wild West shows provided fictionalized accounts of conflicts between cowboys and Indians that served as models for "westerns" on the silver screen. And westerns, in turn, served as models for other action films, especially those about World War II, such as *The Sands of Iwo Jima* (1949), starring one of America's most famous cowboys, John Wayne.

Acceptance of the basic assumptions underlying the western film genre was never universal in American culture. Scholars, activists, romantics, and of course, many Indians themselves resisted the popular stereotypes of Euro-Americans as good guys and Indians as subhuman savages who had to be forced into submission, if not completely exterminated. More positive images of Indians go all the way back to the sixteenth-century Dominican Bartolomé de Las Casas, who criticized the Spanish conquest of North America and spoke out against Spanish plan to enslave Native Americans and to the seventeenth-century founder of Rhode Island, Roger Williams, who compared the moral characters of Native Americans and Europeans to the detriment of the latter. With regard to the Narragansett Indians he lived with, Williams wrote, "I have known them leave their house and mat, To lodge a friend or stranger, When Jews and Christians oft have sent Christ Jesus to the manger."[25]

In northeastern North America, such relatively positive images of Indians as simple and wholesome were heavily outweighed by negative images of Indian cruelty, filthiness, and stupidity until the end of the French and Indian War in 1763, when the threat of Indian attack east of Ohio dramatically declined. Beginning in the late eighteenth century, images of Indians as noble savages gained popularity as numerous historians, playwrights, novelists, poets, and visual artists drew romantic portraits of the charms of Indian life as part of a deliberate effort to create a literary and artistic culture that would distinguish America from Britain and Europe. To some extent, these romantic portraits made the Indian warrior an emblem of America itself, a symbol of the fierce pride, spirit of independence, natural intelligence, and natural skillfulness believed to characterize the proud citizens of the new American republic.[26]

In the nineteenth century, even as Indian fighters such as William Henry Harrison, Andrew Jackson, Kit Carson, and George Armstrong Custer dominated popular notions of American heroism, the Transcendentalist movement contributed to a romantic view of Native Americans that led to condemnation of Indian fighting and calls for the fair treatment of native peoples. In celebrating Indians for their practical knowledge about the natural world and for their supposedly childlike familiarity with nature's spiritual powers, Transcendentalists played a leading role in shaping romantic images of Native Americans as "noble savages" who understood nature as a primary source of religious experience. When he lived at Walden Pond, the Transcendentalist Henry David Thoreau tried to experience the pond as Indians had experienced it in earlier days. In his journal, Thoreau recorded the thrill of hearing a robin "even as he might have sounded to the Indian, singing at evening upon the elm above his wigwam." Later, in the woods of Maine, Thoreau filled his notebooks with information about how Indians actually lived, and he sought inspiration by studying the behavior and personalities of his Indian guides.[27]

Beginning with Helen Hunt Jackson's *Century of Dishonour*, first published in 1881, scholarly studies of the history of encounters between whites and Indians in North America were often critical of Euro-American attitudes and policies with respect to native peoples. By 1965, the historian Robert F. Berkhofer Jr reported, "books upon any phase of American Indian history usually contain, explicitly or implicitly, a denunciation of American policy and express sympathy for the maltreated aborigines whose culture, if not life, was destroyed. Modern scholars," Berkhofer added, "find a delicious irony in the disparity between classic American ideals and the actual treatment of the first Americans."[28]

In the context of the Vietnam War, this long-standing undercurrent of resistance to popular stereotypes of whites as good guys and Indians as bad guys acquired new force. For several reasons, denunciation of American treatment of Indians was more concerted and aggressive than ever before. More people than ever before were being educated to think critically about social institutions and conventions. Thanks to sharp interest in myths and symbols in the academic areas of religious studies, cultural anthropology, and American studies, the idea that there *was* a mythology of America caught on, especially the idea that there was a popular mythology of America as a frontier civilization with a providential destiny that required forcing anyone in its way to submit or die. Disaffection with the war in Vietnam coincided with and stimulated these intellectual trends. Criticism of American policies toward Indians emerged as a framework for denouncing American involvement in Vietnam and for putting that involvement into a broad and shameful historical context.

The discovery that some American servicemen in Vietnam were using cowboy-and-Indian metaphors to describe their relationships to the Vietnamese supported the use of American Indian history as a framework for interpreting Vietnam. In an article first published in February 1970 as part of the initial airing of the Pentagon Papers, the *New York Times* reported that U.S. Navy enginemen assigned to patrol duty on the Vamcotay River near the Cambodian border called the areas surrounding their boats "Indian Country." A subsequent article later in the same month reported that U.S. Marines in the Queson Valley also used the term "Indian Country" to describe "all areas outside their small circular fortresses." The currency of such metaphors among military folk helped establish American Indian history as an interpretative framework for the Vietnam War. And this interpretative framework produced new studies of "the mythology of the American frontier" that looked at the history of warfare between Indians and Euro-Americans through the prism of Vietnam.[29]

Millions of Americans who attended college in the sixties and seventies learned to admire American examples of the prophetic type, such as Roger Williams, and to identify with Henry David Thoreau and his willingness to go to jail rather than pay taxes to support government policies to which he was opposed. They also identified with Martin Luther King Jr. and his civil disobedience and eventual martyrdom in the cause of civil rights. The miscalculations, stupidities, and cultural arrogance that attended American involvement in the Vietnam War fueled identification with the moral resistance of these heroes, as did the terrifying prospect, faced by many young men, of being drafted to fight and die in a war they did not believe in. Through their rejection of American involvement in Vietnam, these young men became prophetic types themselves. And as prophetic types protesting the Vietnam War, they also rejected the mythology of cowboys and Indians they had grown up with. Rejection of this mythology not only exposed its victimization of Native Americans, but also stirred renewed interest in the lives, struggles, and mythologies of Native Americans themselves.

Interlaced with the comparisons between American Indian history and Vietnam, and with discussion of their ethical implications, were streaks of radical outrage and romantic idealism. To some extent, this radical romanticism undermined the very process of ethical reasoning that had generated historical criticism of American policy toward Indians as well as opposition to the war in Vietnam. Thus in his book on Indian-hating in American culture, the revisionist historian Richard Drinnon simply dismissed Alden T. Vaughan's argument that the seventeenth-century Puritans had reason to fear the hostility of Pequot Indians, as he did Francis Paul Prucha's argument that the most egregious violence against Indians was instigated by frontier outlaws in defiance of American law and government policy. Ironically, the commitment to a black-and-white interpretation of Indian victimization was as stereotypical as the game of cowboys and Indians, only now the Indians had all the morality on their side.

The radical idealism involved in this reversal of popular mythology was partly an expression of the prophetic stance these critics assumed with respect to American culture. The tendency of prophetic types to imbue their own feelings of moral outrage with the status of higher law was accentuated by the cultivation of personality in American culture after World War II. But prophetic willingness to stand against society in the name of moral principle was not the only source of the radical idealism evinced in the moral reversal of cowboys and Indians. The enthusiasm for this reversal was also linked to a tendency to sacramentalize the Indian. This tendency was fed by a tradition of nature religion in American culture associated with Transcendentalism, alternative medicine, environmentalism, and modernist appreciation of the vitality of primitive art and ritual. It was also encouraged by a kind of generic sacramentalization of the victim, a long-standing aspect of Christianity that in twentieth-century America was especially characteristic of radical Catholicism. Mixed together as they were in the sixties and seventies, these various elements all contributed to the celebration of Native Americans as both victims and redeemers of American culture. Through this powerful swirl of prophetic criticism, naturalist philosophy, and radical sacramentalism stimulated by the catalytic violence and disillusionment with the Vietnam War, Native Americans came to function almost as Christ figures. In the eyes of many people turned off by cowboy culture, Native Americans were the innocent, righteous, stalwart keepers of moral good. They were America's greatest virtuosos of mystical experience and most venerable masters of spiritual wisdom. They were the ones whose powerful attunement with nature, ancient religious traditions, and cultural lifeways held the keys to American salvation. And this sacramentalization of Native Americans epitomized and helped to carry forward the transformation of American religion that began to occur in the context of the Vietnam War. Opposition to the war in Vietnam sparked new interest in Native American peoples, not only as victims of government policies denounced as genocidal, but also as repositories of religious wisdom long associated with romantic appreciation of nature and the concept of the noble savage.

As a result of this process of sacramentalization, Native Americans became objects of New Age veneration. Hyemeyohsts Storm's *Seven Arrows* (1972), for example, represented Cheyenne culture with psychedelic illustrations of medicine circles that led practitioners into contact with an ancient world where sexuality was a form of sacred initiation and animals and humans spoke the same language. To some extent, *Seven Arrows* represented the updating of a tradition of spiritual esotericism that had been present in American culture at least since the founding of the international Theosophical Society by Madame Blavatsky and Henry Olcott in the late nineteenth century. As Ann Taves showed, Theosophy was a radical offshoot of Wesleyan perfectionism that, along with mesmerism, spiritualism, and Christian Science, flourished in the context of the openness to religious experience and experimentation characteristic of the Methodist tradition and Protestant religious enthusiasm more generally. In their enthusiasm for the scientific mastery of spiritual forces, Theosophists carried forward an interest in explaining the interrelationship of natural and spiritual forces that was also a venerable characteristic of the Wesleyan tradition.[30]

Theosophists devoted themselves to uncovering the spiritual forces working inside the laws of nature and to the knowledge of those forces possessed by mahatmas, or highly evolved souls, residing for the most part in Tibet. While retaining theosophical ideas about the spiritual forces working in nature, Hyemeyohsts Storm relocated the source of this wisdom to North America and discovered mahatmalike sages among the Plains Indians. But more than just recasting theosophical ideas in Native American contexts, Storm and other devotees of American Indian spirituality were also responsive to the radical sacramentalism that burst out of its Catholic shell in the Vietnam era. Arresting images and parodies of sacramental reality (e.g., Day-Glo medicine wheels) characterized this radicalism as that unstable double-sidedness in which, to recall William F. Lynch, "matter is always attending its putative transubstantiation into spirit."

The Bear Tribe Medicine Society, founded by Sun Bear (Vincent La Duke), exemplified the link between the New Age sacramentalization of Indian life and the desire to bring about the transformation of American culture. Beginning in the seventies, participants at Bear Tribe gatherings engaged in a variety of ritual practices—medicine wheel construction, sweat lodge purification, crystal gazing, chanting, dancing, and prayer—intended both to heal themselves and to save the planet. For the most part, these participants were not themselves Native American and the rituals they enacted were Sun Bear's own inventions, inspired by his understanding of Plains Indian religion. In workshops and in various publications, he taught that to cleanse both themselves and the earth, people "have to learn to walk in balance on the Earth Mother," as their ancestors once did, and "use the earth's natural resources in a sensitive and sensible manner, without adding chemicals to everything, and pesticides, and all the other things which destroy the planet's delicate web of life." This return to personal and cosmic harmony involved both the mystical sense that "creation is a part of you" and the belief that "you can move it, you can get it to respond to you. That's why some of us can speak with the animals and have them come to us when we call them," he explained in his book *Sun Bear: The Path of Power.* "We can talk to the trees, to the Earth, to the Creator, and ask for what we need at a particular time," he wrote. "We've been doing it for thousands of years. *It's Not Supernatural. It's perfectly natural.*"[31]

Despite its claim to antiquity, Sun Bear's religion was a recent and, in a certain sense, postmodern phenomenon. A composite religion that first gained attention in the sixties through a series of mimeographed sheets written by Sun Bear under the title *Many Smokes*, Sun Bear's religion represented a self-conscious effort to reenchant a world that had been disenchanted. This deliberate effort to imbue the world with enchantment was different from living in a world whose enchantment was well established and even taken for granted. The New Age sacramentalization of Indian lifeways presumed an ongoing, underlying experience of a disenchanted world.

Efforts to Save the World from Disenchantment

Several prominent scholars of religious studies and anthropology joined the effort to stave off the idea that the world was irrevocably disenchanted by suggesting that disenchantment was not a peculiarly modern problem, as Weber and other sociologists of religion maintained, but part of a more universal process of religious initiation. Thus in his discussion of the ritual initiation of children into the Hopi kachina cult, Sam Gill interpreted the initiation as a process of "religious awareness through disenchantment." Among the Hopi Indians of Arizona, Gill argued, children initiated into the cult heard detailed stories and descriptions of the kachina spirits, who personified powerful aspects of the Hopi world. They learned the correct ways of performing kachina dances and other aspects of kachina ritual. And they received a formalized whipping that symbolized the punishment they would receive if they revealed the secrets of initiation. But the most traumatic aspect of the process, Gill argued, was the discovery that the kachina dancers had human heads underneath their masks, and that the beautiful dancers that they thought were spirits were actually their male relatives. The children learned that they, too, must take responsibility for impersonating the kachinas, and thus were led into a mature and lifelong investment in the ongoing religious life of their community.[32]

Overlooking the likelihood that the Hopi believed in a spiritual infusion that imbued the dancers with kachina power without erasing their human identity, Gill's interpretation partook of a widespread, postsixties tendency to look to premodern cultures for solutions to contemporary problems and, more specifically, for suggestions about how to reenchant a disenchanted world. If Hopi children could go through a process of disenchantment without fundamentally altering religious life for future generations, Gill seemed to be implying, so could we.

Compared to the kind of disenchantment then occurring in American culture, the initiation undergone by Hopi children was really something different, reflective of a culturally more intact society. Even if the children *were* shocked to discover their relatives underneath the kachina clothes, the existence and power of the religious world in which both they and their male relatives participated was never called into question. Indeed, while their understanding of the relationship between Hopi men and kachinas undoubtedly became more complex as a result of the initiation process, the children who passed through it emerged with a deeper sense of loyalty to that religious world and with a clearer and firmer sense of personal responsibility for maintaining it. At least as Gill presented their situation, the Hopi never lost the sense that religious forces undergirded the whole of life, nor did they find themselves in a world bereft of shared cosmic meaning, as many late-twentieth-century Americans did.

Before the Vietnam War ever took place, individualizing tendencies in religious thought and experience, coupled with the enormous growth of technological forces independent of any religious control or value, led many Americans to face the real disenchantment of a world in which religious values failed to hold as forms of cosmic explanation and collective experience. Already in a state of attenuated religiosity, Americans disillusioned by the war in Vietnam found their sense of disenchantment radicalized. Alongside the fear, anger, and sense of betrayal occasioned by disillusionment with America, the radicalism of the Vietnam era often involved a desperate effort to reenchant the world. The tendency to paint the situation in black and white, to reverse the roles of good guys and bad guys, and to extend this revisionist good-guy-bad-guy mythology beyond the war itself reflected this effort at reenchantment, as did efforts to levitate the Pentagon, to find God through LSD, and to rediscover the sacred in Mother Earth or the Goddess within. The rashness of these efforts marks them out as something quite different from the experience of liminality—of being ritually cast out of society into a temporary experience of cosmic chaos—that anthropologists following Victor Turner associated with initiation rituals in tribal societies. Although Turner himself argued for the similarity between sixties radicalism and ritual liminality in tribal societies, his argument was itself an expression of the radical, postmodern effort to reenchant the world that characterized American religious life after Vietnam.

In an interesting extension of this effort, the Jesuit university described in the preceding chapter appropriated Turner's theory of ritual process as a means of student retention and spiritual formation. Students participating in a popular retreat sponsored by the chaplaincy left campus for a weekend designed to take them out of their ordinary lives, attain some distance on what they were doing at college, and help them recombine and reconceptualize the elements of their lives. As one of the chaplains who helped design these retreats explained, the weekends were "based on Victor Turner and the idea of taking the Indian brave into the forest away from the tribe. Then they come back to the tribe having internalized its mythology in an invigorated way." The mythology that students came to understand in a new and deeper way was the mythology of Ignatian spirituality based on postsixties interpretations of the writings of the founder of the Jesuit order, Ignatius of Loyola.

But the ritual process that students underwent during these weekend retreats was actually quite different from what Victor Turner observed among Africans. Among the Ndembu people whom Turner studied, boys undergoing initiation were temporarily pushed outside the familiar structure of their lives into a realm of chaos and symbolic confusion and then brought back into the community with a new sense of respect for its religious and social structures. By contrast, the students at the Jesuit university did not spend their retreat in a ritual passage through chaos and disorder that prepared them to reenter the structured world of their society with deeper religious understanding. Chaos and disorder pervaded their ordinary, everyday life. Their grasp of any mythological structure underlying ordinary life was exceedingly tenuous, if indeed it existed at all. The mythic structure underlying ordinary life was not pulled out from under them during the retreat, as it was for the Ndembu during their initiation, but rather presented as something that could give their lives a structure that they did not possess before.[33]

During the religious upheavals and dislocations of the sixties, many Americans searched for the sense of reenchantment these Jesuits provided as a means of recovering from experiences of a disenchanted world. Pathways to disenchantment were already well established in American culture during the fifties and early sixties. The war in Vietnam, however, was the catalyst for a massive run of disenchantment that brought many to a no-place of disillusion and disaffection. In reaction, the radicalism associated with various combinations of sacramental expression and prophetic outrage led to numerous efforts to reenchant the world. These efforts were deliberate attempts to invest the world with sacred power and thus were quite different from more traditional forms of religious discovery and development. In contrast to traditional types of religious initiation, these postmodern efforts to reenchant the world tended to be manifest in alternative, countercultural forms of religious expression.

Although radical in their opposition to received tradition, these alternative forms of religious expression also carried a profoundly conservative impulse to invest the material world with sacred authority. Their conservative tendency to personalize and sacramentalize material reality gave these new forms of religious expression what Max Weber might have called a priestly dimension. At the same time, their countercultural tendency to stand in tension with mainstream society gave them what he might have called a prophetic edge.

4

Buddhism and the Deconstruction of Selfhood

Thich Quang Duc was the first to immolate himself. On June 11, 1963, the elderly monk sat cross-legged in meditation posture on a street in Saigon. He poured gasoline over himself, lit a match, and continued to meditate as his body was engulfed in flame. As the war intensified, other Vietnamese monks and nuns performed similar acts. In calling attention to the massive suffering occurring in Vietnam, they were also demonstrating the compassion exemplified by the founder of their religious tradition twenty-five hundred years before. In the fifth century B.C.E., according to Buddhist scriptures, Siddhartha Gautama, known as Shakyamuni Buddha, "sage of the Shakya clan," attained enlightenment while meditating under a tree. This enlightenment was a response to suffering and involved the idea that the Buddha's life existed in a continuum with all other forms of life.

In a letter to Martin Luther King Jr. in 1965, another Vietnamese monk explained the meaning of the self-immolations occurring in his country. They were not political protests. The monks and nuns did not support any political party or particular form of government and were not siding with either the American-supported Catholic dictatorship in the south or the Communists in the north. Nor were the immolations acts of suicidal desperation. To the contrary, Thich Nhat Hanh explained to King, they were sincere affirmations of life aimed at protecting the people of Vietnam by "moving the hearts of the oppressors, and calling the attention of the world to the suffering endured by the Vietnamese." Nhat Hanh described this display of determined courage on behalf of the people of Vietnam as "a lotus in a sea of fire."

The two religious leaders met when Nhat Hanh visited the United States in 1966. In a joint news conference, King declared that the Buddhists in Vietnam were engaged in the same struggle as blacks in America. In 1967, on the force of this belief, King nominated Nhat Hanh for the Nobel peace prize. After King's assassination a year later, Nhat Hanh carried on the idea of a religious connection between his cause and that of King's. Inspired by similarities he perceived between King's martyrdom and the burning monks and nuns of Vietnam, Nhat Hanh began to develop the concept of world unity and religious understanding that later he described in his well-known book *Living Buddha, Living Christ*.[1]

In hindsight, the burning monks and nuns that Americans saw in magazines and on television during the Vietnam War can be seen as heralds of a widespread transformation in consciousness beginning to occur in the United States. In addition to being the most vivid pointers imaginable to the suffering going on in Vietnam, the immolations were signs of the deconstruction of cherished notions of selfhood associated with American individualism and with conventional forms of heroism, moral virtue, and salvation. At the time, however, the immolations seemed to many Americans appalling evidence of the distance between Vietnamese and American sensibilities. As an American physician who opposed the war told Nhat Hanh in the sixties, the burnings appeared to be acts of "savagery, violence, and fanaticism, requiring a condition of mental unbalance."[2] At the time, most Americans would probably have agreed with U.S. Army general William Westmoreland, who explained in *Hearts and Minds*, a U.S. propaganda film on Vietnam, that Asians simply did not take human life as seriously as Americans did.

Thirty years later, Americans had become much more familiar with Buddhism and with the critique of metaphysical concepts of selfhood fundamental to Buddhist philosophy. In thirty years' time, this critique, and similar deconstructed notions of personality, had become almost a commonplace in many forms of American discourse. Even if many Americans had forgotten, or never learned about, the self-immolations in Southeast Asia, American culture as a whole had become more hospitable to the ways of thinking that inspired them. While not exactly replicated in the United States, the rejection of autonomous, metaphysical selfhood expressed so vividly by Vietnamese Buddhists during the Vietnam War became much more understandable.

Personalism in the Context of the Vietnam War

In both Vietnam and the United States during the twentieth century, Buddhist concepts of selfhood developed in relation to competing, Christian ideas about the self. In Vietnam, the Buddhist view of selfhood expressed by Thich Nhat Hanh developed partly in reaction against the personalist philosophy championed by the Vietnamese Catholics in the fifties and sixties who supported the police state controlled by Ngo Dinh Diem in South Vietnam.

Catholicism in Vietnam was closely associated with foreign influence and especially with French imperialism. During the "Monks' War" from 1885 to 1898, Buddhists and Confucians had joined together in resistance against the French. When the French regained control, they extended special privileges to Vietnamese Catholics, even though the majority of the population was Buddhist. During the Diem regime, government positions went to Catholics, Catholic refugees from North Vietnam received special privileges, and merchants were required to support Catholic "charities." Diem's brother, the bishop of Vinh Long (later an archbishop), established the Vinh Long Personalist Philosophy Center where all public servants, Catholic or not, were required to receive training in Catholic personalist philosophy, which was presented as the correct alternative to Communist philosophy.

In 1956, when the thirty-year-old Nhat Hanh took over the editorship of *Vietnamese Buddhism*, the journal became a vehicle for criticizing Catholic personalism and its social implications as well as for promoting Buddhism as a form of social engagement worthy of official status as a national religion. In its critiques of personalism, the journal focused on the mystical concept of selfhood advanced by the French philosopher Emmanuel Mounier, who contrasted the spiritual being of the human person with the political individual, which to Mounier was merely a legal abstraction. The journal linked Mounier's personalism with romantic idealizations of medieval feudalism that predisposed people to accept paternalistic and authoritarian regimes, such as the one in South Vietnam.[3]

In the United States, Buddhism also developed in relation to competing forms of personalism associated with Christian theology. But in the United States, personalism was not so firmly tied to religious or social conservatism as it was in Vietnam. In the case of Dorothy Day, who was strongly influenced by Mounier through her Catholic Worker colleague Peter Maurin, personalism was an important factor in her *resistance* to the Vietnam War. And in the case of Martin Luther King Jr., Christian personalism of a different sort functioned as a strong force for progressive social change. King's pragmatic form of personalism did not involve an essentialist, mystical view of the eternal nature of the soul, as was the case in Catholic personalism. It was more compatible with the moral relativism of situation ethics as well as with social progress toward liberal, democratic ideals.

But if the American culture that made King an icon of civil rights was more democratic and progressive than the dominant Catholic subculture of South Vietnam, it was even more fixated on the nature, development, and importance of personality. Socialized both by this American preoccupation with personality and by an African-American heritage that nurtured experiences of Jesus working purposefully in a kind of dialogue with each believer, King had a clear sense of being called by Jesus to stand up for truth and justice. This sense of a personal call from Jesus lacked the passivity of a mystical union with God that legitimated assent to the institutional authority of the Catholic Church and to the political authority of Vietnamese leaders who were affiliated with, and sanctioned by, that Church.

While King's personalism worked as a force for democratic change and as a challenge to social and institutional authority, it also worked to establish a close and self-conscious relationship between his personality and the civil rights movement. The effects of this relationship were complicated. On one hand, it amplified his commitment and sense of responsibility to his people and cause, enabling him to face the constant threat of death with courage. On the other hand, his personality and its fusion with the cause of civil rights overshadowed the community of civil rights workers who surrounded, inspired, and supported him. It may also have sanctioned some dishonesty and some exploitation of the lives and work of others.

King's self-conscious identification with his prophetic role in American society was part of a larger preoccupation with personality characteristic of American culture. But at the same time, important aspects of the personalist philosophy that he shared with many liberal Protestants of his time worked to deconstruct any fixed notion of selfhood. The Protestant variant of Christian personalism typified by King had already begun to break down metaphysical concepts of selfhood by fashioning moral judgment in situational terms and by emphasizing the interdependence of self and society. Caught up in the breakdown of personhood that increasingly pervaded their culture, along with a coinciding cultural preoccupation with personality, Americans found themselves increasingly attracted to Buddhist ideas. These ideas made their way into the mainstreams of American life through this cultural context of simultaneous preoccupation with and deconstruction of personality and set a transforming current into motion.

Buddhism Makes Its Way into American Culture

This is not to say that by the end of the twentieth century, vast numbers of Americans had become familiar with Buddhist scriptures or with the finer points of Buddhist psychology. Indeed, Buddhist ideas seeped into American culture through a wide variety of popular and often unorthodox means. The Ewoks in *Star Wars* spoke high-speed Tibetan, and their goodness and courage caricatured that of the Dalai Lama and his besieged compatriots. The old cartoon character Yogi Bear was smarter than the average bear as a spoofy combination of Asian sage and the famous Yankee catcher Yogi Berra. In the 1990s, commentators perceived that the old catcher himself had attained a certain Zen mastery, evident in his frequent utterance of such enigmatic, koanlike sayings as "You can't hit the ball and think at the same time" and "I'd like to thank you all for making this day necessary." Zen also became popular as a method of improving one's golf game and as a means of recovering from substance abuse and other life problems and painful events. And in their hit song "Bodhisattva Vow," the Beastie Boys "give thanks for the world as a place to learn / And for the human body that I'm glad to have earned." As they proclaimed, "The bodhisattva path is one of power and strength / A strength from within to go the length." And when things did not seem to be going well, not to worry—just "think on the dharma / And the enlightened ones who've graduated samsara."

Many Americans learned about Buddhism not directly from Buddhist scriptures or meditation practices, but from other people who had read or engaged in those things, or from people who knew people who had. The actor and martial artist Bruce Lee conveyed his understanding of Zen Buddhism through the freedom and precision of kung fu. The basketball coach Phil Jackson advised readers of his memoir, *Sacred Hoops*, "If you see the Buddha in the lane, pass him the ball." And the acclaimed American poet Gary Snyder admonished his readers to follow the simple rules outlined by the great forest icon Smokey the Bear, who holds "in his right paw the Shovel that digs to the truth beneath appearances" and with his left offers "the Mudra of Comradely Display." All those who recite the "Smokey the Bear Sutra," Snyder promised, will "help save the planet Earth from total oil slick" and "[w]ill always have ripe blackberries to eat and a sunny spot under a pine tree to sit at."[4]

Through various channels, including psychotherapy, sports, music, film, and poetry, as well as through a wide range of opportunities for formal study and meditation practice, Buddhism filtered into many corners of American culture. This process gained remarkable momentum during the 1990s, partly as a result of the growing number, and growing visibility, of Buddhists and Buddhist resources in the United States. The rapidly increasing popularity of Buddhist ideas in the 1990s was also a result of the effective ways in which Buddhist teachers presented their ideas as antidotes to the dilemmas and stresses of American life.

The process of incorporating Buddhist ideas into American forms of culture and religious life started long before the Vietnam era. In the nineteenth century, the Transcendentalists eagerly read the first English translations of Hindu and Buddhist scriptures. In 1844, Henry David Thoreau translated the *Lotus Sutra* from a French edition for the Transcendentalist journal *The Dial*. His contemporary Ralph Waldo Emerson was even more instrumental in bringing Buddhist and Hindu ideas to the attention of the American public, though his understanding of both was limited and he sometimes confused the two.

Emerson exemplified a general tendency among nineteenth century

American interpreters to view Hindu and Buddhist scriptures within an idealistic intellectual framework that involved a distinctively American combination of German philosophy and English Romanticism. This interpretive framework led nineteenth century Americans to interpret Buddhist ideas in terms of their own beliefs about the connection between individual consciousness and the underlying, spiritual nature of reality. Thus American Transcendentalists and their heirs conceptualized Buddhist ideas about the mind in terms of belief in a divine and universal Spirit underlying nature, history, and art, a belief that they had developed partly from their own religious experiences and partly from their readings in German idealism and English romanticism.

Buddhist conceptions of the mind-stream's flow in all forms of life confirmed the belief held by American Transcendentalists and their heirs that conventional forms of theism popular in revivalism and other areas of American life were intellectually inadequate, excessively moralistic, and insufficiently spiritual. At a deeper level, Buddhist ideas also resonated with some of the Protestant ideas that characterized the spiritual outlooks of the Transcendentalists, their predecessors, and their heirs. In the Anglo Protestant tradition, from which many nineteenth- and early twentieth-century American students of Buddhism emerged, belief in each person's radical dependency on God and notions about God's self-disclosure in the lives of his saints were fundamental principles. Belief in an individual relationship between God and his saints was absolutely central to religious life, to the point of downgrading or even jettisoning mediatory forms of institutional authority. The emphasis on individual experience as the doorway to cosmic consciousness that nineteenth-century Americans found in Buddhist texts worked to confirm and further advance this emphasis on individual experience as the matrix of religious life, which had been developed in Anglo Protestant thought. At the same time, the concern to establish a right relationship between self and world worked to support Transcendentalist criticism of crasser forms of individualism, such as those associated with Daniel Boone, Andrew Jackson, George Armstrong Custer, Kit Carson, and other heroes of victory culture.

After the New England Transcendentalists discovered Buddhism and introduced it to the American public, American Theosophy emerged to recommend Buddhism as a higher stage in a process of spiritual and scientific evolution. The Russian emigré Helena Petrovna Blavatsky and her chum Henry Steel Olcott argued that Buddhism had been mostly hidden from the West until its propitious moment of discovery in their new religious movement, Theosophy, which aimed to unite religion and science on a spiritual plane. At the World's Parliament of Religions, held during the World's Columbian Exposition in Chicago in 1893, the Ceylonese Theosophist and founder of the Maha Bodhi Society, Anagarika Dharmapala, stressed the importance of the Buddha's teaching for the West and its compatibility with both modern science and progress toward universal brotherhood. These ideas were advanced still further by the German-American philosopher of religion Paul Carus, who edited two American journals, *The Monist* and *Open Court*, promoting discussion of Buddhist philosophy and its parallels with both science and humanistic forms of Christianity. Carus also sponsored the Japanese philosopher and translator D. T. Suzuki, who first came to the United States in 1897 to work for Carus and later became an influential exponent of Zen Buddhism in the United States.

According to Thomas A. Tweed's helpful analysis, Buddhism's appeal to Americans in the Victorian era was limited by their relentlessly optimistic outlook and concern for moral activism and by the widespread perception that Buddhism encouraged pessimism and moral passivity. The Americans drawn to Buddhism in the nineteenth century were sufficiently detached from the beliefs of Protestant evangelicalism dominant in their culture to accept Buddhism's rejection of personal immortality and a personal creator. But this dissent from popular religious belief was limited, Tweed argued, by an underlying consent to the values of individualism, optimism, and moral activism characteristic of American culture. As a result, Buddhism did not really catch hold or become firmly established in Victorian America, despite the talents of its spokespersons and its relevance to the spiritual disillusionment faced by many Americans of that time.[5]

Things changed. The distance between American and Buddhist attitudes toward life shrank, partly because religious disillusionment and disenchantment reached new proportions in America. With the defeat of victory culture in the Vietnam era and the proliferation of countercultural movements and revisionist interpretations of American history, dissent from American culture became more pervasive and thoroughgoing. In the context of this unprecedented disenchantment, Buddhism seemed less pessimistic than it once had. To be sure, this greater hospitality to Buddhist ideas also resulted from the availability of more Buddhist teachers, and more and better translations of Buddhist texts, all of which helped to correct misperceptions about Buddhism's allegedly pessimistic, fatalistic, and morally passive outlook. Still, Buddhism came to seem less pessimistic partly because Americans themselves had become less optimistic.

More was involved here than reaching the end of one's tether and thinking that the grass was greener in an alternative religion. Such feelings were an important part of the picture, but they do not explain why during the 1990s Buddhism came to seem not only less pessimistic than it once had, but truly lighthearted. In contrast to the darker face that Buddhism seemed to wear in the past, in the nineties the face of Buddhism in American culture seemed positively upbeat. The friendly smile of the Dalai Lama hailed Americans from numerous book jackets, magazines, and television spots. His frequent writings, utterances, and appearances had a heartening, steadying influence. "The very purpose of our life is to seek happiness," he declared in his best-selling *The Art of Happiness,* "the very motion of our life is towards happiness." This "handbook for living," as the book was subtitled, was coauthored with a psychiatrist and written in direct response to the internal suffering experienced by many Americans. It promised that happiness was readily available through a process of "training the mind." This "inner discipline" involved relinquishing attitudes that promoted suffering while nurturing attitudes that promoted happiness. Not easy, perhaps, but simple, practical, and doable.[6]

Only in the context of the fixation on personality characteristic of American culture and the radical disenchantment experienced by many could this way of interpreting Buddhism take hold. In Victorian culture, the Buddhist concepts of *anatman* (no-self), impermanence, and *sunyata* (emptiness) were too radical to find any kind of general acceptance. But at the end of twentieth century, these concepts came across as something like a relief. In American culture after the second World War, people were more self-conscious about the burden of selfhood and its problems than ever before. And the intensified scrutiny of the human personality and its moods and disorders contributed to a deconstruction of the heroic, autonomous selfhood associated with victory culture.

As this process of deconstruction developed, many Americans started to think of their individual lives less in terms of their souls and more in terms of the various strands of perception and sensitivity working together as their bodies. Often without benefit of formal meditation practice or Buddhist study, many people gravitated to a more symbolic and contingent concept of selfhood that was closer to the Buddhist concept of the five *skandas,* or bundles of perception collected together in each life, associated with the principles of no-self, impermanence, and emptiness. This gravitation was not simply the result of Buddhism's direct or even indirect influence, but also involved the deterioration of traditional and conventional Christian ideas of selfhood, including those involving belief in the soul as a metaphysical essence. Although they certainly did not disappear from the American scene, metaphysical concepts of the soul associated with Catholic personalism and with both German and New England Transcendentalism succumbed to significant critique and erosion, as did their secular counterparts of heroic self-sufficiency and personal autonomy.

Underlying the wild and often happy eclecticism of the process of assimilating Buddhism into American culture at the turn of the twenty-first century, there were important developments in American religious and cultural history that help explain why many Americans seemed open to the fragments, tracings, and shadows of Buddhist ideas, if not entire systems of Buddhist philosophy and practice. Buddhist ideas appealed to many Americans after the sixties because they offered a solution to some of the pressing, internal dilemmas associated with selfhood, or at least the possibility of coping with them more effectively. Buddhist ideas offered ways of thinking about these internal dilemmas that made them seem less insoluble than they once appeared.

During the same period that Buddhism in America left its reputation for pessimism behind and came to be identified with happiness, increasing ethnic and religious diversity in the United States also contributed to the growth of Buddhism. After severe restrictions on Asian immigration were lifted in 1965, Asians became the largest immigrant group in the United States. Buddhists from Korea, Vietnam, Japan, Tibet, Sri Lanka, Burma, Cambodia, Laos, and Thailand established new temples and religious centers in the United States, making this country home to more cradle Buddhists than ever before, as well as to more different forms of Buddhism than any other country in the world.

The increasing diversity and visibility of Buddhism stimulated the development of Buddhist ideas among Americans drawn to the religion from backgrounds in Judaism, Christianity, and agnosticism as well as among those born to its traditions. As Americans moved closer to a Buddhist worldview at the end of the twentieth century, experiencing greater openness to Buddhist ideas as a result of their own history, the growing presence and visibility of Buddhists and Buddhist resources in the United States worked to dispel negative stereotypes about Buddhist pessimism and to stimulate new forms of Buddhist thought and practice.

Mapping the Terrain of American Buddhism

Several authors have proposed schemes for mapping the presence—and diversity—of Buddhism in the United States. Rick Fields drew a distinction between "ethnic Buddhists" and "white Buddhists." For ethnic Buddhists, Fields explained, loyalty to Buddhism was linked to participation in immigrant community life. White Buddhists, on the other hand, were drawn to Buddhist meditation and philosophy from backgrounds in Judaism and Christianity.

Avoiding racial categories and focusing instead on different forms of Buddhist practice, Catherine L. Albanese distinguished between meditative, evangelical, and church Buddhism. Jan Nattier drew a map of American Buddhism quite similar to Albanese's, although she used a self-consciously Buddhist emphasis on modes of transmission to differentiate her subgroups of "import," "export," and "baggage" Buddhists. In Nattier's typology, import Buddhists actively sought to bring Buddhism into their lives from its homes outside their own culture. These elite Buddhists typically had middle-class backgrounds and European ancestry. Export Buddhists, characterized by evangelical efforts to actively reach out and recruit others, had little interest in the meditation disciplines in which elite Buddhists were involved. Baggage Buddhists received their transmissions from their own families, who in many cases had been Buddhists for centuries. Baggage Buddhists brought their religious traditions with them as Asian immigrants to the United States or received them as descendants of these immigrants as part of their ethnic heritage.[7]

For the purposes of this book, a complementary but more expansive typology is in order. To capture Buddhism's wider influence in the transformation of American thinking about selfhood, as well as its more traditional role as a full-blown religion, it is helpful to see how pious, practical, and epistemological aspects of American Buddhism sometimes coincide with one another and sometimes do not. Thus in many forms of American Buddhism, all three aspects are present and mutually supporting, but in other forms, American Buddhism is highly practical but not especially pious. And while most people who are practical or pious Buddhists are probably epistemological Buddhists as well, there are lots of Americans who would not qualify as pious Buddhists, and probably not as practical Buddhists either, but who are Buddhist, or at least Buddhist-like, in their perceptions of knowledge, truth, and reality. In order to appreciate the extent of Buddhism's role in the transformation of American religion and culture, these epistemological Buddhists cannot be left out of the picture. And yet to be interpreted adequately, they have to be seen in relation to the more visible, socially established, and institutionalized forms of pious and practical Buddhism.

Pious Buddhists are people who regard the Buddha, the Buddha-mind, and its manifestations as objects of ultimate devotion and reverence. They celebrate the Buddha's birthday, burn incense, and participate, as members of Buddhist communities, in a variety of formal Buddhist ceremonies. Pious Buddhists include Asian immigrants and their descendants for whom reverential devotion is a family tradition. Pious Buddhists also include some Americans without Asian ancestry who combine these devotional practices with more esoteric meditation practices derived from Buddhist monasticism.

In establishing temples and meditation centers in the United States, many family-tradition and some meditation-centered Buddhists incorporated congregational structures typical of more conventional forms of American religious life. In some cases, they adopted architectural forms, meeting times, clergy-parishioner expectations, and other features characteristic of American churches. In the seventies and eighties, some family-tradition Buddhists grew resentful of the tendency of many Euro-American meditators to view them condescendingly or overlook them entirely, even in places where they shared a facility or the services of a particular priest or monk. During the nineties, the distance between Euro-American meditators and family-tradition Buddhists diminished in response to a variety of factors, including concerns over racial divisions within American Buddhism and efforts on the part of Euro-Americans to look more carefully at Buddhist family traditions and to incorporate some of these traditions into their own family lives. Distance between these groups also diminished as a result of the increasing visibility and authority of Asian-American Buddhist communities in the United States and as a result of the increasing respect commanded by the Dalai Lama and other Asian-Buddhist visitors. To an important extent, then, the phenomenon of pious Buddhism was an increasing blend of two groups that formerly were rather sharply divided between "ethnics" and "whites." While family-tradition Buddhists continued to be less interested in formal meditation practice than many American converts to Buddhism, and converts continued to be less interested in ceremonial functions than family-tradition Buddhists, crossovers were increasingly common. Most important, converts often shared with family-tradition Buddhists a respect for the Buddha's teachings that worked to bring the two groups closer together.

PRACTICAL BUDDHISTS

Practical Buddhists focus on the salutary effects of Buddhism. At one end of the spectrum of practical Buddhism, evangelicals focus on the transformative power of ritual chanting and especially on chanting the *Lotus Sutra*, which they believe contains the essence of Buddhism's transformative power. Moving away from the intense and highly focused devotion of these evangelical Buddhists, many family-tradition Buddhists also combine practical interests in Buddhism with pious devotion. They look to the Buddha for blessings in this life and in the life to come and are often concerned with various means of accruing merit. As the product of good deeds, merit contributes positively to the network of cause and effect action, known as karma, that structure one's situation in this life and the next. Often less saturated with piety than evangelicals, family-tradition Buddhists are as interested as anyone in utilizing Buddhist teaching as a means of escaping suffering and attaining happiness.[8]

Moving further along the spectrum of practical Buddhism, growing numbers of Americans are interested in utilizing Buddhist techniques and philosophy as means to enlightenment without being inclined toward pious devotion to the Buddha and his manifestations. Thus while both evangelical and family-tradition Buddhists tended to be both pious and practical in their orientation to Buddhism, many of the new forms of Buddhism that have sprung up in the United States have a strongly practical but not particularly pious bent. The American tendencies to milk Buddhism for its practical benefits and to define its way of thinking in practical terms are part of a larger tendency toward pragmatism in American culture as well as part of Buddhism's own practical orientation. Many Americans who are intrigued and inspired by the practical benefits of Buddhism do not regard the Buddha and his manifestations as objects of ultimate devotion.

In more than a few cases, these practical Buddhists are pious people, but their piety is directed more toward Judaism or Christianity than toward Buddhism. For example, Rodger Kamenetz is an American Jew who has written eloquently about the contribution Buddhism has made to a renewal of Jewish piety and how his own exposure to Tibetan Buddhism deepened his devotion to Judaism. Father Robert Kennedy incorporated advanced training in Buddhist meditation and dharma transmission from Tetsugen Roshi (Bernard Glassman) within his pious devotion to Christ and his vocation as a Jesuit priest and inspirational Catholic leader. The Zen teacher Ko-un Roshi is also the Benedictine monk Father Willis Jager.

Still further from Buddhist piety along the practicality spectrum, other Americans attracted to Buddhism have little use for pious acts or feelings associated with any form of religious tradition. Many of these people have been drawn to the iconoclastic attitudes toward religion found especially in Zen Buddhism. Criticism of the "stink" of piety is part of Zen lore, like the story of the Chinese poet Han-shan, who laughed uproariously at the fussy and self-important piety of some of his fellow Buddhists. The story of the Zen master who burned a wooden statue of the Buddha, a conventional object of pious devotion, to keep warm while meditating is another instance of the Zen willingness to sacrifice piety for practice, as is the well-known saying "If you see the Buddha on the road, kill him!" Judaism and Protestantism carry strong iconoclastic elements as well, and Americans who have backgrounds in these traditions often embrace Zen iconoclasm with glee, even to the point of seeing it as a welcome relief from what they recall as the superficial observances of piety that they once participated in as Jews or Christians. Thus some Americans have been attracted to the emphasis on practice in Zen Buddhism because it offers a kind of apotheosis of the iconoclasm and practical spirituality familiar to them from their own Jewish and Christian traditions of birth.

Zen traditions focus on the transmission of insight from teacher to student, which occurs in the context of meditation practices that concentrate mind and body on the conditioned nature of existence. The term *Zen* means "meditation" and all forms of it emphasize the necessity of meditation as a means to enlightenment. Thus at one important level, Zen Buddhism is extremely goal-oriented. The ultimate goal of all forms of meditation is satori, or enlightenment, that clear-sighted state of consciousness unmarred by the self's longing for permanence and unconditionedness. For people drawn to this kind of practice, almost every waking moment can be dedicated to attaining enlightenment insight. In this respect, enlightenment is the shore and meditation is the raft that is no longer needed once one reaches the shore.

Of course, many Buddhists who engage in meditation would point to this distinction between using Buddhism and being devoted to it as one of those dualisms that Buddhism calls into question—a variant of the apparent conflict between wanting to get somewhere and already being there. And some American converts to Zen have written movingly about being disappointed in the attempt to reach the escape or ecstasy of satori but having subsequently discovered a greater appreciation for ordinary existence. For example, in *The Three Pillars of Zen,* the founder of the Rochester Zen Center, Philip Kapleau, described his intense effort to experience satori during thirteen years of study in Japan during the fifties and early sixties and his dawning realization that satori and samsara (the endless cycle of death and rebirth) were really the same thing. And in his 1996 memoir *Nothing on My Mind,* Erik Fraser Storlie recalled his desperate effort to attain enlightenment as a young man and his later, more gradualist, and less dramatic approach to enlightenment as a student of the Soto Zen master Shunryu Suzuki. Meditating on the side of a mountain after the death of Suzuki Roshi, Storlie opened his eyes and simply recognized the beauty of the world through which his teacher had passed. Letting his mind's separation from the surrounding world drop away, he whispered, "Nothing on my mind." Amidst the sound of grasshoppers rubbing their legs together, the warmth of the rock, and the coolness of the breeze, "a cloud floats by to the west."[9]

Although the realization that what one is looking for is already there may be fundamental to many forms of Buddhism, the fact remains that many Americans have turned to meditation as a means to the end of spiritual fulfillment. In the context of a culture deeply influenced by the Anglo Protestant tradition and its orientation toward the gift and blessings of grace, Buddhist meditation offers a means to a spiritual goal that, to some extent at least, was already set up in the minds of many Americans before they had ever heard of Buddhism. This goal-oriented approach to Buddhism is hardly without precedent, especially in the Rinzai school of Zen, where proficiency in the arts, especially the martial arts, has received much emphasis. In the context of American culture, it acquired many new adherents, especially among athletes interested in Zen as a way of getting "into the zone" and among mental health practitioners interested in Buddhism as a means of helping patients and clients relieve their mental suffering.

BUDDHISM MEETS AMERICAN DEMOCRACY AND LIBERAL HUMANISM

The development of Buddhist ideas in the United States after the Vietnam War has been characterized by strong and persistent interest in their pragmatic benefits. Thus many Americans have been drawn to Buddhism as a way of learning how to savor, treasure, and make the most of life. But some observers of this American tendency to emphasize the practical and life-affirming aspect of Buddhism point to early Buddhist texts and argue that learning how to make the most of life is not at all what the Buddha had in mind. In their interpretation of these texts, wanting to better appreciate life is the desire that most needs to be destroyed if we are to escape from suffering. In contrast, many teachers of Buddhism in the United States have endeavored to promote the more humanistic interpretation of Buddhism as a practical means to happiness and well-being. Thus in the process of translating and marketing Buddhist ideas to meet American needs, Buddhist leaders have taken the idea that Buddhism is spiritually therapeutic and gone in new directions that incorporate and build on American ideas about spiritual growth, social action, and profitability. Even though

American Buddhist teachers agree that relinquishing attachment to things and to oneself is important, they also have a strong, and typically American, investment in the process of spiritual growth and in the happiness, satisfaction, and appreciation of life that such investment brings.

Of course, Buddhism's practical orientation is of long standing. Its basic emphasis on escaping suffering and enabling others to escape suffering is evidence of that. Moreover, the concept of the middle path of enlightenment and the tendency, especially in Mahayana Buddhism, to conflate the end of enlightenment with the means to it have worked to expedite the process of easing Buddhism into the pragmatic medium of American culture.

In this process of Americanization, Buddhists and people intrigued by Buddhism have not only mined Buddhist philosophy for its salutary and pragmatic benefits, but also recast Buddhist ideas in the context of social frameworks that are more democratic and egalitarian than those associated with traditional forms of Asian Buddhism, which have often been characterized by monastic control of Buddhist doctrine and meditation practice. As a result of democratizing forces within American culture that presume the equality of persons and frown on the institutionalization of social inequality, Americans attracted to Buddhism have criticized and even rejected aspects of Buddhist practice that seem to them to be excessively hierarchical and authoritarian.

This democratization process is manifest most clearly in women's efforts to achieve parity as students and teachers in Buddhist communities and in their criticism of male-dominated Buddhist authority. While women have participated actively in Buddhism since its founding in India in the fifth century B.C.E., they have often been believed to be born to a lower state than men, and any wisdom they may have offered has frequently been presumed to be limited to women's issues. In the Western world today, and especially in the United States, many Buddhists have challenged these traditional assumptions and linked their overturning to the progressive evolution of worldwide consciousness. As one American woman, Karma Lekshe Tsomo, expressed the point: "The Buddha's words were meant to be tested and verified through one's own practice experience." Invoking Buddhist ideas to challenge Buddhist traditions, Tsomo argued, "We are not being asked to believe anything or accept anything (particularly not to buy something simply because a man said it, however enlightened he may have been)." Relying on their own practice experience, "American women, having broken with a patriarchal path, are creating their direction, incorporating wisdom wherever they may find it." If the words of such women "lack some of the weight and depth of tradition," their role in Buddhism's development is crucial, Tsomo argued, because "their viewpoint may be fresher, more personal, more dynamic."[10]

The democratizing tendency has been especially dramatic in Zen, which has been part of American culture since the late nineteenth century and is probably the form of Buddhism most firmly ensconced in the United States. The democratizing of Zen is manifest not only in the emergence of female *roshis,* or teachers, but also in the concept of "everyday Zen," which loosens religious practice and the experience of enlightenment from the formalized structures of monkhood and monastic life associated with Japanese culture. Everyday Zen is the discovery of religious practice and experiences of enlightenment in the ordinary American work of keeping a home, raising children, and holding down a job. Of course, Buddhism has always concerned itself with the meaningfulness of ordinary life and with the "middle way" between denying the needs and pleasures of life and overindulging them. Numerous pictures of the Sixth Ch'an Patriarch, Hui Neng, chopping bamboo at the moment of enlightenment exemplify this respect for mundane tasks. But while monks whose lives were quite different from those of other people studiously cultivated this respect for the mundane, in the American context Zen become an aid to ordinary life. Thus in America, the traditional Buddhist respect for ordinary tasks developed into a more democratic respect for ordinary people. The social and religious distance between monks and the laity shrank. Some of the strict, authoritarian, male-oriented, and male-dominant structures of Japanese Zen weakened in the United States, and both the teaching and the practice of Buddhism became more open and egalitarian.

In considering the development of Buddhism in America, it is important to recognize that Buddhism carries its on focus on the primacy of inner experience. A well-established disposition to psychological analysis has simply been brought to new forms of expression as a result of Buddhism's exposure to American culture. Buddhist and American ideas about the authority of inner experience have combined to create more egalitarian approaches to Buddhist practice, which incorporate respect for women as teachers and for the spiritual value of everyday tasks that women ordinarily perform. Along with this democratizing process, the fundamental commitment to the authority of inner experience has flourished in the context of the historical American commitment to the expression of spirituality in ordinary life. This American tradition of deliberate religious commitment to ordinary life can be traced to the Protestant investment in marriage and family life as the primary locus of religious life, to the Puritan concept of vocation as a religious calling in the world, and to the Puritan commitment to social engagement and responsibility as expressions of religious virtue.

To some extent, then, Buddhist leaders in the United States have adopted a pragmatic approach to religious life that is rooted in the American Puritan tradition. The operative assumption of this approach is that internal forms of spiritual virtue have salutary effects, both in the life of the virtuous person and in the surrounding world. As we have seen, this pragmatic view of religious life can be traced to the Protestant Reformed beliefs that grace enabled moral life and that grace expressed itself in a person's behavior and impact on the world.[11]

BUDDHIST PSYCHOTHERAPY

Practical Buddhism has made its biggest inroads into American culture in the area of psychotherapy. The psychiatrist Marsha M. Linehan attributed her discovery of effective means of treating "borderline" patients to insights gained as a result of Zen meditation. Suffering from one of the least treatable forms of personality disorder and notoriously adept at subverting the therapeutic strategies used to help them, often making the people who try to help them come away feeling cruel-hearted, these (mostly female) patients have often been perceived as essentially incurable. While conventional approaches to treating them have been criticized as being less than helpful, Linehan claimed some success as a result of applying the Buddhist concept of "skillful means" to avoid becoming entangled in her patients' sufferings and to mirror those sufferings in a way that helped her patients work through them.[12]

The best-known advocates of advancing the practice of psychotherapy through Buddhist philosophy and meditation have been associated with *vipassana*, or insight meditation. Originating in Southeast Asia, *vipassana* began as a modernization movement within Theravada Buddhism that aimed to recover Buddhism's original insights in light of the challenges of twentieth-century life. Along with other early developers of this movement, the Burmese monk Mahasi Sayadaw streamlined Theravada meditation practice, dispensing with rituals of chanting, pious devotion, and merit making, and offered it to lay people living in the world, outside of the monasteries where Theravada meditation was traditionally practiced. Focusing almost solely on the development of mindfulness, Mahasi and other *vipassana* teachers led meditation retreats where students learned to label the sensations and thoughts that occurred to them while meditating and to develop the practice of sustained concentration.

Vipassana became an important feature of the American Buddhist landscape in 1974, when the Tibetan Buddhist teacher Chogyam Trungpa and the Hindu teacher Ram Dass (Richard Alpert) invited Joseph Goldstein and Jack Kornfield, two Americans who had studied with Mahasi in Burma, to offer summer meditation courses at the Naropa Institute in Boulder, Colorado. The enthusiasm that greeted their courses at Naropa led Goldstein and Kornfield to collaborate with Sharon Salzberg and Jacqueline Schwartz in founding the Insight Meditation Society in Barre, Massachusetts. (Author of another Buddhist book on "the art of happiness," Salzberg was also a student of Mahasi.) In 1984, Kornfield cofounded a sister institute, the Spirit Rock Meditation Center in Marin County, California. Through meditation retreats held at these centers and also through books, tapes, and lectures, he and other *vipassana* teachers offered instruction in mindfulness meditation, along with a form of loving-kindness meditation *(metta)* derived from the Indian *vipassana* teacher S. N. Goenka.

As Gil Fronsdal pointed out in his helpful essay on the American *vipassana* movement, the meditation centers at Barre and Spirit Rock are not structured in the way that churches, synagogues, and temples have traditionally been structured. Neither do they provide the range of religious and social services that churches and other, more traditional religious institutions do.[13] Students at *vipassana* retreats are less like parishioners than clients who have sought out experts and specialized services. And many of the people attending *vipassana* retreats are mental health professionals of one sort or another, engaged in commitments to their own networks of clients, patients, students, or readers. Their responsibilities to a *vipassana* retreat center are limited and clearly de-fined, as are the center's responsibilities to them. Nevertheless, the re-treats do constitute communities of spiritually minded people, gathered for the purpose of deepening insight and enhancing practical skills. In this respect, *vipassana* centers have the same kind of consumer orien-tation and institutional flexibility as some of the nondenominational churches developed in the United States since the sixties that offer people a variety of different activities and services.

Kornfield's work has functioned as a stepping-stone for a variety of efforts to reconceptualize Western psychotherapy in light of Buddhist philosophy and meditation practice. Beginning in the mid-sixties, after graduating from Dartmouth College with a concentration in Asian studies, he studied mindfulness meditation in Theravada monasteries in Thailand, India, and Sri Lanka. In the mid-seventies he received a Ph.D. in clinical psychology and began work as both a psychotherapist and a Buddhist teacher, convinced that *vipassana* meditation and West-ern psychotherapies had a lot to offer each other. On one hand, he found that the meditation training he received in Asian monasteries did not prepare him for the emotional challenges of American life, especially those of family life and friendship. Because Western psycho-therapies were often geared to these interpersonal realities, Kornfield believed they could supplement Buddhist meditation in useful ways. On the other hand, while working at a state mental institution as part of his training as a psychologist, and toying with the naive idea of teaching meditation to the patients, he "discovered a whole large pop-ulation at this hospital who desperately needed meditation: the psy-chiatrists, psychologists, social workers, psychiatric nurses, mental health aides, and others." While hospital patients were not capable of summoning the concentrated attention required by meditation practice, the clinicians who worked with those patients were. In addition, Korn-field believed, these mental health professionals often lacked precisely the kind of insight that meditation offered. And their patients suffered for it. He was convinced that meditation, by enabling the staff to con-front the forces of greed, fear, and anger within themselves, would help them do a better job of understanding the forces that overwhelmed their patients.

Kornfield's 1993 book *A Path with Heart* presented psychotherapy and insight meditation as complementary endeavors. In addition to explaining the role that psychotherapy could play in clearing the way for meditation, the book also functioned as a guide to integrating meditation into everyday American life. Even if the reader could find time only to focus on a single inhalation and exhalation of breath, Kornfield offered instruction in how to derive benefit from it. At the end of each chapter, the book presented concrete suggestions about how meditation can be usefully infiltrated into ordinary life. For example, at the end of the chapter titled "Turning Straw into Gold," Kornfield coached readers facing difficult problems to sit quietly, pay attention to their own breathing, and pose a series of questions to themselves, such as "How have I treated this difficulty so far?" "How have I suffered by my own response and reaction to it?" "What is the gold, the value, hidden in this situation?"[14]

In this book *Thoughts Without a Thinker: Psychotherapy from a Buddhist Perspective*, the psychiatrist Mark Epstein took Kornfield's understanding of the complementary relationship between psychotherapy and insight meditation a step further. He agreed with Kornfield that meditation required a certain level of psychological integration and that people who lacked it needed to do psychotherapy first. But Epstein went further in arguing that Buddhist meditation could be viewed as a comprehensive form of psychotherapy that superseded previously established forms of psychoanalytic psychotherapy.

In an effort to reconceptualize Western psychotherapy within the context of Buddhist philosophy and meditation practice, Epstein presented the Buddha as the original and, to date, greatest master of therapeutic self-understanding. In this view, practitioners of the Western arts of psychotherapy were working within a field of endeavor whose larger perimeters and ultimate purpose the Buddha long ago discerned. Of course, the Buddha did not anticipate Freud's specific theories about oedipal relationships. Rather, Epstein explained, Freud was working on problems associated with selfhood that the Buddha resolved at a deeper level. While Freud never saw an end to an individual's need for psychoanalysis—indeed, he thought it was interminable—Epstein promoted Buddhism as an effective means of attaining self-realization. Thus Buddhism could resolve some of the dilemmas of Western psychotherapy while at the same time corroborating its insights. Epstein even went so far as to assign the various schools of Western psychotherapy to places within the six realms of existence shown on Tibetan

Buddhist pictures of the wheel of life. As he explained, Freud's theories were especially useful in the Animal Realm, where beings were fixated on sexuality, and in the Realm of the Hungry Ghosts, where oral fixation is a problem. Melanie Klein's theories were helpful for beings stuck in the Hell Realm of rage and anxiety. D. W. Winnicott and Heinz Kohut were good for narcissistic suffering in the Human Realm. And so forth. Each of these Western healers delved into a particular realm on the circle of suffering and provided useful insight there, "but none," Epstein wrote, "have explored the entire wheel." Buddhism provided the holistic view that Western psychotherapy lacked, according to Epstein, because it offered a "comprehensive view of the human psyche" that Western psychotherapy needed, and that Western people needed in order to move ahead in self-understanding and spiritual development.

While the various forms of Western psychotherapy associated with the theories of Sigmund Freud and his students aimed at a narrative "reconstruction" of the formative elements of selfhood, Epstein explained, Buddhist meditation involved a "questioning of the most basic metaphors that we use to understand ourselves" and thus aimed at the "deconstruction" of selfhood. From Epstein's perspective, much of what happened through meditation was therapeutic, in that it promoted "the usual therapeutic goals of integration, humility, stability, and self-awareness." But at the same time, he emphasized that Buddhist meditation "reaches beyond therapy, toward a farther horizon of self-understanding." Because it focused on identifying "the basic cravings that give rise to the sense of self," Epstein concluded that Buddhist meditation led to a transformation in self-understanding "not ordinarily accessible through psychotherapy alone."[15]

Epstein's work provides a clear example of how Buddhism has been utilized in the United States for its practical benefits in resolving problems or advancing solutions beyond the reach of traditional Western resources. Of course, Buddhism has itself been transformed in this process. Thus it was not Buddhism as practiced in Theravada monasteries in Thailand that was transforming American psychotherapy, but Buddhism as reinterpreted by Americans steeped in Western schools of psychotherapy. In the course of this reinterpretation, Americans inspired by *vipassana* reconstructed Buddhism, and spiritual life more generally, as a kind of advanced form of psychotherapy. At the same time, these practical American Buddhists have taken Buddhist meditation practices out of their traditional monastic settings and revised them for use by busy Americans. In this process, Buddhism functioned not as a conventional religion involving ceremonial activities and a stable community, but rather as a spiritual practice designed for individual clients. As part of this transformation of Buddhism into a practice like psychotherapy, the expressions of piety associated with more traditional forms of Buddhist religious life were left behind. In this sense, Americans who engaged in Buddhist meditation for forty minutes before going to work in the morning, during intensive retreats once or twice a year, or at moments snatched during stressful times in a busy day could be said to be practical but not necessarily pious Buddhists.

EPISTEMOLOGICAL BUDDHISTS

By flowing into American culture in such flexible and unorthodox ways, Buddhism expanded not only the range of religious options available to Americans, but also the meaning of the term *religion* itself. As Buddhist practice finds homes in various pockets, corners, and interstices of American life, either we can place it outside the boundary of what qualifies as religion, or we can stretch and otherwise adapt the term *religion* to incorporate it. If the path of exclusion has the advantage of clarity and simplicity, the path of inclusion enables us to see that Buddhism is not just another set of religions in an already crowded marketplace but also a religious movement that is transforming the way that many Americans think about religion and about life.

If practical Buddhism can be difficult to pin down and isolate from other things, epistemological Buddhism is virtually impossible. Ways of thinking about thinking that are compatible with and similar to, if not demonstrably influenced by, Buddhist modes of thought are all over the place in American culture. At the same time, many expressions of Buddhist modes of thought are so fused with other things that any attempt to separate out the Buddhist elements distorts the way in which those elements actually come across. In a world where identifiably Buddhist ideas are increasingly familiar and increasingly mixed into Western thought, it is often impossible—and perhaps finally pointless—to try to distinguish genuine Buddhist influence from its look-alikes. A closer look at this fuzzy coupling of Buddhist epistemology and Buddhist-like epistemology enables us see how crucial aspects of American culture have become open and receptive to, if not already transformed by, Buddhist thought.

An excellent example of this phenomenon is the highly acclaimed book *Emotional Intelligence*. Drawing on studies of behavioral research, brain architecture, and human biology, psychologist Daniel Goleman argued in this book that people who excel in the emotional areas of life tend to excel in other areas of life as well. In fact, Goleman found that success in developing close relationships was a better predictor of success in the workplace than IQ. If they were emotionally balanced and open, Goleman argued, even people with modest IQs tended to be more productive contributors to society than people with much higher IQs whose emotions were less well-trained.

For our purposes, the most interesting aspect of Goleman's book is its lack of any reference to Goleman's background in *vipassana* meditation. Once you know about this background, its inspirational force is evident throughout the book—for example, in the analysis of the "anatomy of rage" in the chapter "Passion's Slaves," and in the terminology of a later chapter, "Managing with Heart." But there is no explicit mention of Buddhism anywhere. Readers who warmed to his ideas could have their worldviews altered without the slightest idea that they had been influenced by Buddhism. As Goleman said of an earlier work, "The Dharma is so disguised that it could never be proven in court."[16]

Other instances of the relationship between Buddhist influence and Buddhist-like thought are even more difficult to sort out. Take, for example, the form of textual analysis known as deconstruction and its popularity among many academics in France and the United States. Jacques Lacan, Gilles Deleuze, Jacques Derrida, and other French developers of poststructuralist and deconstructionist theory challenged Freudian ideas about the omniscience of the psychoanalyst and the autonomy of the patient. In broader scope, they emphasized the artificial and porous nature of subjectivity, questioned the idealization of creative originality, and challenged assumptions about the objectivity of texts and the authority of authors. Thus Derrida conceptualized each person's life as a text with a life of its own, largely free of authorial control, and every text as an ongoing narrative that is subject to innumerable forms of influence and interpretation.

This deconstructive analysis of texts emerged out of French psychoanalysis and especially out of the theoretical work of Jacques Lacan. In his 1960 paper "The Subversion of the Subject and the Dialectic of Desire," Lacan rejected the term *psychology* because "its criterion is the unity of the subject." With reference to one of Freud's cases involving a patient's dream of his dead father, in which the father did not know himself to be dead, Lacan asked, "If the figure of the dead father survives only by virtue of the fact that one does not tell him the truth of which he is unaware, what, then, is to be said of the *I*, on which this survival depends?" Remarking on the insubstantiality of the patient's "I," Lacan concluded in a typical flash of arcane terminology, "Being of non-being, that is how *I* as subject comes on the scene, conjugated with the double aporia of a true survival that is abolished by knowledge of itself, and by a discourse in which it is death that sustains existence."[17]

This sounds like the antipsychologism of the post-Freudian school of French psychoanalysis. It also sounds rather like Buddhism. In fact, Lacan mentioned Buddhism in passing in this article and, as a French intellectual, he was certainly familiar with Buddhist ideas. But it is impossible to measure, isolate, or prove Buddhism's influence on Lacan and his "subversion of the subject." Nevertheless, the idea that Lacan's deconstruction of selfhood is Buddhist-like is a useful way of seeing deconstruction as something more positive than a mean-spirited countercultural effort to overthrow Western epistemology by exposing its shaky underpinnings.

No less important, the recognition that deconstruction is Buddhist-like points us to the colonial and postcolonial context out of which French deconstruction emerged. Connections between French and Buddhist intellectuals were established in the sixteenth and seventeenth centuries by French Jesuits engaged in missionary activity in Southeast Asia and subsequently developed further in the context of French colonial rule in Vietnam, Cambodia, and Laos. As we have seen, the philosophy of French personalism played a crucial role in the Diem regime in Vietnam and its suppression of Buddhist nationalism. In 1960, during the presidency of John F. Kennedy, the center of support for the Diem regime shifted from Paris to Washington. But the French were largely responsible for the structure of this colonial arrangement. And beginning in the 1930s, Buddhists played an important role in challenging this structure and its religious and philosophical underpinnings in Catholic personalism. As a result of the increasing presence and visibility of Buddhist refugees in France, the development of Buddhist studies and Buddhist centers in France, and the coinciding development of postcolonial theory, French intellectuals became increasingly attuned to Buddhist philosophy.

Poststructuralism and deconstruction can be seen as part of a larger challenge to Western philosophy developed by French intellectuals critical of the imperialism of Western civilization and especially of French colonialism. After the Vietnam War, and in the context of American receivership of much of the legacy of Western imperialism, many American intellectuals became attracted to these developments in French psychoanalytic and literary theory. As the chumps in the Vietnam War, having played out, with much vainglory, a scenario set in motion by the French, Americans were ready for deconstruction and its fusion of cultural criticism and Buddhist-like epistemology.

American Zen

The Beat Zen of Gary Snyder, Allen Ginsberg, Jack Kerouac, Alan Watts, John Cage, Kenneth Rexroth, Diane Di Prima, and others is an important part of the story of Buddhism's seepage into American culture. These artists and intellectuals were disaffected from Western civilization and American culture before the Vietnam War broke out and they found inspiration for their disaffection in Buddhism's deconstructive force. They also found a welcome alternative to conventional forms of American religious life in Buddhism's emphasis on spiritual enlightenment and respect for all forms of life. And they were drawn especially to the spontaneity of Zen and to its demand for an intuitive grasp of things that broke through intellectual categories and the logical procedures of systematic thought. The Beats relished the iconoclasm of Zen as a way of breaking free of what they saw as the spiritual restrictiveness of American culture. Like the New England Transcendentalists of the previous century, they sought an immediate relationship to the universe beyond what they perceived as the confines of conventional religious life and its moralistic prescriptions and second-hand reports of spiritual experience. Like many American Puritans before that, the Beats looked beyond the moral authoritarianism of the institutional church to the grace that enabled moral life and brought happiness as well.

As American military intervention in Southeast Asia escalated during the 1960s, the Beats encouraged disaffection from the violence and greed of American culture in a younger generation and pointed to Buddhism and Hinduism as worthy spiritual traditions and welcome alternatives. Of course, the Buddhism celebrated by the Beats was rather different from many forms of living Buddhism in Asian countries—Sri Lanka, Burma, Thailand, Tibet, India, Cambodia, Vietnam, Laos, Korea, and Japan—where Buddhism had been practiced for centuries. As Buddhist immigrants from these countries to the United States found, American adaptations and appropriations of Buddhism were often novel.

Alan Watts, the Beat Anglican priest and freelance author-lecturer whose *Way of Zen* (1955) did much to popularize Zen for Americans, was so free in his interpretation of Zen that he believed that a person could practice Zen and even attain enlightenment while at the same time dispensing with *zazen,* the practice of sitting meditation taught in Zen monasteries by the *roshis,* or officially recognized teachers, who carried the lineages of traditional Zen authority. In Watt's view, Japanese monastic training was "Square Zen," which he compared unfavorably to the early Chinese Buddhists, whose Ch'an Buddhism was a combination of Indian Buddhism and Taoism. In the context of the militaristic and feudal culture of the Japanese samurai, Watts argued, the natural and simple spontaneity of the early Chinese masters had degenerated into Square Zen.[18]

The Beat poet Allen Ginsberg also took a novel approach to Buddhism. In his poem, "Why I Meditate," he made a list of reasons why he sat, reasons ranging from "because Buddha saw a Corpse in Lumbini" to "because the Yippies whooped up Chicago's teargas skies once" and "because I read about it in the Funny Papers." In another poem, "Ego Confession," Ginsberg wrote, "I want to be known as the most brilliant man in America," the man who "Prepared the way for Dharma," the man with the "extraordinary ego, at service of Dharma and completely empty. . . . " In an interview with Jack MacKenzie conducted in 1982, Ginsberg linked Buddhism's insight into the Big Mind of enlightened consciousness with the insights of the American Transcendentalists, calling attention to the legacy of Walt Whitman "announcing large magnanimous full-consciousness of American person" and to the legacy of Henry David Thoreau "pondering in the woods about the overgrowth of competitive materialism" and "going to jail not to pay war taxes for the Mexican War." Ginsberg vowed to transmit this legacy, and its connection with Buddhism, to the next generation. Linking the Beats' role as catalysts of the transformation of American culture in the twentieth century to their discovery of Buddhism, he credited his friend and fellow poet Jack Kerouac, whose experiments with automatic writing led him to the realization that Buddhist enlightenment was similar to insights gained through poetic inspiration. In pursuit of this inspiration, Ginsberg took the Bodhisattva vow, "sentient beings are numberless, vow to illuminate all; attachments are inexhaustible, vow to liberate all; nature gates, Dharma gates are countless, vow to enter every one; Buddha path limitless, endless, vow to follow through."[19]

Among all the artists and intellectuals usually associated with Beat Zen, the poet Gary Snyder made the most effort to become a serious practitioner of Buddhism by immersing himself in a living tradition of Asian Buddhism. Beginning in 1956, Snyder studied Zen in a Rinzai monastery in Japan for several years and became a disciple of Oda Sesso, head abbot of Daitokuji in Kyoto. But while devoting himself to an extremely arduous and highly orthodox form of monastic Zen Buddhism in the context of Japanese culture, Snyder discovered that his Beat appreciation of Zen was pretty idiosyncratic. Even more difficult to cope with than Rinzai practice itself, he recalled, was "the incomprehension of Japanese poets of my own generation with whom I could share a few hours' comradely talk until the subject of Zen came up, and then I lost them." While Snyder had been attracted to Zen at least partly because it offered a liberating alternative to what were to him the oppressive and unnatural features of American life, he found that this view of Zen was not widely shared in Japan. Indeed, many Japanese viewed Zen as a reactionary force connected with samurai culture.

While Snyder, Watts, and other artists and intellectuals played a crucial role in popularizing Buddhism for Americans, their own appreciation of Zen was inspired by D. T. Suzuki, the Japanese scholar-translator who laid the groundwork for Beat Zen. As Snyder explained, "Suzuki's presentation of Zen [was] in many ways a creative leap out of the medieval mentality" that had locked Zen inside a culture of "authoritarianism, feudalism, and militarism." It was "a personal way of pointing Zen in a fresh, liberating direction, without even saying so." Although he met Suzuki only once, at a dinner party in Kyoto in 1961, Snyder acknowledged that with respect to the influence of Suzuki's writing on his whole outlook on life and, more specifically, his decision to study Rinzai Zen in Japan, "D. T. Suzuki gave me the push of my life and I can never be too grateful." He also recognized that Suzuki's interpretation of Zen had a significant impact on American culture more broadly. "Now, living again in America," Snyder wrote in 1986, "I see evidence of his strong, subtle effect in many arts and fields, as well as in the communities of Americans now practicing Zen."[20]

In 1963, in his introduction to the reissue of Suzuki's *Outlines of Mahayana Buddhism,* Alan Watts credited Suzuki with being "the first great scholar-interpreter of the East to the West to come out of Asia." With regard to Suzuki's extraordinary influence on Western culture, especially in the United States, Watts referred to the remark made by James Bissett Pratt in the late twenties, after Suzuki had published *Essays in Zen Buddhism,* that "there are two kinds of cultured people: those who have read Suzuki and those who have not." And by the early sixties, Watts could say that Suzuki's ideas were "in the air" and that people could "catch them without [even] knowing their source."[21]

In her study of Zen in the United States, Helen Tworkov made a similar point about the pathbreaking nature of Suzuki's interpretation of Zen and its widespread influence in American culture. Tworkov noted that both D. T. Suzuki and Watts, who was Suzuki's first major popularizer, were criticized for identifying Zen as a kind of experience at least somewhat separable from formal meditation. At the same time, she emphasized that "in neither case can their influence in the United States be overestimated." And this influence laid the groundwork for the subsequent development of Buddhist meditation in American culture. Thus Tworkov argues that "it was precisely their liberal, visionary commitment to transmit Zen independent of its cultural identity that eased Zen into the intellectual life of the West and directly inspired the (more formal) training that followed."

Born in 1870 in Kanazawa in the Ishikawa Prefecture of Japan, Teitaro Suzuki first came to the United States in 1897 to assist Paul Carus in translating the *Tao Te Ching* into English. The year before, he had published an essay on Emerson and translated a draft of Shaku Soen's address to the World's Parliament of Religions. When Carus met Soen in Chicago, he asked Soen's help in finding a translator, and Soen recommended Suzuki. Suzuki spent ten years working at Carus's publishing company in LaSalle, Illinois. After attending the World Congress of Faiths in London in 1936, he visited the United States again to lecture on Buddhist philosophy at several universities. In 1949, he attended the East-West Philosopher's Conference in Honolulu; the following year, at the age of eighty, he moved to New York and embarked on a series of lectures entitled "Oriental Culture and Thought" sponsored by the Rockefeller Foundation at Princeton, Columbia, Harvard, Chicago, Yale, Cornell, Northwestern, and Wesleyan Universities. He lectured at Columbia as a visiting professor from 1952 to 1957, when he moved to Cambridge, Massachusetts, and lectured at Harvard, MIT, Wellesley, Brandeis, Radcliffe, and Amherst. Suzuki died in Tokyo in 1966, having made various forms of Buddhism, especially Zen Buddhism, accessible to many American intellectuals.

In contrast to the emphasis on gradual enlightenment taught by the Soto Zen roshi Shunryu Suzuki in the San Francisco Bay area beginning in 1958, D. T. Suzuki emphasized the experience of sudden enlightenment. He identified Zen with satori, or enlightenment, and with *kensho,* the experience of seeing into one's own nature that provided a taste of satori. D. T. Suzuki introduced the Rinzai commitment to the quest for sudden enlightenment that, as we have seen, appealed to athletically-oriented, outcome-minded Americans who were conditioned by the pragmatism and materialism of their culture to want to strive for something. However much it had a tendency to fall into what the Tibetan teacher Chogyam Trungpa called "spiritual materialism," the Rinzai emphasis on the breakthrough experience of sudden enlightenment was something that Americans could relate to and, in some cases, even feel that they had always been preparing and looking for.[22] Satori came across as what the American psychologist Abraham Maslow called a "peak experience." It also came across as an apprehension of the living presence of God.

In bringing Rinzai Zen into American culture, D. T. Suzuki presented the experience of satori as something more universal than Japanese culture and even independent of the formal regime of meditation. He also reconstructed the meaning of satori by conceptualizing it in terms of Western philosophical theology and by comparing it with the experience of God in Christianity. Thus in an essay on satori, Suzuki began by equating this breakthrough experience with the essence of Zen. "To understand Zen," he wrote, "it is essential to have an experience known as *satori*, for without this one can have no insight into the truth of Zen." Then he invoked well-known terms from Continental European philosophy to explain the nature of this experience. "[G]enuine satori is at once transcendental and immanental." But, he went on to caution, satori is not "a mere intellectual discipline." Indeed, "satori is existential and not dialectical, as Kierkegaard may say." Moreover, Suzuki explained, satori was an existential leap analogous to Christian faith in which the end result was the same. "Kierkegaaard says that faith is an existential leap. So is satori." Even though "[f]aith has a Christian ring, while satori is specifically Zen, both are experientially identifiable."

Later in the same essay, Suzuki pointed to the idea of "the Absolute Present" in both Zen Buddhism and in the sayings of Jesus. Quoting from the King James Bible, he focused on Matthew 6 34: "Take therefore no thought for the morrow, for the morrow shall take thought for the things of itself. Sufficient unto the day is the evil thereof." While Zen and Jesus each had a distinctive way of saying things, Suzuki explained, the experience they pointed to was one and the same. But in many cases, he went on to argue, Christians did not really understand what Jesus was saying, or experience the Absolute Present as he had. Christians tended to think of God as having "many ethical and spiritual appendages, which in fact keep him from them." As Suzuki explained, Christians failed to experience the Absolute Present, or naked God, because "they somehow hesitate to appear before him also in their nakedness, that is, take hold of him in the Absolute Present." But "[w]hen Christians stand all naked, shorn of their dualistic garments," Suzuki promised, "they will discover that their God is no other than the Absolute Present itself."[23]

As these quotations reveal, D. T. Suzuki did not import Rinzai Zen to the United States in an unexpurgated way. He translated Rinzai Zen into the categories of philosophical theology familiar to American religious intellectuals. And more than that, he used this existential Zen to tell them what Jesus was talking about. The transcendental-immanent reality of satori *was* the God of the Bible. But the naked reality of the biblical God was hidden from many twentieth-century Christians because they had not made the existential leap of faith beyond the dualisms of subject and object, self and world, consciousness and God.

In his introduction to Suzuki's *Outlines of Mahayana Buddhism*, Alan Watts observed that "there is an almost uncanny affinity between some of the major trends of modern Western thought and Buddhist philosophy." But Suzuki's own familiarity with Western thought made the tendency of twentieth-century Continental and American philosophers to "think like Buddhists" less weird and inexplicable than Watts believed. Buddhism's attractiveness to Western intellectuals was partly the result of Suzuki's adeptness in handling the categories of Western thought and his sensitivity to the spiritual thirst and theological dilemmas that Westerners experienced.

In presenting Zen to Christians as a means to better understanding of their own tradition, and as a means of apprehending the God of their own scriptures and traditions, Suzuki was working, at least partially, as a Christian or post-Christian theologian. Utilizing concepts of the existential, transcendental, and immanent that derived from Continental European philosophy and New England Transcendentalism, he was speaking to Europeans and Americans about their own religious lives, which of course were shaped by their own religious and philosophical traditions. Suzuki reconstructed Buddhism in terms of concepts that were largely derived from liberal Protestantism and post-Protestant philosophical theology. He was familiar with both Kant and Emerson and with the work of a variety of philosophical theologians working in the twentieth century, including Alfred North Whitehead, John Dewey, Martin Heidegger, Carl Jung, and Paul Tillich. Like many of these thinkers, Suzuki was skilled in addressing people with backgrounds in Protestant Christianity. Also like these thinkers, he was interested in going beyond the confines of Protestantism, Christianity, and even religion itself in order to grasp the most basic dynamics of human experience and their connection to ultimate reality.

This deliberate effort to reach beyond the structures of particular denominations, cultures, and religions to more basic and universal forms of spiritual experience was a strategy that, in the modern era, emerged out of liberal Protestantism and post-Protestant philosophical theology. Indeed, the effort to reach beyond particular religious structures to a large extent defined liberal Protestantism and post-Protestant philosophical theology. As this strategic effort developed, many of the specifically Protestant elements associated with it receded in importance, and people from other traditions joined in, contributing to the development of this way and making it their own. Thanks in no small part to D. T. Suzuki, Buddhism came to play an important role in the process of lifting up universal forms of spiritual experience underlying particular religions. Moreover, as Suzuki offered it up, the Zen experience of satori also represented the goal of this universal spiritual process. In America especially, thanks to Suzuki's influence here, the Zen experience evolved into something like a nonsectarian form of grace, available not only to seasoned meditators, but also to motorcyclists, basketball players, victims of addiction, and anyone else who wanted to live fully and happily in the moment.

Jewish Buddhism

One of the most interesting aspects of Buddhism's merger with American religious and intellectual life is its disproportionate appeal to people with backgrounds in Judaism. If liberal Protestantism and post-Protestant philosophical theology played the leading role in defining the intellectual context in which Buddhism came to popularity in the United States, Jews often took the lead in the subsequent development of American forms of Buddhism.

Between the early seventies and the early nineties, Jews constituted between 6 percent and 30 percent of Americans affiliated with Buddhist groups who had not been born into Buddhist families. Since Jews were approximately 2.5 percent of the population of the United States, this meant that they joined Buddhist groups at a rate between two and twelve times that of other Americans. Moreover, a significant and disproportionate number of officially recognized American-born teachers of Buddhist practice in the United States came from Jewish backgrounds, including the Zen teacher, entrepreneur, and author Tetsugen Roshi (Bernard Glassman), the Tibetan Buddhist nun, meditation teacher, and author Thubten Chodron (born Cherry Green), and all four founders of the *vipassana* Insight Meditation Society—Jack Kornfield, Joseph Goldstein, Sharon Salzberg, and Jacqueline Schwartz. The statistics on Jewish involvement in Buddhist scholarship are equally impressive. In the eighties and nineties, a significant and disproportionate number of scholars of Buddhism teaching at colleges and universities in the United States came from Jewish backgrounds, including Alex Wayman, Matthew Kapstein, Anne Klein, Charles Prebish, Steve Heine, and a number of others. In many cases, these scholars of Buddhism also practiced Buddhist meditation and belonged to Buddhist communities.

Several factors contributed to the high presence and visibility of American Buddhists from Jewish backgrounds. For one thing, the emphasis on intellectual training and the study of religious texts served as a bridge between Judaism and elite forms of Buddhism. In its elite and, in many cases, monastic forms, Buddhism was highly intellectual, rational, and psychologically oriented. These elite forms of Buddhism attracted a number of people whose familiarity with Jewish traditions of scriptural and scholarly study and religious debate prepared them to find Buddhist philosophy stimulating.

In addition to this bridge of intellectual training and religious study, both traditions focus on suffering and its implications for religious and spiritual life. A disproportionate number of Jews work in professions dedicated to healing suffering, including the mental health professions. To a significant extent, Jewish history is a history of suffering, and Jewish history is the predominant framework of Jewish identity. Since World War II and the Nazi effort to systematically exterminate the Jewish "race," Jews have been preoccupied with the religious and spiritual implications of the massive suffering endured by Jews in the Holocaust. In this context, the First Noble Truth of Buddhism, that existence is suffering, was something to which Jews could certainly relate.

But Buddhist approaches to the nature of suffering have not always met with Jewish approval. As Rodger Kamenetz's description of the 1989 dialogue between Jews and the Dalai Lama and other Tibetan Buddhists in Dharamsala revealed, some of the Jews who made the trip to Dharamsala could not accept the Buddhist idea that karmic action and one's own desires caused suffering. But Buddhism appealed to other Jews in the group precisely because it addressed their own doubts about the necessity of suffering and offered a way to become free of its power.

In addition, the nontheistic aspect of Buddhist philosophy provided a way around the problem that more than a few American Jews had with God. For these Jews, belief in a theistic God—the man upstairs who loved and protected people like a father—was impossible. If such a deity existed, his apparent decision to stand by idly during the Holocaust would seem to convict him of the grossest kind of moral negligence. Buddhism's understanding of ultimate reality as the mind-stream, or universal flow of consciousness, offered another way to think about God, or a way to experience and think about the sacredness of reality without having to resort to a theistic deity, and without having to accept the ethical outrage that belief in such a deity created.

Similarly, the emphasis that many Buddhist teachers placed on the universal truth and relevance of Buddhist thought and practice appealed to Jews frustrated with the Jewish emphasis on ethnic particularism. In the United States, Kamenetz argued, many Jews tended to think of Judaism as the property of their own particular ethnic group. This tendency functioned to minimize the spiritual and mystical aspects of Judaism, the very things that Jews attracted to Buddhism were hungry for. Most Jews attracted to Buddhism, Kamenetz explained, "grew up with a Judaism heavy on ethnic pride, obsessive about preserving itself, about maintaining Jewish identity at all costs." But such an emphasis on ethnic identity, Kamenetz went on to say, "seems to contradict the very universalistic prophetic messages Judaism also teaches." Because of their impatience with Jewish particularism and their underlying investment in Jewish universalism, Kamenetz suggested, "some JUBUs [an acronym formed from the sounds of the words *Jew* and *Buddhist*] left Judaism *because* of their Jewish ideals."[24]

Putting this tension between ethnic pride and the universalistic prophetic messages of Judaism in the context of American religious history, it is useful to note that Judaism in the United States developed in relation to a larger cultural mix shaped by Anglo Protestant habits of thought and that, to some extent at least, trends in American Jewish history reflect some of the trends of this larger cultural mix. More specifically, the tendency to define Judaism in terms of ethnic pride and tribal chosenness can be seen as part of a larger inclination within American religious history to define religion in moralistic terms at the expense of its wisdom, beauty, and inclusive spiritual qualities. This tendency toward moralism has often generated a countertendency to revitalize spiritual vitality, as in the case of the New England Transcendentalists who looked to German philosophy, English Romanticism, and Asian religions for inspiration. More recently, Jews have looked to Buddhism for help in recovering the inclusive, spiritual aspects of their own religious tradition.

If a number of Jews have been drawn to Buddhism because it offered ways of developing their own spirituality, it is equally true that Buddhism in the United States has been shaped by the Jews it has attracted. The high Jewish presence among students, teachers, and scholars of Buddhism has affected the intellectual, cultural, and spiritual development of this tradition in the United States. The late founder of the Naropa Institute in Boulder, Colorado, the Tibetan teacher Chogyam Trungpa, adopted Jewish expressions to explain Buddhist concepts, and joked that he learned to teach with a Yiddish accent. Trungpa interpreted the Buddhist precept "Existence is suffering" in terms of the Yiddish concept of *tzuris,* or troubles. And with reference to the large number of Jews at Naropa and their special combination of *tzuris* and self-deprecating, parodic humor, Trungpa referred to his students as "the Oy Vay school of Buddhism."[25]

In addition to the many specific contributions that individual Jews have made to the development of American Buddhism, some characteristic Jewish sensibilities may have made their way into American Buddhism and shaped its development in a profound and general way. Perhaps the most important thing Jews have brought to Buddhism is *menschlichkeit. Mensch* is a Yiddish term of honor for a decent man or person, but a mensch is not necessarily a pious individual. Nor is a mensch defined by investment in the ethnic particularism or chosen-peoplehood aspect of Judaism. Rather, the mensch represents the universalist aspect of Jewish life and thought, the nonsectarian, humanistic embodiment of Judaism's ethical force.

In theory at least, any truly decent person, regardless of religious background, could be called a mensch. At the same time, the term *mensch* derives from Jewish religion and Yiddish culture. As a living expression of good-heartedness and fair judgment, the mensch epitomizes the realism of Jewish thought and the humanistic thrust of Jewish ethics.

One way to think about Jewish influence in the development of Buddhism in the United States is in terms of a shift from monkhood to menschhood or, one might say, in terms of a tendency to define Buddha-hood as a *menschlichkeit* kind of thing. Instead of monkhood being the most exemplary form of Buddhism, as it is in Asia, human decency, compassion, and self-understanding in more ordinary human terms have come to represent what many American Buddhists think of as exemplary expressions of Buddhist life. Partly as a result of Jewish Buddhists who have brought their appreciation of human decency into Buddhism, Buddhism has become more identified with the common touch. If some people rolled their eyes at Buddhist philosophy and thought of it primarily in terms of naive idealism, the extinction of righteous feeling, and the austerities of shaved heads, brown rice, and carrot tops, the *menschlichkeit* dimension of American Buddhism functioned as a corrective.

Taking a step back from this fertile blend of *menschlichkeit* and dharma, we can see a larger historical and cultural context enabling this blend. In the post-Protestant and even post-Christian world of contemporary American religious life, a simple, pragmatic notion of sainthood has persisted, merging with other religious traditions to define a kind of basic standard for personhood. In the guise of a variety of different religious and doctrinal wardrobes, the dharma mensch is defined not by position in a religious hierarchy or by the kind of extraordinary religious virtuosity that might be associated with displays of supernatural power, but rather with the personal expression of what, in a down-to-earth and unpretentious way, might be called grace.

5

Gender Consciousness, Body Awareness, and the Humanization of Religion

What has been termed a monotheistic ordering—expressed in the self-referentiality of language, the narcissistic patterning of the autonomous individual, the self-preservation of the state—must be uncovered and resisted . . . Conceived in this way, feminist theology is good news, good news to the desperate world, to the hungry masses, to desiring individuals, to the diseased planet . . . The hope is not that feminism can give all the answers but that feminism can hold fast to tracing the possibilities of questioning anew.

Rebecca Chopp, *The Power to Speak*[1]

I was in a feminist consciousness-raising group. We talked a good deal about our problems . . . about being women, students, lovers, and working women . . . We talked about whatever it was that was going on in our lives at that time, but we never really were able to formulate anything beyond or larger than ourselves . . . We were good at defining negatives.

I needed something that spoke to me directly about being a woman . . . decisions about my sexuality, for instance. I had enough of one night stands . . . I wanted to know how sexuality would fit into my life, you know, over the long haul. Orthodoxy had an answer to that . . . When I learned about the family purity laws . . . they immediately made sense to me.

Two Newly Orthodox Women, *Rachel's Daughters*[2]

As well as undergoing the experiences of disenchantment and self-analysis that accompanied the decline of victory culture in the decades following the Vietnam War, people in the United States also became intensely self-conscious about gender. Indeed, awareness of the social construction of gender was part of the process of disenchantment, and part of the process of deconstructing selfhood, that engaged many Americans in the last decades of the twentieth century. Traditional, religiously sanctioned patterns of gender role differentiation could no longer be taken for granted. Ideals of manhood and womanhood once accepted as universal models fell under critique.

As many Americans learned, the term *gender* referred to socially constructed norms for males and females. Gender was something above and beyond biological sex. In other words, society imposed elaborate and often oppressive gender role expectations on individuals simply because of their sex. Gender role expectations were present in and part of the basic structure of every human society.

But if gender role expectations were a fundamental aspect of all forms of human culture, it was only in the latter decades of the twentieth century that these expectations became a frequent subject of conscious reflection and open discussion. Of course, attempts to lift restrictions on women's activities and promote greater equality between women and men were not new. Such efforts were common in the nineteenth century, when American, British, and European social reformers called for the extension of women's influence in society and, in many cases, for the extension of their political rights. More roundabout approaches to elevating the status of women certainly existed in many times and places before that, as did special allowances for particular women of genius. But not until the last part of the twentieth century did the idea really take hold that gender was a means of social control and that, consequently, gender was an essential element of social change open to strategic manipulation.

The religious implications of this new self-consciousness about gender were profound. People interested in analyzing gender roles kept running into religion, as did people who wanted to change those roles. And people involved in studying or advancing religion kept running into gender. Beginning in the 1970s, it became increasingly apparent that religion played a major part in defining and sanctioning gender roles. It also became apparent that religion was subject to deconstruction as part of the analysis of gender in any given society. Advocates of changing, loosening, or expanding gender roles saw the deconstruction and reformulation of religion as a means to their goal. And for those who resisted more flexible and porous gender roles, it was clear that religion's role in defining and sanctioning traditional gender roles needed to be more deliberately and tactfully supported than ever before.

In the course of these interesting and multifaceted developments, religion became more open to strategic manipulation from all sides. The social functions of religion were increasingly recognized and increasingly subject to various forms of tinkering. In this process, religion came more and more to be viewed as a cultural and thoroughly human phenomenon.

Mary Daly Sums It Up

The renegade American Catholic philosopher Mary Daly was a pioneer in pursuing the connection between religion and gender. The briefest tracing of the progression of ideas in her first four books illuminates the inner logic of the growing awareness of this connection. In the spirit of reform that swept through American Catholicism in the wake of the second Vatican Council, Daly's first book, *The Church and the Second Sex* (1968), argued that the Catholic Church was a contributor to women's oppression and that the time had come to face up to that and move the Church beyond it. Daly's second book, *Beyond God the Father: Toward a Philosophy of Women's Liberation* (1973), was less hopeful about reform. Defining the central thrust of the whole Judeo-Christian tradition as a means of instantiating patriarchy, Daly argued that belief in God's paternal nature, and the rituals and institutions that inculcated that belief, established women's subordinate status. Images of God's paternal oversight created a picture of the cosmic structure of reality that sanctioned men's control of women and perpetuated women's submission to men.

In her third book, *Gyn/Ecology: The Metaethics of Radical Feminism* (1978), Daly went further, arguing that patriarchal religions functioned not only to legitimate women's subordinate status in society, but also to legitimate violence against both women and nature. Patriarchal religions, Daly argued, exploited the powerful perceived analogy between women's bodies and the natural world. Women's bodies were seized, possessed, and domesticated as if they were plots of land—and plots of land were subjugated as if they were women's bodies. In her fourth book, *Pure Lust: Elemental Feminist Philosophy* (1984), Daly urged women to take control of the metaphors linking their bodies to the natural world. Not only should they throw off the Father God, but they should embrace the Goddess and see her as a metaphor for themselves and for the invigoration and ascendance of their own "elemental" powers.

Of course, Daly was not alone in constructing a feminist theology— or thealogy, as some preferred to distinguish their enterprise from the patriarchal sort—nor did she represent its most commonly agreed upon conclusions. More numerous feminist theologians continued to identify with Christian or Jewish traditions while subjecting those traditions to critique and revision. Thus Christian feminists strove to separate the gospel from patriarchal interpretations and to emphasize its egalitarian message and support for people who were suffering and oppressed. Jewish feminists strove to recast both the ethical force of Judaism and its commitment to live in harmony with the created world in ways that emphasized the importance of women's religious lives. Although fewer in number, Islamic feminists embarked on a somewhat similar path, affirming respectfulness toward women in the Qur'an and Hadith and criticizing oppressive regimes in the Islamic world for distorting the truth about Islam's regard for women.

Sticking with their traditions of birth and struggling to reform them, these feminist theologians did not follow Mary Daly on a path of rejection that never returned home. But if Daly did not sway the ultimate loyalty to tradition that would define the work of most feminist theologians, she did play a pioneering role in calling attention to two groundbreaking insights of gender analysis, namely, the inherent connection between religion and gender and the related connection between images of women and images of nature. Daly was among the first theologians to see that one of the principal functions of religion was to define and sanction gender roles. She was also among the first to see that religion's contribution to defining gender depended on the construction and maintenance of belief in a fundamental connection between womanhood and nature.

Daly's realization that some version of this connection between womanhood and nature lay at the heart of virtually all religions led her to encourage women to exploit it for their own benefit and for the health of the planet. In other words, she saw more clearly than anyone before her that religion's role in constructing gender could be manipulated and reimagined. Of course, women in earlier times and places had manipulated religious symbols and participated in the construction of gender. But even when that participation enabled women to develop religious symbols in ways that generated female solidarity and pride, it presumed their assent to the defining myths of their culture, which inevitably explained and sanctioned women's subordination. As the anthropologist Michelle Rosaldo argued, women in every known society achieved social influence by exerting pressure on men, controlling information, rewarding those who enhanced their influence, and establishing female subcultures that promoted their own strength and their own interpretations of reality. But even in the most egalitarian societies, women have been subordinate to men.[3] As Mary Daly was one of the first to see, religion functioned to define and establish that subordination.

What distinguished Daly and other feminist theologians from women in more traditional societies was not their exertion of pressure on society through religion, but their understanding of gender as a social construct mediated by religious symbols, myths, and rituals. In this understanding, not only was gender a plastic and relativistic social construct, but to a large extent so was religion. Thus Daly and her cohort did not stop with analysis of myths of male dominance and the mystique of femininity, but pressed on toward a thoroughgoing reinvention of religion. They used gender analysis as a kind of blueprint of how religion actually worked to construct human society, and they employed this blueprint in endeavors to create better religions, which they hoped would create better societies and better relationships with the natural world.

Widespread awareness of the constructedness of gender played a key role in the larger transformation of American religion because it made that constructedness more apparent, in turn making religion more malleable, more vulnerable, more subject to correction, and more humane than ever before. In many cases, feminist theologians led the way in insisting that religion conform to the standard of what the Catholic feminist Elizabeth A. Johnson called "human flourishing." Like other feminist theologians, Johnson claimed that women's emancipation was the prime measure of this flourishing and that no aspect of religion should be overlooked or set aside in the process of working toward it. As Rosemary Radford Ruether put it, "[T]he critical principle of feminist theology is the promotion of the full humanity of women. Whatever denies, diminishes, or distorts the full humanity of women is, therefore, appraised as not redemptive." On the other hand, "this negative principle also implies the positive principle: what does promote the full humanity of women is of the Holy, it does reflect true relation to the divine, it is the true nature of things, the authentic message of redemption and the mission of redemptive community."[4]

Once this criterion of human flourishing, measured in terms of promotion of the full humanity of women, became explicit and paraded out in the open, then every religion—feminist or not—became subject to it. After all, no group of people wanted to think that its religion worked *against* human flourishing or the full humanity of women. Once the pragmatic criterion of benefit to humanity was in the air, it was hard to resist reconstructing every living religion in its terms.

This pragmatic, humanistic, and sometimes masterminding approach to religion altered religion in a fundamental way. As we saw at the end of Chapter 3, once the religious, cultural, and ideological structure of reality was dismantled, subsequent efforts to put the world back together left the internal structures of that world more fully exposed. Humpty Dumpty could be put back together again, but afterward, his constructedness was more far apparent than before. Thus awareness of the constructed nature of religion became difficult to escape, and the principal reason for this difficulty was the popularity of gender theory, which led repeatedly and inevitably to the discovery of how deeply religion was interlaced with social constructions of gender. For some, awareness of the constructed nature of religion dogged the peripheral edges of religious vision despite efforts to deny it or brush it away, while others openly and even gleefully celebrated it. Perhaps the majority of Americans came down somewhere in between, aware that religious life had become more tenuous, more human, more in need of help, and more responsive to change, but not entirely sure why or how this transformation happened or whether it was a good thing.

Gender Consciousness

Although the term *gender* did not enter common parlance until the 1970s, American intellectuals were already familiar with the theory behind it. The idea that men's and women's roles were socially constructed first took shape in the context of Marxist analysis of the economic function of beliefs about women and the family in a capitalist society. In *The Origin of the Family, Private Property and the State* (1884 in German), Friedrich Engels argued that an ideology of womanhood and family life functioned to legitimate private ownership of property. This ideology, and the capitalist economic system underlying it, required women's subordination to men and implied that women belonged to men as part of their private property.

Feminism emerged as a more general theory about the social construction of women's roles partly as a result of such Marxist analysis of the role of womanhood in capitalist ideology and partly as a result of political efforts to promote women's rights, which were increasingly supported by this sort of analysis. The emergence of sociology as an academic discipline at the turn of the twentieth century and its more general interest in the interdependence between expressed values and underlying structures also stimulated the development of feminism. Along with Marxist analysis, theories advanced by Max Weber about the relationship between the social values and social structure, and theories advanced by Emile Durkheim about the function of belief and ritual in maintaining social order, contributed to the early development of feminism.

Although many historians point to the women's movement of the mid-nineteenth century, with its activism in support of women's rights, as the "first wave" of American feminism, the term *feminism* itself did not enter intellectual parlance in the United States until the second decade of the twentieth century. As Nancy F. Cott discovered in her study of feminism's early development, Hubertine Auclert, the organizer of the first woman suffrage society in France, coined the terms *féministe* and *féminisme* in the 1880s. In writings published in the United States, the term *feminism* was first invoked in 1913, when proponents of sexual equality introduced it to mark a new approach to women's equality based on analysis of the social construction of women's roles.

Like the social reformers associated with the women's movement in the nineteenth century, the feminists of the early twentieth century advocated greater rights for women. But the first feminists distinguished themselves from participants in the earlier women's movement by rejecting the argument that women should have equal suffrage, or other opportunities to contribute to public life, because of special, God-given moral instincts that were inherent in their nature as women. In rejecting this naturalist argument, feminists maintained that traditional ideas about womanhood were not as firmly grounded in biological reality or divine decree as many people believed. As social activists interested in the most strategically effective means of reform, the early feminists believed that women were more likely to succeed in their efforts to attain greater equality with men once womanhood came to be perceived as a social construct. And they believed that more women would be motivated to work for equal rights once they came to perceive themselves as members of a social as well as biological group.[5]

Interest in the social construction of women's roles declined during and immediately after the Second World War, when Americans invested considerable effort in pulling their society together and Marxist analysis gained a reputation as blasphemous and incendiary. In the sixties and seventies, when Marxist analysis became popular again and widespread interest in the human personality encouraged many women to feel dissatisfied with the social and psychological restraints imposed on their development as individuals, feminism sprang back to life with new vitality. The democratic idealism of the civil rights movement contributed to this revitalization of feminism by stirring general enthusiasm for political equality and stimulating recollection of nineteenth-century American women whose involvement in the cause of abolition led them to become advocates of women's rights. This political enthusiasm coincided with a psychological enthusiasm for unlocking human potential by freeing personality from obstacles that hindered its development. At the same time, the disillusionment with American culture occasioned by the Vietnam War contributed to a general distrust of conventional norms and expectations, which in turn provided a hospitable context for rediscovering the early-twentieth century feminist idea that women were members of a social group whose subordination was part of an oppressive social system.

With her widely influential book *The Feminine Mystique* (1963),

Betty Friedan led the way in generating enthusiasm for the feminist idea that women's roles were in large part social constructions. The popularity of *The Feminine Mystique* was partly due to its timeliness— Friedan's argument that femininity was an oppressive social ideology fell on receptive ears—and partly due to its success in exploiting current theories about the human personality and its psychological development. Sidestepping any explicit engagement with Marxist analysis, Friedan zeroed in instead on the concerns about psychological development that preoccupied many Americans. Utilizing the concept of self-actualization advanced by Abraham Maslow to describe the process of healthy psychological development, Friedan argued that the ideology of femininity caused many women to forfeit self-actualization and full individuality. Thus *The Feminine Mystique* succeeded in popularizing gender analysis by locating it in the context of the widespread postwar American fascination with personality.

Freidan's argument that traditional roles for women were ideological constructs hampering self-actualization figured importantly in the consciousness-raising (CR) groups of the 1970s. CR groups usually comprised less than a dozen (mostly young) women who gathered together on a more or less regular basis to discuss their lives as women. For the most part, the women who joined these groups were already critical of American involvement in Vietnam and at least somewhat disaffected from American culture. CR meetings focused this disaffection onto women's issues and encouraged participants to interpret their personal difficulties and frustrations in political terms. The National Organization for Women (NOW), along with the New York Radical Feminists and other CR pioneers, played an important role in generating enthusiasm for these groups by promoting them in writing and speeches and by suggesting discussion topics for group sessions and guidelines for facilitating them.[6]

Also in the seventies, women's studies programs were established in many colleges and universities. Typically, these programs had two purposes. On one level, they were intended to promote and support women and protest discrimination against them both within academic institutions and in the larger world. In this regard, women's studies programs carried forward much of the same agenda as CR groups. On another level, these programs were established to promote the neglected but important study of women's roles in society and thus to advance understanding of human culture and society across all areas of the humanities and social sciences. By the nineties, both of these agendas had succeeded to the extent that some faculty even entertained the question of whether women's studies programs needed to exist any longer. As many people agreed, significant strides had been made in challenging discrimination against women within American colleges and universities. At the same time, the feminist idea that social expectations for women should be scrutinized as ideological constructs had become well established and figured importantly within many areas of academic theory and subject matter.

The term *gender* became popular in the context of this feminist success. As a subfield within many disciplines and departments in the liberal arts, gender studies developed out of feminist theory as a way of broadening the implications of the social construction of sex roles to incorporate analysis of men's values and behavior as well as women's. Gender studies also developed as a way of encouraging more cutting-edge forms of social and textual analysis, such as queer studies and the study of pornography. In academic circles, then, gender analysis became partially separated from the social activist side of feminism and its commitment to constant and direct political pressure on behalf of the advancement of women's equality. Of course, the development of gender studies as a phenomenon distinct from women's studies occurred in institutional contexts familiar with and friendly toward the egalitarian ideals of feminism that had been promoted through women's studies. Nevertheless, as gender analysis became more widespread across the academy it also began to float free of the political interpretations and restraints that some feminists wanted to impose.

In her book *Hard Core: Power, Pleasure, and the "Frenzy of the Visible"* (1989), film studies scholar Linda Williams challenged feminists who flatly condemned all pornography as men's sexual exploitation of female victims. Gendered expressions of power and submission were often quite fluid in pornographic film, Williams found. In playing off stereotypical categories of male power and female submission, pornography often challenged, inverted, or merged those categories. As an important cultural product that exposed the plasticity and permeability of gender roles, Williams argued, pornography was more deserving of dispassionate study than across-the-board moral condemnation.

In the expanded edition of her book, published in 1999, Williams admitted that she had geared herself to defend the book against anti-porn feminists—who, it turned out, mostly ignored it—and had found herself unprepared for the enthusiastic interest with which others greeted it. In addition to gay men who welcomed her investigation of pornography as an art form that did not deserve to be cast out of serious discussion for its alleged abuse of women, Williams found her most appreciative readers to be "pro-sex" feminists, whom she defined as "women who are interested in sexuality and who do not see masculine sexuality as the root cause of the oppression of women."

Williams's failure to predict positive interest in her book represented more than a lapse in judgment about American feminism. Her book reflected and contributed to an important shift toward examination of the body that occurred in feminist theory during the eighties and nineties. As both an outgrowth of the sexual revolution of the sixties and seventies and a critical assessment of it, this shift in feminist theory played a leading role in a larger cultural trend toward increased attention to the body and public discussion about it.

During the nineties, pro-sex feminism became increasingly visible in American culture, as did both pornography and public condemnation of pornography. As pornography was increasingly marketed to women and available to anyone on the Internet, women showed more open interest in it than ever before. Meanwhile, opponents outraged by its accessibility also joined the discussion and contributed to the unprecedented publicity for pornography. When Jesse Helms displayed pornographic photos on the Senate floor and the penis of the president of the United States became an object frequently referred to in the American media, the very nature of obscenity was transformed. No longer "off-scene" as part of stag culture and its "secret museums," as Williams explained in 1999, obscenity came "on/scene"—visible and available to all. As a result, pornography could no longer be summed up in "sweeping generalizations about the phallic mastery of a disembodied 'male gaze. ' " Even if pornography had originally been "designed for a male subject to play with a female object," Williams observed, "in an era of on/scenity, there is really no limit to who will play the game."[7]

Both pornography and religion deal with the limits of human experience and humane behavior, and both are concerned with reaching and transcending those limits. In American culture at the end of the twentieth century, both religion and pornography were very much on scene, more visible and open to public examination than ever before and more subject to reinterpretation. Increasing sophistication about how religion and pornography were constructed affected the way people participated in and understood these phenomena. As a result, Americans did not become any less committed to religion, or any less involved in pornography, than they were in the fifties. But increased self-consciousness about these things, and increased understanding about how they were constructed, altered their nature.

Attitudes toward gender and the body played a central role in the public exposure that both religion and pornography underwent. Awareness of gender as a social construct figured prominently in the explosion of open discussion of pornography, whether it was gay men celebrating pornography as an art form that broke free of oppressive stereotypes about gender or members of the Christian Right working against pornography in the media. Similarly, awareness of gender also figured prominently in the transformation of American religion and its subjection to the criterion of human flourishing. And all this self-consciousness about gender precipitated a new level of attentiveness to the body. As part of the larger cultural changes affecting both religion and pornography, the body came to be seen as a important site of cultural construction and religious concern.

From Feminist Ideology to Body Awareness

While debates about gender could be highly ideological and abstract, they also cleared the way for a new attentiveness to the body, which by its nature could never be viewed as wholly ideological or abstract. As an important part of the transformation of American religion, discussions about the intertwining of religion and gender helped to clear the way for discoveries about the important role of the body in religious life. These discoveries attended to the realities of corporeality, sensation, and life and death, even as they incorporated analysis of the body's social construction. With increasing frequency, discussion of these realities came to anchor ideological and doctrinal debates about gender. To appreciate the significance of this turn toward the body, it is helpful to look back at earlier, more thoroughly ideological discussions of gender to see how their idealizations have been complicated and transformed.

In the early stages of its development in the United States, proponents of feminist theory concerned themselves with identifying and exposing social constructs that fostered female subordination. Religion often figured prominently in what they uncovered and, in many cases, became a target for attack. The most prominent forms of this attack developed out of Marxist theory. Exponents of Marxist forms of gender analysis were often merciless in their analysis of religion, especially modern Christianity, which they inevitably interpreted as an agent of female oppression. But at the same time, Marxists tended to define religion as ideology and thus to view it as nothing more than an intellectual superstructure that existed for the purpose of legitimating economic order. Thus while they often criticized Christianity as an ideological force legitimating female oppression, Marxists viewed capitalism as the real culprit. In this scenario, Christianity finally played no more than a supporting role. While offering great insight into the construction of society, Marxist theory relegated religion to the ideological realm and overlooked its grounding in the body's sentience and vitality.

As we have seen, among liberal and radical Catholics in the seventies, Marxist analysis contributed to a revitalization of the longstanding Catholic critique of modernism and its manifestation in capitalism and Protestant culture. Blending the Marxist critique of capitalism with the social gospel message derived from liberal Protestantism and the Catholic critique of modernism, proponents of liberation theology targeted American culture as the main foe, identifying it as the epitome of oppression. At the same time, these theologians also attacked the Catholic Church for its failure to side with the poor. Beginning in the seventies, Rosemary Radford Ruether led the way in focusing this liberationist critique onto women's issues, holding up an egalitarian model of the Church and Christianity as an alternative to their complicity in women's oppression, and arguing that the virtue of any religion could be measured by its promotion of women's full humanity.[8]

The work of the anthropologist Eleanor Burke Leacock offers a more straightforward example of the Marxist approach to religion and gender, unadulterated by any loyalty to Christianity. Advancing Marxist

theory in the clearest terms, Leacock argued that women's status declined under the influence of capitalism and its Christian superstructure. Her work is particularly useful here because it shows how Marxist
feminism led to an idealization of Native American societies. In fur-
thering her critique of Western culture and its subjugation of women,
Leacock turned to Native American societies for examples of precap-
italist egalitarianism.

Leacock held up the Montagnais-Naskapi people of Labrador as an
example of a relatively egalitarian society that had managed to resist,
to a considerable extent, the myth of male dominance introduced by
Western society. Among the Montagnais-Naskapi and, by extension,
people in all simply organized ancient societies, leadership was infor-
mal, class and status divisions were lacking, and, as Leacock put it
ideologically and idealistically, "unquestioned acceptance of respect for
each individual" was the norm. Although formal distinctions existed
between men's work and women's work, in actual practice, Leacock
argued, men and women shared in many forms of labor, each according
to his or her individual ability, and received support from the community, each according to need.

As Leacock explained in the preface to her collected articles, she
first became aware of the Western myth of male dominance as a young
anthropologist, mother, and political radical in New York in the 1950s.
She was drawn to anthropology party because of the pioneering analysis
of the social construction of sex roles in Margaret Mead's early work
Sex and Temperament (1935), which examined the contrasting roles
played by women in three different societies in New Guinea. Women's
roles in the three societies were sufficiently different from one another,
Mead argued, that they could not be interpreted simply as manifestations of some inherent biological trait or emotional or intellectual inferiority. While Leacock approved of the "progressive" implications of
this early study, she was an outspoken critic of Mead's subsequent work.
In a review of Mead's *Male and Female* (1949) published in the *Daily
Worker* in 1952, Leacock distanced herself from Mead's new emphasis
on the indirect but important connections between women's biological
and social roles. Leacock attacked Mead's understanding of the universal tendency in males to play more active roles in society than females as well as her advice to women to "turn inward" and "heighten

their 'femininity' " as a way of supporting men's activism and thereby strengthening society. Looking back thirty years later, Leacock attributed Mead's loss of a progressive spirit with regard to women's equality to her participation in "the reactionary culture of the 1950s."[9]

In several important respects, Leacock's anthropology paralleled the critique of women's roles in American society that Betty Friedan advanced in *The Feminine Mystique*. Both Leacock and Friedan emphasized the social construction of women's roles, and both criticized what they perceived as Margaret Mead's overemphasis on the connection between women's social roles and their biological sex and reproductive capacities. Both attacked the ideology of femininity that flourished in the United States after World War II as many returning GIs and their wives moved to the suburbs, where women were expected to stay home and not pursue careers. Both viewed this ideology of femininity as an excessive and oppressive valorization of women's biological nature. And neither anticipated the extent to which nature would become a source of inspiration for feminists interested in creating myths and rituals that empowered women.

NATURE SPIRITUALITY

By the 1970s, discussion of the social construction of women's roles had become deeply complicated by the increasing popularity of religious reverence for nature and by the increasingly widespread conviction that, for their own sakes as well as for the sake of the planet, human beings needed to improve their spiritual connections to the natural world. This growing interest in nature-friendly forms of spirituality was part of a more general enthusiasm for things countercultural. Reverence for the natural world, and for women's bodies as essential parts of the natural world, emerged as a form of resistance to the oppressive, patriarchal structure of the Judeo-Christian tradition, alleged to be rooted in an underlying hostility to nature.

This enthusiasm for spiritual attentiveness to nature—and concern about the despoilment of nature under capitalism—offered a way to be religious while still pursuing gender analysis and its critique of patriarchy in Christianity and Judaism. At the same time, the increasing popularity of nature-based spirituality expressed a new kind of investment in an older and more ubiquitous tendency to link the fertility of nature with that of women and to define womanhood in terms of nature.

While Marxist theory was a major contributor to gender analysis of all types, its approach to religion as a form of ideology and its fundamental animus against capitalism led to a tendency to idealize premodern, non-Western cultures as egalitarian, utopian societies. Ironically, this highly positive view of premodern cultures led to closer examination of gender in those cultures, which in turn led to discovery of the virtually universal connection between women's biological and social roles and to religion's role as a mediator of that connection. As many Americans came to see, the valorization of femaleness, however limited, often occurred by investing femaleness with the same kind of sacredness perceived to flow through the natural world. To some extent, then, the valorization of women in the nature religions of the late twentieth century involved a conservative impetus to affirm this ancient and pervasive connection between femaleness and nature. Of course, it was precisely this connection that earlier feminists, in their efforts to challenge the assumption that women's social roles were a natural extension of their biological functions, had tried to overturn.

But the postsixties investment in the connection between womanhood and nature was not simply an extension of the ideology of femininity that Leacock and Friedan decried. As a result of its exposure to the concept of gender associated with feminism, this phenomenon also represented something new. Exponents of the new approach to that old connection imputed positive, salvific meaning to both womanhood and nature, thus challenging tendencies in Christianity and Judaism to link women to nature in ways that imputed inferiority, impurity, and evil to both. At the same time, advocates of feminist spirituality lifted up tribal religions, long condemned by Christians and Jews as pagan cults that deserved to be destroyed, as exemplars of the kind of religious respect for women and nature that ought to be recovered.

Neopagans and Goddess thealogians drew on anthropological studies that showed how religion and society were closely identified in premodern, preindustrial cultures. As these studies often argued, tribal peoples conceptualized their economic resources and productivity in terms of spiritual forces controlling the natural environment, rather than in terms of impersonal rational and mechanical forces, as was more often the case in modern society. Anthropological studies showed that gender roles in non-Western cultures were defined through religious rites and symbols that linked males and females quite differently to the natural world and its spiritual forces.

But neopagans stood on shaky ground as far as their assertions of the high status enjoyed by women in tribal regions were concerned. For example, many advocates of Native American spirituality argued that belief in Mother Earth was common to the native cultures of North America and that this belief was an integral part of the high respect and egalitarian treatment accorded to women in native societies. Upon closer investigation, however, it appeared that Mother Earth was not really an ancient deity with an ancient ritual cult. As Sam Gill showed, Mother Earth was a modern deity who originated as a figure of speech used by pan-Indian religious leaders in the nineteenth century to convey to Euro-Americans the religious feeling, expressed differently by native people of different tribes, for the land that Euro-Americans were claiming as their own. Only in the nineteenth century, in the context of colonization, did Mother Earth come to be incorporated into prayers and other ritual performances as a pan-Indian deity accessible and impressive to whites.

Romantic idealizations of women's roles in traditional native societies were also part of neopagan lore. But scholarly studies showed that these roles were more complex than many neopagans and other admirers of Native American spirituality believed. For example, the Iroquois were often cited as prime examples of the ancient system of matriarchy indigenous to pre-Christian, tribal society. But as Elisabeth Tooker demonstrated, while Iroquois women did inherit and control farmland, and did play important roles in naming new chiefs and in contributing to decisions about whether to kill or adopt captives and whether or not the men should go to war, they were rarely chiefs themselves and were generally assumed to have inferior status to men. Indeed, Iroquois warriors referred to the tribes they conquered as "women." Furthermore, the important roles and relatively high status that women enjoyed in Iroquois society seem to have developed at least to some extent in the colonial period, when men were often away fighting and women needed to take on greater responsibility at home.[10]

While proponents of various forms of postsixties nature religion romanticized women's roles in pre-Christian tribal societies and appropriated native symbols with little regard to their historical development, this freewheeling interpretive process reflected the inventive, creative spirit of these proponents and their new religions. A strategic and politicized self-consciousness often drove neopagan and New Age enthusiasm for indigenous religions. While overlooking or downplaying the negative association with natural forces that could stigmatize women in these religions, neopagans and others attracted to Native American spirituality embraced the sacralization of womanhood in these religions and elaborated upon their symbols associating women's fertility with the spiritual forces of the natural world.

This investment in nature-based spiritualities involved deliberate efforts to reconstruct and even invent religious rituals that empowered women by celebrating their sacred connection to nature. Thus Starhawk, one of the most influential proponents of witchcraft, or Wicca, as a Goddess religion, encouraged her followers to create their own ceremonies and provided how-to exercises to stimulate their imaginations. Although enthusiastic about the many ways in which contemporary ideas and institutions could find a home within the "ancient" Goddess religion, she also encouraged her followers to reconstruct that religion in a radically contemporary way. Thus she defined a "coven" as "a Witch's support group, consciousness-raising group, psychic study center, clergy-training program, College of Mysteries, surrogate clan, and religious congregation all rolled into one." The ceremonies conducted by covens should be no less eclectic or encompassing, she maintained, and no less well directed or choreographed than any other deliberately staged event. "A ritual," as she put it, "like a theater production, needs a director."[11]

Gender analysis moved to the fore in new forms of ritual associated with the ancient rites of Wicca. For example, the spiritual director of the East-West Healing Arts Center in Oakland, Wendy Hunter Roberts, incorporated feminist analysis as part of the ritual process itself. In her handbook for constructing neopagan rituals, Roberts outlined the steps one might take to devise and conduct a maypole ritual and advised readers how to handle the ritual's erotic energy. "The purpose in designing and executing the Maypole ritual," Roberts explained, "was to fundamentally alter the power relationship of male to female" by "remov[ing] all implications and aspects of the subordination of women from the celebration of Eros. This," she admitted, "was no small task." In one maypole ritual that Roberts conducted, "the men had rushed into the circle with the Maypole and, like adolescent boys in the backseats of cars, tried to jam it hastily into the ground, once even breaking the statue of Pan on the altar. Upon discussing the matter later," Roberts reported, "a few men said that they could not help it, that the Maypole had 'a life of its own'!" Belittling the men's efforts to interpret their behavior in religious terms—"Where have we heard this before?"—Roberts interpreted the incident as a ritual rape of the Goddess. She subsequently redesigned the ritual in a way that "raised consciousness among female and male participants about the nature and effects of sexism in their lives."[12]

A similar combination of inventiveness and didacticism was evident among those feminists who were committed to reforming Judaism and Christianity by transforming negative interpretations of the connections between womanhood and nature into positive ones. In *She Who Dwells Within: A Feminist Vision of a Renewed Judaism* (1995), Lynn Gottlieb criticized the tendency of Jewish authorities to hold up Abraham's worship of the monotheistic God of the Bible as a great breakthrough in human history that lifted Jews above the level of pagan superstition, nature worship, and sexual lewdness. This sort of understanding of Jewish history functioned to endorse negative stereotypes about nature, women, and sexuality, Gottlieb argued, and these stereotypes, in turn, functioned to justify women's subordinate status in much of Jewish history and culture. As an alternative to this patriarchal construction of Jewish history and theology, Gottlieb imputed positive value to Tiamat and other female images of God in ancient Near Eastern culture. She argued that YHVH incorporated these images and thus might be described as a mother giving birth to her people as well as a father looking after them. Like Starhawk, Gottlieb provided her readers with guidelines for creating ceremonies that consoled and empowered women by identifying their own nature with that of the Goddess.

Christian feminists took a similar tack. For example, the Catholic feminist theologian Elizabeth A. Johnson pointed to the connection between Jesus and Sophia, the female figure of Wisdom represented in the Bible as the Spirit of God. In her focus on the effectiveness of female imagery as a means of representing the mystery of God, Johnson identified Sophia with the *shekinah,* or presence of God, in medieval Jewish cabalistic writing and also with Mary, the Mother of God, who had been at the center of Catholic piety for centuries. As she emerged in the wisdom literature of Hellenistic Judaism, the figure of Sophia incorporated the characteristics of the Egyptian goddess Isis, Johnson argued, who was worshiped throughout the Hellenistic world by rich and poor alike. In Johnson's interpretation, this meant that Sophia was "the female personification of God's own being in creative and saving involvement with the world." As the "functional equivalent" of the biblical God, Johnson claimed, "Sophia fashions all that exists and pervades it with her pure and people-loving spirit." In addition to her fundamental role in creation, "she also works in history to save her chosen people, guiding and protecting them through the vicissitudes of liberating struggle."[13]

CONSERVATIVE GUARDIANS OF WOMEN'S ROLES AND BODIES

In religiously conservative circles, there was strong resistance to this kind of inclusive, female imagery for God. Furthermore, feminism was often targeted as the prime example of what had gone wrong with American culture and religious life. In her study of conservative Protestant evangelicals, Margaret Lamberts Bendroth observed that by 1980 most evangelicals had become convinced that feminism and Christianity were "antithetical." Feminism "not only clashed with historical attitudes toward feminine submission but rejected the self-abnegating tone of much evangelical piety." In addition, Bendroth pointed out, the feminist critique of patriarchy "was laden with negative implications." These negative implications involved suspiciousness about the heavy-handed imposition of male dominance in received traditions. Once people became alert to this way of thinking, "demands for more women leaders only served to underline the socially vulnerable position of evangelical men in a largely female-dominated constituency."

Conservative Protestant evangelicals were not immune to increased self-consciousness about gender, and even among them, this self-consciousness had a transforming effect. The demonization of feminism itself marked a repositioning of evangelical faith that presumed a high degree of gender consciousness. Before 1970, evangelicals did not define Christianity in terms of its opposition to women's social equality. Moreover, even as they redefined Christianity in opposition to feminism, evangelicals also appropriated many of the emotional and ethical values associated with it. Testimonies and inspirational books linking evangelical Christianity with women's personal fulfillment abounded, and evangelicals proudly claimed that their religion promoted self-realization and personal fulfillment, even while attacking feminism for excessive emphasis on those values. Evangelical efforts to define and attend to the "masculine soul" also became prominent. The Promise Keepers movement, founded by University of Colorado football coach Bill McCartney, focused very deliberately and strategically on reconstructing a certain traditional concept of manhood, along with a religious and cultural system to support it. Without feminism and its success in drawing attention to the social construction of gender, the Promise Keepers never would have come into being. Awareness of gender as a social construct, and awareness of the importance of religion in defining gender, was no longer something of which evangelicals were innocent.[14]

In the context of American Judaism, a new kind of self-consciousness about gender contributed to the growth in Orthodox communities during the last decades of the twentieth century. In her analysis of religious commitment among newly Orthodox Jewish women, sociologist Debra Renee Kaufman found that many *ba'alot teshuvah* (women who deliberately chose Orthodoxy) were both reacting against feminism and inspired by it. Many of the *ba'alot teshuvah* Kaufman interviewed associated feminism with materialistic and self-interested behavior, which they condemned. They were often hostile to feminism because they thought the effect of claiming equality for women was simply to leave women sexually unprotected and vulnerable to men's predatory behavior. They were strongly committed to Orthodox rules for regulating marital sexuality as well as to defining their religious identities as women in terms of their sexual and reproductive lives. But this devotion to Orthodoxy was profoundly shaped by their exposure to feminism. Several of the women Kaufman interviewed had turned to Orthodoxy after trying out feminism, which they rejected when they found themselves alone and uncared for. A number of these women concluded that women's liberation simply meant that men were freer to exploit women and freer to take advantage of greater opportunities for sex without having to invest much commitment in sexual relationships. In this respect, some *ba'alot teshuvah* expressed a fundamental distrust of men that was reminiscent of the hostility to male behavior characteristic of "militant" feminists. Many of the women Kaufman interviewed also seemed inspired by feminism in their self-conscious advocacy of women's interests, deliberate efforts to raise women's status within Orthodoxy, and explicit attempts to nurture men's roles as husbands and fathers. While deeply invested in being "Torah True," which meant being invested in the inviolability of Jewish law, many of these religiously conservative and even fundamentalist Jewish women were also committed to strengthening networks of female support, exploring new forms of female mysticism, and supporting women's increased involvement in religious study.[15]

A similar combination of ideas and feelings could be found among Muslim women who affirmed their religious tradition as an alternative to what they perceived as the materialism, self-absorption, and blatant marketing of sexuality characteristic of Western culture in general and American culture in particular. For many newly Muslim women, wearing clothes that covered skin and hair and obscured the outlines of the figure was a public statement of sexual virtue and respectability. Covering the body was a way of establishing one's distance from the hedonism and decadence perceived in the surrounding culture. At the same time, it was also a way of empowering oneself and elevating one's status with respect to both men and women. Many Muslim women believed that, in its essence, Islam was a way of life that was respectful of women and liberated them from oppression. As Islamic feminists argued, Islam was essentially and truly feminist. From their perspective it was an effective antidote to the exploitation of women as sexual objects and to what they perceived as the dishonest lip service paid to women's liberation in American society.[16]

THE SOCIAL CONSTRUCTION OF NATURE

As these conservative religious concerns about sexual protection and modesty make clear, increased awareness of gender led to a new degree of self-consciousness about the body. And increased scrutiny of the relationship between gender and nature led to increased awareness of the universal tendencies to ascribe femaleness to nature, to define women in terms of their bodies, and to associate the female body with the forces of nature. Thus gender awareness became an important part of the transformation of American religious life after the sixties. The whole spectrum of attitudes toward religion and its relationship to both the human body and the natural world was deeply affected by self-consciousness about the socially constructed aspects of women's and men's roles. And attitudes toward nature were themselves altered in the process.

In her 1994 book *Changing the Subject*, Mary McClintock Fulkerson focused on the undeniable fact that everything we think and say and believe about reality is socially constructed. As Fulkerson asserted, "Realities are coded, socially signified, not natural." Thus it followed that nature itself and all the things associated with nature, such as women's bodies, their "natural" relationship to children and men, and their God-given gifts or divinely appointed roles in life, were mediated through social expectations about proper human behavior. This was not to say that bodies lacked material reality or that the world "out there" did not really exist. But Fulkerson argued that every one of these things, insofar as it entered human consciousness, was inscribed, filled, and shaped by social expectation.

Awareness of the signs that encode social norms and expectations within all forms of reality did not originate with feminists, but this kind of analysis acquired new importance and credibility as a result of feminist attention to gender. Semiotics became more commonplace once feminists popularized the discovery that, as Fulkerson put it, "historical practices of attaching 'natural' meanings to women's bodies [had] allowed them to be subjected to uses perceived as natural." Conversely, revealing the social codes hidden within ideas about nature provided a way of confronting "imbalances in power" between men and women that were sustained by previously unquestioned acceptance of these codes.

Once the socially constructed codes connecting women and nature came to be seen as vulnerable to decoding and reconstruction, the implications of this malleability for religion were hard to avoid. Again, the idea that religion was socially constructed had been around a long time, but widespread acceptance of this idea in American culture was due in large part to feminist gender analysis, which popularized the discovery that religion played a major role in defining and sanctioning the coded connections between women and nature. This widespread discovery led not only to criticism of religious patriarchy, but also to awareness of the more general role that religion often played in essentializing things. And once this essentializing power was discovered, it was broken. When it became apparent that religion authorized men to regard women in much the same way they regarded nature, then religious people began to see that it was up to them to either shore up this mechanism or replace it with something new.

In the context of this new self-consciousness about the human nature of religion and its dependence on human support and intervention, it became apparent that every aspect of religion was subject to a continual process of interpretation. As Fulkerson explained, "[T]he lens of gender criticism has made it impossible to assume the liberating character of Christian tradition as such"—or, one should add, of any religious tradition. At the same time, "the mirror image to that assessment, the judgment that Christianity is essentially patriarchal, is also a dead end." The ground to stand on to be able to claim that Jesus was essentially a feminist, or conversely, that Christianity was essentially opposed to women's equality or to women's ordination, shrank dramatically and indeed completely disappeared for many people. In the context of this dawning realization of the human contingency of religion and its pronouncements about gender, it was perhaps no wonder that Pope John Paul II forbade Catholics, and especially American Catholics, to participate in any discussion of women's ordination.[17]

The Body as a Site of Religious Imagination

While the social constructedness of our categories of womanhood, nature, and religion became increasingly apparent—and increasingly subject to critique, revision, or deliberate reconfirmation—we also grew increasingly attentive to the embodied realities in which those categories were inscribed. Interestingly, our increased awareness of the ideological structure and agency of these things led to a growing appreciation not only of their corporeality, but also of the marvelous fusion of this corporeality with its intellectual and, ultimately, social construction.

This is not to say that debates about the relationship between nature and culture, materialism and idealism, genes and environment, or flesh and spirit ceased. But the real story with regard to the development of American intellectual opinion lay beyond these debates. Dichotomous thinking itself fell under critique. The unity of mind and matter was in the public eye. And with regard to religion, the embodied nature of both religious practice and religious experience came to the fore. It was no longer sufficient to speak about religion as a system of idealization, as Marx and Freud and their followers did. As we became increasingly aware, the idealizations associated with religion were powerful because of how they functioned in corporeal practice and sensory experience.

In the context of religion, this awareness was often mediated by the gender analysis associated with feminist theology. For all their differences, most feminist theologians agreed that dualisms of body/spirit and nature/spirit should be rejected. Goddess theologians were often in the forefront of these efforts to reconceptualize the spirit in naturalistic and embodied terms, but Christian and Jewish feminists did not lag far behind. As one Catholic feminist argued, Catholic feminism "bases its critique of these dualistic conceptions on a retrieval of the Incarnation, seeing God's taking on the condition of humanity as God's own self-expression." From this perspective, "sacramentality grows out of human embodiment and its connection to the natural world, not in contrast to it." Thus Catholic feminism "argues for a closer connection between nature and history, body and soul."[18]

In her helpful analysis of the relationship between religious imagination and the human body, Paula M. Cooey argued that the body was both necessary and ambiguous with respect to all forms of imagination, because it was the "site for the imagination as well as the object of the imagination." Religious imagination, Cooey suggested, was a collective phenomenon that played a central role in creating and sustaining human culture. Furthermore, as maps of human existence, religions were distinct from other kinds of maps, such as primarily political ones, in that they not only attempted to define human existence, but also tried "to extend and transcend the limits of human existence." As both site and object of the religious imagination, the body and its feelings constituted the "battleground or theater" not only "for making real and continually reproducing cultural meanings and values," but also for attempting to define, extend, and transcend the limits of those cultural meanings and values. And with regard to this attentiveness to the limits of human culture and existence, Cooey said, "it is precisely in this area that religious institutions, life, and practice can manifest both their most revolutionary and their most totalitarian aspects."

Cooey argued further that while religions almost always carried "a deep awareness" of the importance of the body and its feelings of pleasure and pain, only in recent years have we become aware of the extent to which the teachings of the great religious traditions of the world have overlooked or denigrated the body's importance for religious thought, practice, and experience. Indeed, as Cooey pointed out, the very idea that the body and its capacity for pleasure were central to religious life "flies in the face of the dominant religious traditions, both Western and Eastern." For all of their differences, most religious traditions "have tended through much of their recorded histories to ignore or to devalue the body's relevance, to view its relevance as almost exclusively negative, or to relegate any positive value to the purely instrumental role of altering consciousness." In other words, "the body, connected directly to an economic context and the constant reminder of mutability and lack of individual control, suffers, at best, lack of attention and, at worst, outright denigration within these various symbolic frameworks." Thus the recent discovery and affirmation of the body's role in religion marked a major transformation, or at least the point of departure for a major transformation, in human culture. If the function of religion was not only to map human existence but also to attempt to extend and overcome the limits of human existence, then discovery of the body's centrality to religious life might be said to qualify as one of those transcendent breakthroughs in cultural meaning for which religion is deservedly famous.[19]

To deliberately claim the body's centrality for religious life, and to promote awareness of the connection between religious symbols and human feelings of pleasure and pain, has had the effect of making religion a more openly and explicitly human affair. Heightened awareness of the relationship between the symbolic frameworks of religion and the corporeal experiences of pleasure and pain led to greater exposure of the symbolic frameworks that legitimated or encouraged human pain. At the same time, heightened awareness of the body's central role in religious life opened up a new understanding of the role that religion often played in easing human suffering. And it also opened up new possibilities for utilizing the symbolic frameworks of religion as strategic means of relieving pain, stimulating pleasure, and promoting well-being.

HEALING THE BODY

The importance of religion as a means of healing has, of course, long been recognized, and healing may be one of the first and most basic uses of religion. Indeed, religion's relatively high degree of effectiveness as a means of relieving both suffering and pain may be one of the chief reasons that the human species has evolved with a strong predisposition toward religion. If religion is a universal human phenomenon, as many scholars of religion believe, then biologists would insist that it can be understood in terms of its contribution to human survival. Viewed in this way, religion's universality surely has much to do with its capacity to make people feel better and stronger.

Although our knowledge of premodern religions is spotty and easily subject to distortion, it seems to be the case that shamanic healing is one of the earliest and most basic forms of religion. Shamanic healing figures importantly in the simplest known tribal societies and often exists in more elaborate forms in more complex premodern societies. In Western societies today, shamanic healing still flourishes in cultural pockets here and there and even exists, in attenuated forms, inside the culture of modern medicine.

In its purest and simplest forms, shamanic healing works through the performance of symbolic utterances and actions that locate a patient's suffering in terms of a mythic framework. In such a performance, the shaman dramatizes a relevant piece of the larger mythic framework of his or her culture in a way that stimulates a salutary, psychobiological change in the patient. Thus in Claude Lévi-Strauss's famous example of the Pima shaman who specialized in helping women through difficulty in childbirth, the shaman sang and acted out the story of an expedition to Muu's abode, imagined as a kind of command center for the spirits of unborn children. The way to Muu's abode was fraught with peril, and the shaman encouraged his patient at every step as they made their way along passages filled with demons and whirlpools. Through words and probably through touch as well (although Lévi-Strauss was interested only in words), the shaman mapped a terrain that mythologized the patient's vagina, cervix, and uterus as landmarks on the journey to Muu's abode. After undertaking this dramatic journey and calming every whirlpool and demon found in the woman's body, the shaman and the woman sometimes succeeded in bringing out a baby.

In addition to providing the dramatic structure for an intense, one-on-one relationship between a woman in pain and a therapeutic specialist, this shamanic ritual also affirmed the larger symbolic framework of Pima culture, which was made up of many stories, dreams, prejudices, and forms of ritual performance. Anytime one of those stories came to full embodiment, as in the case of a successful shamanic performance for childbirth, the whole network of stories, behaviors, and attitudes characteristic of Pima culture was affirmed and strengthened. In a limited but nevertheless profound way, the woman's body represented Pima culture. Her successful delivery of a child underscored the legitimacy, authority, and power of that culture. As a manifestation of cultural authority, the performance in and on the woman's body was not only a highly social event, but also one of great danger for the woman herself. Her death in childbirth, or the death of her baby, was an immediate possibility, and if she survived and her baby died, there was also the subsequent possibility of her being scapegoated as a representation of communal vulnerability and disorder.

As this ritual and the various scenarios that might be played out in conjunction with it illustrate rather nicely, religion's effectiveness as a means of relieving pain and suffering could be extended but also complicated by its effectiveness as a means of defining and strengthening human culture. In many situations, these two roles worked together quite effectively—the cultural weight borne by shamanic rituals added to their credibility and authority and thus contributed to their therapeutic power. In other situations, however, the desire to strengthen or purify the culture could overshadow and even obliterate compassion for the body and its pain. To take an example from a different Native American culture, when Inuit hunters and fishermen failed to bring home sufficient food for the community, a shaman might journey, via dramatic performance in a state of trance, to the underwater home of Sedna, the spirit who controlled big fish and water animals. To placate Sedna, who was prone to fits of anger ever since her father had dumped her off a fishing boat when she was a human girl and chopped off her fingers so that she could not hold on, the shaman combed her hair with his fingers. Upon his return to ordinary consciousness, the shaman reported to the community that one of Sedna's taboos had been violated. He reported further the perpetrator of this violation should be found and punished so that Sedna would release fish and animals to be hunted and killed. Often, a woman accused of aborting a fetus or hiding a miscarriage was identified and then beaten, cast out of the community, or killed.[20]

Since the seventies, scholars of religion have become increasingly interested in the mechanisms of religious sacrifice and scapegoating and have pointed to their effectiveness in drawing communities together and creating a sense of collective strength.[21] At the same time, increased awareness of the gendered aspects of religion has made it difficult to avoid seeing how common it has been to make women's bodies objects of, and subject to, these mechanisms. On the therapeutic and more salutary side of things, however, advances in other areas have enabled us to better understand how religion works to relieve suffering and pain. And many, if not most, of the advocates and beneficiaries of these advances have been women.

Through studies in medical anthropology, it has become increasingly apparent that modern medicine carries at least some vestiges of shamanism. More than a collection of experts, instruments, pharmaceuticals, treatments, and procedures, modern medicine also functions as a therapeutic culture with symbols of authority—white coats, stethoscopes, M.D. degrees, the title "Doctor"—that encourage feelings of hope, loyalty, and sometimes intimidation in patients. While fear of what can happen in a hospital or doctor's office can increase people's blood pressure and even make them break out in hives, trust in a doctor's authority, knowledge, and power can also have profoundly salutary effects. As doctors themselves are beginning to understand, the potential for helping patients to feel better through the noninvasive interaction of a medical interview or examination is so significant that these basic procedures can be practiced as forms of therapy as well as diagnosis. And through the performance of symbolic utterance and action within the context of a medical interview or examination, doctors can stimulate a healing process that, at least in a partial way, is similar to that of shamanism.

In addition to increasing the awareness that the culture of modern medicine involves symbolic actions that can function in ways similar to shamanic healing, there have been advances in medical research that have begun to explain healing as a psychobiological process in which the suggestions delivered by doctors play an important part. With respect to the transformation in American religious understanding, some of the discoveries most relevant to the psychobiology of healing have clustered around the so-called placebo effect. First discovered as a kind of side effect that had to be discounted in order to measure the actual results of medicines being tested in scientific procedures, placebos became a subject of research in their own right beginning in the sixties. As researchers found, placebos worked by generating positive expectations about relief from pain that actually functioned to produce that relief. Thus a significant percentage of patients in a control group would always report a lessening of negative symptoms after taking simple sugar pills, which they had been told might contain medicine designed to remedy their ailment. In negative forms, placebos could cause pain rather than take it away; voodoo death might be an extreme example.

In his classic work *Persuasion and Healing* (1974), Jerome Frank compared the healing that could occur in modern psychiatry with various forms of traditional religious healing, and he urged psychotherapists to maximize the placebo effect they could produce through suggestion. Benefiting from subsequent advances in biological psychiatry and brain chemistry, more recent research focused on how placebos actually work at a biological level. Herbert Benson and others showed that by decreasing psychological stress, placebos can reduce heart rate, lower cholesterol, and boost immune functions compromised by psychological stress. Thus placebos can alter a person's whole biological system. In other words, "feeling better" is a unified corporeal process involving the brain and its capacity for hopeful thought and imagery of positive outcome, along with the other biological systems connected to the brain.

Religion, Benson went on, has often figured importantly in this healing process. More specifically, belief in God and in God's power to heal has been one of the most common and effective forms of placebo known to humanity. Indeed, Benson argued, human beings have found such belief to be so productive of well-being and relief from stress that, as a species, humans have evolved as animals predisposed to this belief—or, as Benson put it, "wired for God."[22]

This biological way of thinking about religious beliefs and their placebo effects complements recent anthropological discoveries about the inseparability of mind and body in rituals of religious healing. In his study of healing rituals among Catholic charismatics, for example, Thomas Csordas called attention to the central role of the believer's body in the healing experiences that were often associated with, and apparently triggered by, the religious experience of being seized by the healing power of the Holy Spirit. Csordas found that the body of a suffering member of the religious community became the central object of both imaginative concern and physical interaction during a healing ritual. As the body of the believer fell backward into the arms of others, who set the body on the ground and prayed and sang and moved around it, healing sometimes occurred. Csordas found a strong correlation between the healing experienced by believers and the passing of the body's handling and control to members of the community who functioned as assistants and surrogates for the Holy Spirit. In this ritual, as in many other forms of religious healing, the believer's body was the site of a transformative event that was simultaneously imaginative and biological. The transformative power of the ritual centered on the body and on breaking through the body's self-control and its social and tactile isolation from other bodies.

Thus while Herbert Benson and other medical researchers found that symbolic language and behavior played an important role in the biological process of relief from pain and recovery from illness, anthropological investigators of religion such as Thomas Csordas found that the body played a crucial role in experiences of religious transformation and healing. At the same time, Paula Cooey and other feminists working in the area of philosophical theology found gender to be a basic element of religious experience that was always located in relation to the body and its pain or pleasure. As biological, anthropological, and theological studies of religion began to converge in this way, researchers became increasingly aware of the central place that the body occupied in religion. They also became increasingly aware of deeply ingrained habits of mind that have led to overlooking or denigrating the body's religious importance.

POPULAR RELIGION TAKES ON THE SCIENCE OF HEALING AND WELLNESS

In the arena of everyday American religious life, increased interest in the relationship between religion and the body may be even more remarkable. To take one example, a significant number of American Catholics have become involved in the Centering Prayer movement, which integrates yogic meditation and Christian prayer. Meeting in parish halls, chapels, monasteries, and private homes, participants in this movement sit in mediation posture and focus on their breath and its movement through their bodies as a means of intensifying their awareness of God and awakening spiritual insight. Like believers in other religions, Catholics have long used prayer as a means of coping with sickness and pain. And the effigies of the crucified Christ so often associated with Catholic worship have provided images of the body as inspirations for prayer. But while the suffering, broken body has long been an object of compassion and an inspiration to prayer, the healthy body deeply attuned to its own vitality has not, until recently, been viewed by Catholics as a means of attunement to God. Indeed, negative images, ideas, and attitudes toward the body have characterized a great deal of Catholic thought and practice over the centuries. And extreme instances of starving, flagellating, and otherwise punishing the body have often been associated with sanctity. The Centering Prayer movement represents a reversal of this powerful negative trend. Even if some practitioners long for a union with the Spirit that ultimately transcends the body, the body is honored as the point of departure.

Since the sixties, Americans have expressing growing interest in various forms of medication, yoga, tai chi, and dance that connect spiritual insight with corporeal movement. While some of these practices, such as Centering Prayer, occur in more or less traditional religious settings among members of a religious community, others occur in classes and workshops that students enroll in and pay to take. Almost every American city has at least one yoga center where people take classes. Alternative health centers have sprung up everywhere, offering massage therapy, aromatherapy, acupuncture, and instruction in various dietary regimes, most of which embrace the concept of spiritual respect for the body as a means to health.

In many cases, these body-affirming spiritual practices carry Eastern and countercultural associations. They stand, in important respects, as self-conscious alternatives to the dualism of mind and body perceived to characterize both Western medicine and the Judeo-Christian tradition. At the same time, however, they are not unmodified transplants from other cultures but products of modern, Western, and often American imagination. Thus many ideas and practices from Asian cultures have been selected, rearranged, and reinterpreted for Western and especially American consumption. In this process, affirmations of the positive connection and underlying harmony between spirit and body have come to the fore, and often in ways that significantly alter traditional Asian thought and practice. For example, Kriya Yoga, one of the most influential forms of yoga in the West, is an adaptation of yogic principles for Westerners created by Swami Paramahmsa Yogananda. First taught through Yogananda's Self-Realization Fellowship (SRF) in the United States, Kriya Yoga offered a scientific approach to God-realization. As well as reconstructing yogic practice to fit Western enthusiasm for science and scientific technique, Yogananda also selected from and readjusted Indian religious thought to conform to Western idealism. Thus he advanced a particular form of Advaita Vedanta monism as the epitome of Hindu philosophy, even though a great deal of yogic philosophy was much more dualistic.[23]

The strongly American cast to body spirituality is especially clear in the area of popular interest in the connection between spirituality and health. Not only do spiritual support groups of various kinds help victims of illness and their families, but wellness itself has taken on spiritual dimensions. Aerobics, dance, hiking, football, horseback riding, massage, and cooking have all been associated with spiritual experience at least partly because of their connection to health, wellness, and life itself.

In American culture especially, the scientific and technical aspects of these activities are an important part of their appeal. The focus on effective techniques for attaining both spiritual and physical well-being reflected a general American tendency to see things in practical terms and to except beneficial results from investments of time and energy. Americans have often expressed their religious expectations in such practical terms, and these practical expectations frequently have worked against tendencies within many of the universalist religions of the world to define the divine as a transcendent reality apart from the world. Although it has led some outsiders to consider Americans the least religious people on earth, American enthusiasm for the practical benefits of religion has imparted a kind of engineering mentality to various aspects of religious life. Many Americans have worked systematically to bring God down to earth and to build practical knowledge about how to tap into the divine and make it work for human well-being.

Of course, belief in underlying connections linking religion, health, science, and practical application is not new to American culture. One of the most interesting new religions of the nineteenth century, the Church of Christ, Scientist (also called Christian Science) emerged as an effort to recover the healing ministry of Jesus and utilize the idea that God is love to eradicate disease and suffering. The founder of Christian Science, Mary Baker Eddy, combined popular interest in mesmerism with the conviction that the principle of love described in the New Testament was the essence of God. Positing a kind of mental osmosis through which thought was transmitted from one mind to another, she urged her followers to concentrate on the principle of love as a means of doing battle with the evil thoughts that made them and other people sick.

Christian Science is probably the most well-established form of New Thought, which is an approach to religion that became popular after the Civil War and continues to impact the American religious scene in the form of New Age religions. Proponents of New Thought affirm the objective reality of positive and negative thoughts, and the power these thoughts have to affect the material world. While traditional religious thoughts did not venture to explain the supernatural, proponents of New Thought approach the nature of God and other forms of supernatural reality as mental forces and claim that their effects can be scientifically measured and understood. Like other forms of New Thought and New Age religion, Christian Science was at once a highly idealistic system of religions belief and one that promised real practical benefit. Sickness could be cured and injuries healed, Eddy and others in the New Thought/New Age traditions believed, by invoking the powerful force of positive spiritual thought.

Eddy herself went so far into idealism as to maintain that the material world itself did not really exist. Even though her approach to Christianity was strongly focused on relief from sickness and pain, she also believed that these infirmities and the bodies containing them were finally unreal. Thus while the pragmatic orientation of Eddy's thought is an important precursor of the widespread investment in the connection between spirituality and health characteristic of American culture at the turn of the twenty-first century, her radical idealism and ultimate denial of the body's reality have been replaced, at least to some extent, by a new kind of attention to the ways in which various kinds of social and psychological meaning are inscribed within the body's corporeality.

While the eclecticism of New Age spirituality and its inclusion of various forms of neopaganism makes for a strong contrast with the exclusive scriptural focus on the New Testament in Christian Science, their efforts to join religion and science and to make scientific claims for religion are similar. Crystal gazing, telepathic healing, analysis of past lives, communion with the spirits of nature, and belief in guardian angels are similar to Christian Science and New Thought, and grow out of these older traditions. All these religions involve efforts to advance spirituality by connecting it with science. And all these religions claim that the symbolic objects of religious belief have the kind of existence that is, or eventually will be, scientifically verifiable.[24]

To some extent, the schools of psychoanalysis founded by Sigmund Freud and his students and followers have functioned similarly to Christian Science, New Thought, and New Age spiritualities. While more closely linked to the medical establishment than the theories associated with these explicitly religious traditions, the psychological theories promoted by Freud and his successors (such as Freud's oedipal complex or Jung's anima) often functioned as myths invested with metaphysical reality. And like Christian Science, New Thought, and New Age spiritualities, psychoanalysis developed largely in response to the sufferings of women and their yearnings for personal transformation. In the late nineteenth century, psychoanalysis emerged primarily as an explanation for, and a means of treating, female "hysteria," an emotional disorder believed to be caused by dysfunction of the uterus. While Freud himself never relinquished the belief that mind and body were inseparable or that mental illness had a biological context, his successors abstracted his psychological theories from that context. As a result, patients with psychosomatic illness were often treated as if their illness were "all in their heads." But since the 1970s, advocates of a return to biological psychiatry have challenged this highly idealistic and guilt-provoking approach to psychosomatic illness. Leading proponents of recent advances in biological psychiatry have claimed that "the new neuropsychiatry is an integration of psychology and biology, of nurture and nature, and of mind and body." In its transcendence of dualistic thinking, one spokeswoman affirmed, "neuropsychiatry offers tremendous hope—hope that new, more effective treatments will be found, hope that by understanding the biological causes of these disorders, we will be able to prevent our daughters from suffering, and hope that patients soon will be told, 'It's *not* all in your head.' "[25]

To the extent that they treat psychosomatic problems through symbolic utterances and actions, all forms of psychiatry are like shamanism. And in this regard psychiatrists are similar to practitioners of Christian Science, New Thought, and New Age spiritualities who utilize the power of suggestion and positive thinking to alleviate illness and suffering. But biological psychiatry diverged from more idealistic forms of treatment in its greater attention to the corporeal context and functions of symbolic thought and behavior. And in this focus on corporeal context, recent developments in biological psychiatry paralleled some of those in anthropology and feminist theory.

The healing traditions of New Thought, New Age spiritualities, and psychoanalysis all contributed to new efforts to integrate religion and health. But at the same time, some of the most important new advances in understanding the relationship between religion and health diverged from these traditions in rejecting metaphysical idealism. These new advances focused instead on the fusion of mind and body and on the corporeal matrix of psychological function and religious understanding. As part of this shift, the spirituality movement became less countercultural and more mainstream with respect to established health care institutions. And the connection between religion and health became more open to methods of scientific investigation that did not presuppose the independent existence of God, the anima, or any other object of religious or psychological belief.

The body and its important role in religious life became increasingly appreciated as part of the growing recognition of religion's relevance to health, and as part of the shift from making scientific claims for the existence of metaphysical forces to opening religious belief and practice up to investigation based in established forms of scientific method. This increased appreciation of the body's role in religion was partly a result of new advances in biology and biological theories of religion. It was also the result, as we have seen, of converging interest in the body and its centrality to religious life among both scholars and practitioners of religion. And growing interest in the body among scholars and practitioners of religion was largely the result of self-consciousness about gender and analysis of its role as a social construct deeply intertwined with religion.

CONCEPTUALIZING RELIGIOUS EXPERIENCE
IN PRAGMATIC TERMS

Viewed in the context of long-standing trends in American religious history, interest in the healthful benefits of spirituality reflected not only the universal tendency to utilize religion as a means of obtaining relief from suffering and pain, but also a distinctively American tendency to conceptualize religion in pragmatic terms. In one of the classic formulations of this distinctively American tendency, the philosopher William James linked the will to believe to the active resolution of problems, arguing that the viability of any belief could be measured in terms of its effectiveness in producing outcomes that enabled people to manage their worlds. James also linked the effectiveness of religious beliefs to their therapeutic benefits, especially with regard to mood. While acknowledging that some people were born with a temperamental inclination to optimism that made belief in divine assistance easy and natural, he was particularly interested in individuals who struggled with hopelessness. Enervated by a lack of will to believe, these individuals required a conversion-type experience to infuse them with hope and enable them to live productive and happy lives. Thus James viewed religious experience as a fundamental aspect of human psychology, one that was ultimately associated with emotional strength and well-being.

Like many other American religious thinkers, James did not draw a firm distinction between the analysis of religious life and its pursuit. Indeed, in fusing psychology and religious experience to a certain extent, James enlisted religious experience in the aid of psychological health. Many other religious thinkers in late-nineteenth- and early-twentieth-century America were working in same vineyard, although not always with the same understanding of and respect for scientific method. Proponents of New Thought were equally interested in the therapeutic benefits of religious experience and in explaining those benefits in a way that bridged the gap between religion and science. Like their New Age successors at the end of the twentieth century, proponents of New Thought during James's era incorporated divine reality into the cause-and-effect, mechanistic framework they associated with scientific thinking. They performed experiments designed to harness divine reality, produce therapeutic benefit, and emulate the scientific practice of discovery and validation. While James stood apart from them in understanding that scientific method could be applied only to the effects of religious belief and not to its objects, he stood with them in appreciating the healthful benefits of religious experience and in believing that the investigation of those benefits, and a better understanding of how they were produced, would not weaken those benefits or make them disappear.

The roots of this kind of psychological orientation in American religious thought can be traced back to the Anglo Protestant tradition through Jonathan Edwards and John Wesley. While Edwards's emphasis on the will, the power of self-deception, and the terrible beauty of God attracted Emerson, Melville, Hawthorne, Dickinson, and Thoreau, Wesley's understanding of the interdependence of nature and religion exerted great influence on popular ideas about religious experience and contributed to enthusiasm for a wide range of activity, from revivalism to mesmerism, spiritualism, and Theosophy.[26]

American intellectuals amplified their psychological orientation to religion through the study of German theologians who located the essence of religious life in emotional feeling. Beginning with the German theologian Friedrich Schleiermacher at the beginning of the nineteenth century, liberal Protestant theology in Europe moved away from the business of formulating statements about the objects of religious belief and their operations and into the business of describing religion as an essential dimension of human experience. Immanuel Kant's earlier argument that all knowledge was preconditioned by the structures of the human mind laid the groundwork for this inward turn toward human experience in European Protestant thought and for Schleiermacher's understanding of religion as a universal human phenomenon characterized by feeling.

The Schleiermachian tendency to define religion in terms of human experience and feeling influenced the academic field of religious studies as it emerged in the United States. Religious studies, in turn, contributed to growing interest in the therapeutic benefits of spirituality and the body's role in religion. While neither religious studies nor current American interest in the therapeutic benefits of spirituality is by any means limited to people who identify themselves as Protestants, they carry important vestiges of Protestant thought and thus exemplify its shaping role in the larger context of American religious thought.

The distinctly American tendency to focus on and attempt to manage the beneficial effects of religious experience can be seen as part of the pragmatic trend in American religious thought that can be traced back not only to William James and his New Thought contemporaries, but to the Anglo Protestant tradition in America out of which much of their thinking emerged. The New England Puritans expected the fruits of grace to manifest themselves in public life as well as in the Christian households that were celebrated as the building blocks of Puritan society. While some descendants of the early Puritans complained that prosperity was killing the grace that mothered it, underlying belief in the salutary benefits of religious life persisted. And more was involved here than the universal tendency to turn to religion for help in times of need. An Anglo Protestant preoccupation with conscience and right intention contributed to the later idea that religion was essentially a matter of will and experience. It also contributed to the American tendency to be moralistic about people who lacked prosperity or good health.

And finally, this whole process of humanizing religion—of understanding the benefits, mechanisms, and nature of religion in human terms—was linked to gender and to a historical process of increasing awareness of the interdependence of gender and religious life. This process has accelerated dramatically since the 1960s, but it had earlier roots as well, not only in Marxist theory, which contributed significantly to the emergence of feminism, but also in the Anglo-Protestant tradition and its heavy emphasis on affectionate marriage and "well-ordered" family life as embodiments of grace. In rejecting belief in celibacy as a superior form of religious life and in celebrating marriage and family life as earthly types of divine life, Puritans and other early Protestants endorsed a strongly patriarchal social order. But in affirming marital sex, and even conceptualizing it as a typological reflection of divine grace, they brought the body into the picture of Christian life in a new way. And in revitalizing the biblical image of God as a bridegroom devoted to his bride, the Puritans offered women and their bodies a kind of privileged status. This privilege was not the same as equality, and not without a downside, but it served as an important step in the larger process of humanizing religion, which came to fruition in the United States in the late twentieth century.

6

The Pragmatic Role
of Religious Studies

Congress shall make no law respecting an establishment of religion, or prohibiting the free exercise thereof.
—First Amendment to the Constitution of the United States

What William James said about pragmatism might be applied equally
to religious studies:

> [I]t lies in the midst of our theories, like a corridor in a hotel. In-
> numerable chambers open out of it. In one you may find a man
> writing an atheistic volume, in the next someone on his knees praying
> for faith and strength, in a third a chemist investigating a body's
> properties. In a fourth a system of idealistic metaphysics is being
> excogitated, in a fifth the impossibility of metaphysics is being shown
> But they all own the corridor, and all must pass through it if they
> want a practicable way of getting into or out of their respective
> rooms.[1]

The academic study of religion contributed to the transformation of
American religion in several ways. Introductory courses in religious

studies stimulated many American college students to sample, reflect on, and experiment with new forms of belief and ritual practice. The distinction between the study of religion and its practice, which many instructors emphasized, played an important role in this process. By involving many young Americans in studying a variety of different religious traditions and at the same time relieving them of the requirement of loyalty to any particular tradition, religious studies contributed to the rise of eclectic forms of spirituality characteristic of American culture since the sixties, to a lowering of barriers between religious groups, and to a tendency to tailor religious beliefs and practices to meet personal needs.

While contributing to a consumerist approach to religious life and indirectly stimulating increasingly sophisticated forms of religious marketing, religious studies also had a stabilizing effect on religion's role in American public life. By promoting a better understanding of the nature of religion and its various manifestations and effects, religious studies encouraged respect for religious difference along with increased self-consciousness about how religious symbols work and a general tendency to understand religion in humanistic terms. Through discussion of the social effects of various religious traditions, religious studies contributed to greater understanding of the ways in which religion functioned to divide people from one another and the ways it could function to promote equality and build community. Partly as a result of the widespread existence and popularity of courses in religious studies, religious difference was used less often to stigmatize people than in the 1950s and served less frequently as a hindrance to professional, public, and personal interaction. Some commentators interpreted the general decline in the importance of religious difference in American culture as a sign of religion's lamentable retreat into a sphere of private life and, consequently, as an indication of its waning influence on public life. But this decline in the social importance of religious difference was also a sign of the lowering of barriers between religious groups in the United States and a reflection of religion's increasingly benign role in public life. In this regard, religion came to function less as an agent of ethnic identity and tribal solidarity and more as a catalyst for individual concern about social issues.

In the context of American political history, this tendency for religion to play a smaller role in cementing group difference and a more explicit role in personal development can be seen as an outcome of the ideas about the relationship between religion and public life that informed the framing of the First Amendment to the United States Constitution. The tendencies toward increased respect for religious difference and personal choice can be viewed as an extension of religious freedom.

The academic study of religion has contributed to this new freedom. Although some critics interpret the multitude of methods and sub-agendas within the field as evidence of an "unfortunate" state of "disarray," in its overall effect, religious studies has served as a vehicle for open and informed discussion of the varieties of religious belief and practice.[2] Through its approach to religion as a universal human phenomenon manifest in a variety of different cultural forms, religious studies has contributed to the respect for religious difference that distinguishes the United States from countries where religious difference feeds violence and civil war. And through its analysis of the social functions of religion, religious studies has indirectly encouraged the development of benign forms of religious belief and practice.

Both in the academic study of religion in the United States and in American culture more broadly, the tendencies to value freedom of religious expression and to criticize religious establishment are really two sides of the same coin. These closely related tendencies are so deeply ingrained in American culture that scholars of religious studies in the United States are primed to see violations of religious freedom and to focus on the ways in which de facto religious establishments have excluded some people from participation in public life. The tendency to rap religious authority on the knuckles for infringing on religious liberty or prohibiting the full exercise of religious feeling is an old and distinguishing habit in American thought. Scholars in religious studies carry this habit onward when they criticize American Christians for their historical failures to respect Native American religions, empower women, or be otherwise inclusive and democratic in supporting every believer's full engagement in public life. These criticisms can obscure certain achievements, such as women's disproportionate involvement in Christianity, the high degree of respect that Native American traditions command among many Christians today, and the fact that the vast majority of Native American traditionalists are professing Christians. Such criticisms can also obscure the considerable efforts that have been exerted, and continue to be exerted, to make the practice of Christianity live up to expectations about the inclusive, democratic, and socially responsible implications of its gospel. But if attention to lapses and shortcomings sometimes obscures achievement, it also reflects a powerful, underlying respect for religious difference and an equally powerful, underlying tendency to link access to religious expression with the strength of society and limited access with social failure and weakness.

Implications of the First Amendment for Thinking About Religion

The American system of government and, more specifically, the protection of religious freedom guaranteed in the First Amendment supported and even stimulated the American tendency to openly criticize religious authority. The chief author of the amendment, James Madison, identified religious freedom as the most basic of all the rights guaranteed in the Constitution. The state could "sweep away all our fundamental rights," Madison claimed in 1785, including freedom of the press, trial by jury, and the right to vote, if it did not "leave this particular right untouched and sacred." Thus Madison viewed religious freedom as the prerequisite for the freedom of all other forms of expression. He also believed that religious liberty involved more than the prohibition of religious oppression. By guaranteeing individuals the right to pursue the responsibilities associated with religion without having to conform to any external or institutional standard of religious belief, religious freedom shifted responsibility for religious life to the individual conscience, where Madison believed it belonged.

Madison was under no illusion that religious freedom would guarantee moral virtue or ensure responsible citizenship. But he did believe religious freedom would produce greater moral virtue and more responsible citizenship than any form of religious establishment. He held, furthermore, that religious freedom was consonant with the fundamental principles of Christianity and that it would facilitate the growth of Christianity within the United States and throughout the world. Conversely, nothing would retard the healthy growth of Christianity more than official ties to government. Noting that "during almost fifteen centuries has the legal establishment of Christianity been on trial," Madison claimed that the results of this establishment, "more or less in all places," have been "pride and intolerance in the Clergy, ignorance and servility in the laity, [and] in both, superstition, bigotry and persecution." On the other hand, a form of government based on the idea that it was "the duty of every man to render to the Creator such homage and such only as he believes to be acceptable to him" would stimulate the growth of Christian virtue, retard the growth of cruel and divisive forms of religious life, and prevent the chilling effect on religious vitality that he associated with the establishment of government-sanctioned religious authority.

Madison was aware that religious freedom would often contribute to political disorder and complexity. But he believed that the suppression of religious freedom would cause even more trouble. In addition, he believed that any attempt by the government to suppress religious freedom would ultimately be ineffective and thereby conducive to disrespect for law. All in all, he argued, the imposition of restrictions on religious liberty would "slacken the bands of Society." Moral virtue and civic responsibility would flourish best, Madison asserted, under a system of government in which religious authority was completely divested from the state.[3]

The academic study of religion does not involve any sort of credo supporting First Amendment rights. But as a general enterprise, it fits within a larger cultural paradigm that incorporates First Amendment principles. While a variety of approaches to understanding religion exist within the field, along with many disagreements about what constitutes effective understanding, few if any exponents would contest the general statement that the purpose of religious studies is to increase understanding of different forms of religion and their social functions. This increased understanding works to decrease religious animosity, lower barriers between religious groups, and stimulate freedom of religious expression.

As part of the process of understanding religion, assessing the social functions of religion often involves students in distinguishing religious beliefs, practices, and institutions that enable democratic participation in community life from those that do not. Analysis of the social functions of religion involves some understanding of how religion empowers people and of how it often works to empower some people at the expense of others. Subtle or not, this analysis encourages criticism of exclusionary, divisive, and hierarchical forms of religion and often has the effect of holding religion to standards of humaneness and human flourishing. And this process of assessing religion in humanistic terms has the indirect effect of encouraging religious reform. Once students begin to compare the social functions of their own religions with those of others, and once they begin to think about their own religions in terms of standards of human flourishing, the urge to revise, reinterpret, and reform is almost inevitable.

RELIGIOUS NEUTRALITY AS A FRAMEWORK FOR RELIGIOUS FREEDOM—AND RELIGIOUS STUDIES

While the framers of the Constitution were more concerned about government and politics than they were about religion or theology, Reformed Protestant theology exerted a strong indirect influence on their construction of a legal guarantee of religious freedom. Most of these men were liberal Protestants influenced by Enlightenment ideas about the compatibility of reason and Christian virtue. While many of them held ideas about revelation and free will that separated them from strict Calvinists, they shared with more conservative members of the Reformed Protestant tradition the conviction that Christian virtue was centered primarily in the individual, that individuals should be nurtured in religion by their families, churches, and schools, and that nurturing individual virtue was the best way to create and sustain a just and harmonious society. While liberal and conservative Protestants at the end of the eighteenth century disagreed about the extent to which disestablishment should be carried out and religious liberty allowed, they all believed that this matter was a proper subject for thoughtful study and informed public discussion. And while they disagreed about the extent to which traditions other than Protestant Christianity deserved to be acknowledged as genuine forms of religion, they agreed that religious study and understanding were important aids to religious virtue.

James Madison became convinced of the necessity of religious freedom as a result of his observation of the condescending way that Baptist "dissenters" were treated in Virginia while the Church of England was established there. As an Anglican influenced by liberal trends within the Puritan tradition, Madison disliked the system of religious establishment in Virginia not only because he sympathized with the dissenters, some of whom he counted as friends, but also because he believed that it enervated and corrupted the Christian religion. Much like Roger Williams in the seventeenth century, Madison believed that religious establishment worked against the exercise of individual conscience, which in his mind stood at the core of the Christian religion. Like Williams, he believed that the system of government most compatible with Christianity, and under which Christianity would flourish best, was a secular state.

In its efforts to think about religion objectively and dispassionately, religious studies is somewhat analogous to a secular state. Of course, complete objectivity and dispassion are impossible—our own experiences and inclinations shape everything we see. But religious studies is strongly characterized by expectations of nonpartisanship with respect to particular religious traditions. While scholarly judgments are often made about the virtues or inequities of particular traditions, there is tacit agreement that such judgments must be reached on the basis of accessible evidence and not simply be expressions of religious preference or assent to religious authority. This does not mean that practitioners of religious studies are subject to any restriction on expressions of personal assent to religious authority, although being a practitioner of religious studies admittedly complicates one's personal religious life. But it does mean that religions other than one's own must be treated fairly and that, within the context of comparative work, one's own tradition should not be treated under different rules or special privileges.

Like the religious neutrality of the state, the presumption of neutrality in religious studies works against favoring one religious tradition over the other by prejudgment. And like the effect of religious disestablishment as a stimulant to the religious pluralism of American culture, the scholarly construction of a neutral arena for religion has stimulated interest in a variety of religions and thus contributed to the eclecticism and experimentalism characteristic of American religious life. Much as James Madison saw that a secular state was consonant with the fundamental principles of religion as understood in the liberal Reformed Protestant tradition of Christianity, we can see that the open neutrality toward particular traditions cultivated in religious studies contributes to the development of some of religion's most positive benefits.

PROTESTANT ORIGINS OF RELIGIOUS FREEDOM—AND RELIGIOUS STUDIES

While Enlightenment interpretations of Reformed Protestant thought shaped the political and legal framework of the larger culture within which religious studies developed in the United States, evangelical interpretations shaped many of the earliest efforts to understand the actual content of non-Christian traditions. In their effort to bring Protestant Christianity to people of other nations, some American missionaries endeavored to acquaint themselves with the beliefs and practices of the people they hoped to convert. To be sure, most nineteenth-century Protestant missionary accounts of other religions were full of gross prejudice and misinformation. But among all the effusions of self-justifying rhetoric, a steadily growing number of more circumspect and scholarly accounts of other religions began to appear. By the 1930s, these efforts to treat other people and their religions respectfully had contributed so significantly to an ecumenical concern for world understanding that, as we saw in Chapter 1, the whole idea that non-Protestants were heathens or infidels in need of conversion was called into question by a large cohort of liberal Protestants. As a result, some of the people who followed this train of thought invested their desire to improve the lives of other people in humanitarian enterprises. Others invested their hopes for world understanding in the fledgling enterprise of religious studies.

Catholic missionaries, especially those representing the Society of Jesus, were among the earliest Christian missionaries to make any attempt to understand the religious traditions of non-Christian peoples, with Matteo Ricci in China and Robert di Nobli in India standing out as early modern exemplars of Christian universalism. But as we saw, Protestants were the first to make the transition from missionary work to modern ecumenism and its developing commitment to world religious understanding. This transition from missionary work to ecumenism laid important groundwork for the subsequent transition to religious studies. Ecumenism led to the development of theories of religion that treated non-Christian traditions on an equal basis with Christianity, stimulated interest in the training of scholarly personnel to lead the way in developing better understanding of non-Christian traditions, and helped to promote the idea that religion was a universal human phenomenon.

In addition to their role in drawing attention to the need to understand religion as a universal phenomenon, liberal Protestants introduced assumptions about the centrality of religious experience and the secondary importance of institutional authority into the emerging field of religious studies. While early exponents of religious studies did not neglect the institutional embodiments of religion, neither did they associate the fundamental essence of religion with either the ideal concept of "church" or the institutional reality. The absence of a strong doctrine of the church in Protestant theology led instead to an emphasis on the essential importance of personal experience in religious life. And it was through this Protestant emphasis on the priority of religious experience that religious studies developed.

In this regard, the writings of the German theologian Friedrich Schleiermacher stand as an early landmark in the history of Protestant thought leading up to the emergence of religious studies. As we have seen, Schleiermacher located the essence of religion in human feeling and, more specifically, in the feeling of dependence on a higher power. His theory about the essence of religion represented an important breakthrough in the process of conceptualizing religion as a universal human phenomenon. And this conceptual breakthrough was the direct result of a climate of religious opinion conditioned by the Protestant break away from the Catholic Church. Thus Schleiermacher stood on the shoulders of earlier Protestant Reformers who had been intent on defining Christian life in a way that focused on the connection between grace and faith and that excluded, or at least downplayed, allegiance to the Catholic Church. Protestant Reformers had emphasized the centrality of the individual in religious life, not only to justify their departure from the Roman Church but also, and more positively, to express their faith in the saving power of God's grace within the individual. As many scholars explained, the Protestant turn to the individual as the centerpiece of Christian life was part of a larger historical process in Western culture associated with the rise of capitalism, the invention of the printing press, the emergence of nation-states, the decline of medieval feudalism, and investment in the nuclear family as the building block of society.

With regard to subject matter, religious studies was by no means limited to Protestant forms of religious experience. If anything, exponents of religious studies were more interested in non-Protestant and indeed non-Christian experience than in Christianity. Until the 1970s, many scholars of religion even shied away from examining Christianity with the same methods to which other religions were subjected. If some still regarded Christianity as normative and thus exempt from deconstruction, most scholars in the field wanted to remedy existing ignorance about other traditions. And many emphasized the role that Protestant self-righteousness played in supporting that ignorance.

The scholars who secured a place for religious studies as part of most institutions of higher learning in the United States turned a good deal of their attention to the question of what Americans could learn from religious experiences of people in primitive and non-Western cultures. In their emphasis on individual experience and in their tendency to view institutions of religious authority in a negative light, exponents of religious studies carried forward some of the most cherished assumptions of liberal Protestant thought. This liberal Protestant orientation helps to explain the tendencies in religious studies after the Second World War to conceptualize religion as a means of expressing and answering existential need and to turn toward non-Christian religious as a means of expanding individual religious consciousness.

Paul Tillich, Mircea Eliade, and Their Enthusiasm for Other Forms of Religion

The idea that religious experience was a universal phenomenon at the heart of virtually all forms of human culture supported the academic study of religion. Although not everyone in religious studies believed that such a universal phenomenon existed, some of the best-known and most influential scholars were intent on organizing the field around this theory. Here again, Protestant ideas about religion defined the conversation. Even though non-Christian religions often provided the subject matter, the assumptions and theories driving the analysis of those religions were tied to theories about the transcendental nature of religious experience that derived from Continental philosophy, and especially from the work of Schleiermacher, Schelling, Hegel, and Heidegger. Influenced by the concentration on feeling, esthetic idealism, and transcendental phenomenology associated with these thinkers, a significant number of liberal Protestants turned their attention to the study of non-Christian cultures in the hope that acquaintance with religious experience in those cultures would revitalize the religious lives of modern men and women. At one level, this desire for inspiration was the opposite of the missionary desire for conversion and represented a progressive concern for world understanding. At another level, as we shall see, it could still involve a somewhat predatory approach to other religions and to the people who participated in them.

While many Protestant theologians in the United States after World War II participated in discussions about the transcendental quality of religious experience, no one was more influential than the German expatriate Paul Tillich. His definition of religion as "ultimate concern" freed the essence of religion from any particular doctrine or culture and correlated the essential principles of Christianity with forms of religious experience outside the boundaries and explicit manifestations of Christianity. His definition of religion as ultimate concern also encouraged seekers to look for spiritual life outside of churches and other customary institutions and to find it in art, literature, and anyplace else where human beings expressed their vitality, passions, and deepest emotional commitments. It was there that the ground of being and the God beyond theism were to be found.

In addition to provoking religious discussion about modern art and literature, Tillich's approach to religion stimulated a new kind of emotional and esthetic interest in other religions. As expressions of ultimate concern analogous to Christianity, non-Christian religions could function as new sources of inspiration for Protestant who were jaded, bored, or disaffected by the moralism of their own religious traditions. Tillich's approach to religion encouraged more than a few Protestant theologians and their students in Protestant divinity schools to venture outside of church history and Christian theology for inspiration. In their desire to expand religious thought beyond its Protestant and Christian boundaries, these scholars participated in efforts to make religious studies an established part of the humanities curriculum in many American colleges and universities. In many cases, these developers of religious studies envisioned a future in which the study of ultimate concern, advanced through courses in religion, would eventually permeate all of academic life.

Tillich's approach to religion exerted a profound influence on Protestant thought in the United States and his celebrity during the last decade of his life was remarkable. In 1959, his picture appeared on the cover of *Time* magazine. In 1963, he delivered the keynote address at the magazine's fortieth-anniversary party to an audience that included Adlai Stevenson, Francis Cardinal Spellman, Douglas MacArthur, and 280 other people who had been featured on the cover of *Time* throughout the years. In 1965, within an hour of his death on October 22, the news of his passing was broadcast on major television and radio networks, and the next morning his photograph appeared on the front page of the *New York Times*. The obituary noted that "Protestant theology in this country is profoundly different as a result" of Tillich's work and that he had achieved his long-term goal of anticipating "a new form of Christianity."

The article in *Time* magazine described Tillich's popularity in terms of the unorthodox character of his theological ideas, explaining that he administered "a kind of shock treatment" to people that drove them "to re-examine the basis of their own faith." The article attributed at least some of Tillich's allure to the "razzle-dazzle paradox of his ideas," which included the theory that "sin is not something one commits, but a state of 'estrangement' from one's true self," along with the invitation to "rejoice with Nietzsche that 'God is dead.'" The article also noted that Tillich's approach was criticized by some who argued that "his theology comes close to draining the meaning from all traditional Christian concepts." One of these critics, the philosopher of religion Nels F. S. Ferré, called Tillich "the most dangerous theological leader alive."[4]

At Harvard, where he taught between 1955 and 1962, the student newspaper investigated Tillich's popularity. On the basis of a survey it conducted in 1959, the *Harvard Crimson* reported that the "undergraduate speculation about religion" stimulated by Tillich at Harvard did "not represent a return to the faith in which [students] or their forefathers were raised." In contrast to the upsurge in church attendance occurring contemporaneously in American suburbs, the interest in religion at Harvard was far more evident "in campus discussion than in church attendance." Students chose such phrases as " 'trivial,' 'mundane,' and 'unworthy of a religious person's interest' " to describe organized religious activities, while at the same time demonstrating "great epistemological concern." The *Crimson* linked this concern to Tillich's teaching and observed that as a result of this teaching, "Harvard's main effect" on Protestant students "seems to be one of 'reshaping' " their beliefs.[5]

Tillich's theology was a contributing factor to many of the new theological movements that emerged in American culture in the 1960s. Participants at the 1965 civil rights protest in Selma invoked his notion of *kairos* as a historical moment of religious crisis and fullness. James H. Cone, the originator of black theology, drew heavily on Tillich's theology in calling Americans to correlate being Christian with being black. And the influential feminist theologian Mary Daly based the argument of her seminal book *Beyond God the Father* in Tillich's theology. Although she later chided him for calling Christ the "final revelation" and went far beyond him in attacking Christ as a symbol of the patriarchal religious and social systems that oppressed women, she drew heavily upon his understanding of ultimate reality as the erotic, ecstatic, and antiauthoritarian nature of being at the vital center of human life and experience. Other feminist theologians, including Valerie Saiving, Judith Plaskow, and Carol Christ, were also indebted to Tillich. By shifting attention from doctrine and history to ultimate concern as the proper focus of religious thought, these and other feminist theologians utilized Tillich's theology to incorporate women's experience as a basis for religious and theological reflection.[6]

Tillich's view of historical events and interpersonal relationships as expressions of the Absolute and occasions for revelatory ecstasy complemented much of the religious and political radicalism that swept American campuses when Lyndon Johnson escalated the war in Vietnam in 1965. Tillich's theology encouraged a totalistic emotional rejection of American society by disdaining middle-class morality and by interpreting it as the spiritually impoverished product of capitalism, technology, and bureaucracy. Moreover, Tillich held forth the possibility of constructing superior kinds of social relationships based primarily on intensity of feeling. In the third volume of his *Systematic Theology*, published in 1963, Tillich described the kind of social life that might be taken up by individuals who were truly grasped by ultimate concern, and wrote about "spiritual community" in a way that presaged some of the countercultural communes of the later sixties and seventies. For Tillich, "spiritual community" was "latent" outside of churches and came into being wherever persons participated together "in the holiness of Divine Life." In the passionate relationships that Tillich described, there was little self-restraint and ultimately "no conflict . . . between *agape* and *eros*, between *agape* and *philia*, between *agape* and *libido*."[7]

Tillich interpreted depth psychology and religious faith in terms of each other, arguing that the process of working through denial and emotional pain was common to both and that spiritual experience of the "power of being" defined both religious salvation and the goal of psychotherapy. In 1941, while teaching at Union Theological Seminary, Tillich organized the New York Psychology Group, which included Ruth Benedict, Erich Fromm, and Rollo May, along with a number of Jungian therapists. Through this group, which convened a series of well-publicized seminars over the course of five years, and through the Religion-Psychiatric Movement at Columbia, which drew together ministers and psychiatrists interested in bridging psychotherapy and pastoral care, Tillich was an important participant in the development of pastoral psychology.[8]

In American academic life, where Tillich's influence was greatest, the Tillichian approach to theology as ultimate concern harmonized nicely with the approach to religion advocated by the Romanian phenomenologist Mircea Eliade. Along with Tillich, Eliade and his colleagues and students in the history of religions at the University of Chicago played major roles in defining religious studies in the seventies. Eliade wrote approvingly that Tillich "was interested in the existential meaning of history," which Eliade identified with inherently religious structures behind historical events, in contrast to the study of the "modifications of changes" in history that were merely results of the mundane "flowing of time."

Tillich found his own existentialism confirmed and enlarged when he cotaught seminars with Eliade in 1964 and 1965 after joining the divinity school at Chicago following his retirement from Harvard. Tillich credited Eliade with expanding the implications of his theology and believed it would be carried forward through Eliade's approach to the history of religions. Asian and primitive religions, as Eliade taught them, brought "a new intensity of meaning" to the doctrines and practices of Christianity that Tillich taught.[9]

Eliade, who taught at the University of Chicago from 1956 until his death in 1986, analyzed experiences of the sacred in yoga and shamanism and compared the vital role of myth in primitive societies with what he regarded as the decadent but still persisting role of myth in modern society. While primitive people were intrinsically religious by virtue of being centered and saturated in mythic reality, Eliade believed, modern people found themselves adrift in the flux of time. But the terrible sense of meaningless that modern people suffered could be remedied by imaginative experiences that stimulated the archaic capacity for mythic experience.

For Eliade, myth and history were opposite and antagonistic ways of understanding reality. While history represented a chronological sequencing of more or less distinct events, myth represented the underlying dynamics of human experience that human events always recapitulated. In a mythic view of the world, nothing was ever really new. Moreover, myths that recounted the persisting dynamics of life were deeply tied to experiences of the sacred. Inspired by Rudolf Otto's *The Idea of the Holy* (1923, original German, 1917), Eliade believed that the sacred was a nonrational experience shared by religious adepts in many non-Western cultures. He derived his concept of the transconscious, which he defined as a universal human capacity for experience of the sacred, from Otto's idea that human beings had an awareness of divine reality beyond rational comprehension, or *sensus numinis*. Tillich was similarly indebted; he incorporated Otto's idea of the holy "as a constitutive element" of his theology and correlated Otto's categories with his own. Thus he argued that when Otto "describes the mystery of the holy as *tremendum* and *fascinosum,* he expresses the experience of 'the ultimate' in the double sense of that which is the abyss and that which is the ground of man's being."[10]

Competing Forms of Transcendentalism

In some respects, the transcendental approach to religion represented in the work of Paul Tillich and Mircea Eliade dovetailed with ideas associated with New England Transcendentalism that were already influential in American religious life and thought. Both forms of transcendentalism drew from German idealism, and both defined religion in terms of human experience and, more specifically, human responsiveness to the larger currents of life. Both forms of transcendentalism enabled Protestants to look beyond the special claims and exclusionary practices of Christianity to appreciate other religions and draw inspiration from them. And both forms of transcendentalism encouraged people to celebrate the esthetic aspect of religion and to discover the religious dimensions of esthetic experience. Both served as alternatives to rationalistic and rule-oriented conceptions of religion and to the judgmental moralism characteristic of many forms of both liberal and conservative American religious life.

While both groups celebrated the esthetic quality of religious experience, however, they differed on the question of how this esthetic quality was related to moral virtue. As heirs to the Puritan tradition in religious thought, epitomized by the eighteenth-century theologian Jonathan Edwards, the New England Transcendentalists regarded the esthetic dimension of religious experience as primary and morality as ancillary. But while ancillary, moral virtue was a necessary and inevitable consequence, they believed, of genuine religious experience. Thus Edwards argued that the internal beauty of a virtuous heart was always expressed through a person's life. A hundred years later, Emerson expressed a similar belief, claiming that the moral sentiment of righteousness suffused the religious sentiment of assent to the beauty of the universe. He believed that the steady pursuit of moral obligation and honesty helped to remind people of and prepare them for experiences of spiritual beauty.[11]

Like Emerson, Henry David Thoreau linked reverence for spiritual beauty in nature to moral virtue and simplicity. Like Margaret Fuller, Theodore Parker, Bronson Alcott, and most other New England Transcendentalists, Thoreau was deeply interested in politics and social reform. And like their Puritan predecessors, these Transcendentalists believed that the spiritual development of individuals was the best means to the creation of a just and harmonious society.[12]

Tillich and Eliade, on the other hand, tended to divorce religious experience from moral virtue. Tillich was especially intent on a transvaluation of ethics into ecstasy. He accepted the "moral element" in biblical teaching only insofar as it could be interpreted as a symbol of an existential situation. Thus sin for Tillich was existential estrangement, not violation of one's neighbor, disobedience to God, or transgression of moral law. Indeed, he explicitly rejected the authority of any person, idea, or law outside the self. Tillich's commitment to the normative status of his own existential experience contributed to the confidence with which he interpreted all human beliefs and experiences as illustrations of his own categories of thought. It also contributed to the aggressive and seductive quality of his personal "presence," which his former graduate student Rollo May described as "an experience of being psychologically and spiritually penetrated." May observed "a great deal of libido in this presence, especially felt by women." Tillich "had a way of looking not *at* but *into* a woman," May maintained, and was constantly involved in enterprises of "spiritual seduction." According to his wife's biography, Tillich was a self-absorbed and often cruel womanizer. May explained that Tillich deliberately aroused anxiety in his listeners, and justified himself in doing so, on the grounds that "anxiety is present in every authentic encounter." Tillich claimed that he was simply giving others "the dizziness of freedom" recommended by Kierkgaard.[13]

Tillich's celebrity in America can be understood partly as an example of the problem that Christopher Lasch described in *The Culture of Narcissism*. Lasch argued that developments in media technology fostered an increasingly consumerist orientation in American society, which encouraged narcissistic behavior and drew narcissists into the public limelight. While at one level, this "culture of narcissism" reflected the apparent freedom and abundance of American life, at a deeper level, Lasch worried, it reflected diminished expectations about social cooperation and belonging. In psychological terms, Lasch focused not on the primary, healthy narcissism of young children but on the secondary or pathological narcissism first identified by Otto Kernberg and other ego psychologists in the forties and fifties. While he could be high-functioning and charming, the narcissist's "devaluation of others," Lasch explained, "together with his lack of curiosity about them, impoverishes his personal life" and reinforces the "subjective experience of emptiness" that fueled a need "for constant infusions of approval and admiration."[14]

Whatever their psychological origin, Tillich's ideas provided a response to and means of coping with the social and emotional stresses of the Cold War era, the debacle in Vietnam, and the transformation of America from an industrial society to a technological one. During several decades of rapid social change, recurrent unrest, and fear of nuclear holocaust, Tillich's emphasis on anxiety and the terror of non-being struck a responsive chord in many Americans. The popularity of his existential ontology was a sign of the stress involved in living under the shadow of the bomb and of disenchantment with victory culture and conventional forms of religious life.

At the same time, Tillich's theology and its popularity among American intellectuals also signaled a new era of religious vitality characterized by rediscovery of the power of religious experience, its esthetic quality, and its emotional benefits. Tillich's subjective idealism might be seen as an extreme version of the rejection of external religious authority and the corresponding investment in individual experience characteristic of American religion in general and of the post-sixties era in particular. If this radical idealism quickened an already profound thirst for religious experience in American culture, it was eventually criticized and modified by many of the people who relied on other aspects of Tillich's theology in the process of breaking away from more conventional and restrictive forms of religious thought.

The relationship between Tillich's theology and feminist theology fits this pattern. In their development of Tillich's ideas about religion as ultimate concern and God as the ground of being, Valerie Saving, Mary Daly, Judith Plaskow, and other pioneers of feminist theology avoided his manipulative attitudes toward women and sexuality and whittled his subjective idealism down to something more self-critical and democratic. Thus while Mary Daly acknowledged Tillich's ideas as "springboards" for her own, she also presented him, in her inimitable way, as chief among "the philosophers of phallicism, huddling behind the bastions of reified *being* . . . know[ing] that they are living . . . in a house of cards." With reference to his Heideggerian concept of the "grasping-and-shaping-self," Daly accused Tillich of promoting "the 'hairy claw' view of ontological reason." She claimed, furthermore, that the pathological aspects of his thought were so obvious that they could easily be isolated from his useful critique of religious rationalism and discarded. Thus she argued that feminists should be grateful to Tillich because the "pornography" of his thought was so thinly veiled.[15]

A similar observation could be made about the larger transformation of American religion since the sixties in which Tillich's theology played a part. Evidence could certainly be found for Lasch's point about the way in which the media-driven and consumerist orientation of American culture gave narcissistic personalities new opportunities for self-expression—Jim Bakker and David Koresh come to mind as well as the brilliant, cosmopolitan, and highly educated Paul Tillich. But the larger transformation of American religious life since the sixties cannot be fully comprehended by Lasch's theory of a culture of narcissism. In contrast to the always unsatisfied preoccupation with self-aggrandizement characteristic of narcissism, the upsurge of interest in new and old forms of spirituality and much of the innovative blending of different forms of religious practice were often concerned with social benefit. And if narcissists had greater access to the limelight than ever before, they were also more subject to the spotlight of public scrutiny and to the pragmatic test of beneficence.

The tendency to invest states of feeling with ontological reality was an important development in Protestant thought that contributed to awareness of the body's centrality in religious imagination and experience. In the United States, this equation of human feeling with God (or, as Tillich preferred, the God beyond God and the ground of being itself) dovetailed with the preoccupation with personality that characterized American culture after World War II. In the fifties and sixties, considerable professional effort and public attention were directed to the development of personality and to understanding and treating the various pathologies that hindered this development. This effort and attention coincided with, and were responsive to, feelings of anxiety and alienation among many people resulting from terror of the bomb, increased urbanization, and the decline of consensual communities and social cohesion. The war in Vietnam added to these stresses by giving rise to moral protests against the policies of the United States government and by stimulating criticism of and disaffection from many of the perceived values underlying American society. Of course, these protests were also expressions of long established American commitments to democratic reform, freedom of individual expression, and impatience with established authority. But whatever the exact degree to which they expressed or rejected American values, the outrage over Vietnam and accompanying disaffection from contemporary American society exacerbated the already prevalent psychological stress.

Tillich's theology had the effect of radicalizing the emphasis on situation ethics characteristic of the liberal personalism already influential in Protestant circles. Indeed, the Tillichization of Protestant personalism lifted situation ethics out of its original context as an aid to social responsibility and linked the value of particular historical situations to their capacity to serve as vehicles for revelatory insight and ecstasy. If this gave narcissists a green light for their preexisting tendency to manipulate situations for personal advantage, it also contributed to major breakthroughs in black theology and feminist theology and freed many people from equating religion with oppressive forms of hierarchy and rule mongering. The radicalization of situation ethics in terms of human feeling also led to increasing self-consciousness about the body's central but often hidden role in religious life. And this new self-consciousness about the body's place in religious life worked to expose hurtful forms of religious sacrifice and fed the pragmatic tendency to judge and reform religion with regard to its salutary and therapeutic effects.

Joseph Campbell, C. G. Jung, and Catholic Imagination

In investing ontological reality in religious experience, Tillich's theology was similar to the mystical personalism associated with neo-Thomism and, at least to some extent, with the Catholic Worker movement. But theologically conservative Catholics had little interest in either the relativism of situation ethics or the conflation of spirituality with emotional feeling. In addition, assent to set rules for personal behavior grounded in the official teachings and transcendent authority of the Church prevented them from equating sacramental reality with subjective experience.

But for theologically liberal Catholics, the story was quite different. For many liberal Catholics, the transcendental approach to religious experience as a universal human phenomenon contributed to a new appreciation of the mystical aspect of religion in general and of Catholicism in particular. Even where Tillich's own theology may have had little impact, theologies like his made great headway. Especially important in this respect were theories about the meaning of religion advanced by Joseph Campbell and C. G. Jung. During the same decades when Tillich and Eliade made their greatest impact on American religious thinking, the psychological theories of the American mythographer Joseph Campbell and the Swiss psychoanalyst Carl Gustav Jung became popular among an even wider American audience.

An Irish Catholic from New York who attended a Jesuit high school, Campbell acknowledged that his interest in mythology originated in the symbolism that suffused his life as a Catholic boy. But he grew tired of what he called the "stupid liberalism" of Catholic doctrine and the institutional rigidity of the Catholic Church and its practices. Campbell's personal irritation at the Church declined in his later years when, according to his wife, Jean Erdman, "it became easier for him to reinterpret the symbols of his original Catholic faith in a mystical way."

A professor of literature at Sarah Lawrence College for thirty-eight years and a national celebrity at the time of his death in 1989, Campbell had a lifelong fascination with American Indian myths and Arthurian romance. Building on Jung's theory of the collective unconscious and its archetypes, and also on the German psychologist Eduard Spranger's emphasis on the importance of myth in adolescent development, Campbell argued for the supreme importance of the hero's journey in both individual and cultural life. Although the hero had many faces and the journey took many forms, Campbell believed that all these variants resonated with one another as particular expressions of a monomyth that was universal and fundamental to the human psyche. Campbell's theory of the hero's journey contributed not only to the burgeoning interest in spirituality among Americans after the 1960s, but also to renewed interest in Christian mythology, especially among Catholics, more than a few of whom returned to the Church with a new appreciation of Christ inspired by Campbell. His approach to myth also influenced George Lucas, the creator of *Star Wars*, who drew his ideas for the film series from Akira Kurosawa's 1958 film *The Hidden Fortress* and from Campbell's 1949 book *The Hero with a Thousand Faces*.

At a conference on the implications of the "Campbell phenomenon" for Catholicism held in Washington, D.C., in 1991, "many of those at the conference," according to reporter Pythia Peay, "credited Campbell's thinking with revitalizing the rituals they celebrate and for bringing them a more mystical awareness of Christian symbols." As conference participants agreed, Campbell's work helped disaffected Catholics see the Church as something more than a bastion of outmoded law and repressive authority. Campbell's approach to the symbols and stories of the Church as expressions of a universal hero myth enabled many Catholics to accept those symbols and stories as metaphors for their own emotional struggles and personal journeys. At the same time, Campbell's work helped many Catholics see beyond the division—imposed by some of the official teachings of the Church—between themselves and people of other religions. As one participant, Joanne Eiglesbach, claimed, "Campbell has been able to show us the *spiritual* meaning of those rituals performed in other cultures. This has softened the lines between the 'pagans' and the 'enlightened ones.' In fact," Eiglesbach went on, "the tables have turned, and these religions are now perceived as being more spiritual than our consumeristic Western society."

But critics of Campbell's influence on American Catholicism were suspicious of what they perceived as a tendency to separate the highly personalized meaning Catholic symbols may have for individuals from loyalty to the Church and its teachings. Thus Peay quoted the sociologist William Dinges, who claimed that Campbell's most famous saying—"Follow your bliss"—functioned too easily among American Catholics "as a narcissist's call to arms." Without denying that his existential approach to myth and symbol could be exploited in this way, Peay also quoted Campbell's friend Eugene Kennedy, who took a more generous view of the implications of Campbell's theory. According to Kennedy, following your bliss "means you must follow your innermost voice." Whether this led "to a vacation or a calling which is extremely difficult," Kennedy asserted, it should engage "the deepest recesses of your being."[16]

Campbell's appreciation of myth was, in part, an outgrowth of the archetypal approach to depth psychology advanced by C. G. Jung. A student of Sigmund Freud, Jung came to disagree with Freud's view of religion as a form of illusion. Utilizing a transcendental approach similar to Eliade's, Jung argued for the existence of a collective unconscious, a mental realm common to all humanity that provided the underlying dynamic structure for the ordinary consciousness of each individual. Jung understood the collective unconscious to be populated by archetypes that surfaced within individual consciousness, most clearly in dreams, but also in waking consciousness through the individual's projection of archetypes onto ordinary events and people. Religion attracted Jung because of its similarity to dreams. As far as he was concerned, myths were the most important aspect of religion because they represented the archetypes of the collective unconscious in vivid and compelling forms.

In the context of the reforms of the second Vatican Council and the revitalization of American Catholicism, Jung's way of thinking struck a resonant chord in many Catholics. Jung argued for the existence of a psychic realm underlying the conscious life of every human being, which motivated virtually all aspects of human feeling and behavior. He claimed that Jews and Protestants had consigned themselves to an endless task in seeking manifestations of this sacred realm in conscious life. Catholicism, however, succeeded in drawing forth some of the most important areas of the "collective unconscious." While objecting to the psychological authority that the Catholic Church presumed to exert over its members, Jung nevertheless asserted that "the timeless and the eternal" reality of the collective unconscious was always "available and present" to the Catholic "in the Holy of Holies on every altar."[17] Sympathetic both to Jung's criticism of heavy-handed religious authority and to his appreciation of the underlying sacrality of life and the disclosure of that sacrality in the mass and its mythology of a death-defying hero, more than a few American Catholics embraced his psychological interpretation of religion.

The Jungian approach to religion also stimulated interest among other American seekers. Because of the supposed connection between the individual psyche and the myths of all the world's religions, Jungian psychology led many Americans interested in exploring the depths of their own psyches to look to the myths of various cultures for personal inspiration. This eclectic but highly personalized interest in myth contributed, in turn, to the growing interest in spirituality that swept through many areas of American religious life in the 1970s. The Jungian approach to myth fueled the tendency to distinguish between spirituality, often perceived in terms of deep personal engagement, and religion, often perceived less positively in terms of institutional organizations and impersonal rules.

Religious Studies as a Corridor of Public Discourse

In the academic study of religion, debate about the merit of ideas advanced by Tillich, Eliade, Campbell, or Jung takes place in the context of a larger question about the role of theory in religious studies. Theories of religion provide frameworks of interpretation to help organize the massive jumble of religious stuff—symbols, rituals, artifacts, stories, doctrines, communities, institutions, and histories. And theories often provide valuable insight into the meaning of these things. But theory can also overshadowed the stuff of religion and, in some cases, even function as a substitute for it.

Tillich's theory about religion as ultimate concern, along with Eliade's theory of sacred space, Campbell's hero myth, and Jung's archetypal symbols, proved useful as means of sorting through religious stuff and organizing and interpreting it in a way that brought it to life. In religious studies courses, these theories enabled many students to think about religion as a universal human phenomenon, to learn about religions other than their own, and to appreciate certain aspects of their own traditions in new and often exciting ways. But at the same time, the utilization of these theories led some to make theory the object of study in a way that oversimplified the nature of religion and denigrated some of its most prevalent and important aspects.

In the case of Tillich's theory of ultimate concern, this problem was exacerbated by the subjective idealism implicit in the theory. Tillich's theory encouraged the interpreter to read his or her own feelings of ultimate concern into other people's lives, which was not always a bad thing, and in any case not entirely unavoidable. It also invited students to make their own feelings the primary object of concern. Making correlations between these feelings and the stuff of other religions could then function as a means of mining the world's religions in order to describe one's own feelings and stimulate their development and expression. While much could be said in favor of developing religious self-expression, and in recognition of the indirect but important role that religious studies could play in that process, the appropriation of other people's religious symbols as metaphors for one's own psychic expression could be deceptive, manipulative, and exploitative.

Of course, religious symbols are not private property. If they are vital parts of people's religious lives, they are always being appropriated, revised, and reinterpreted. But for a university professor to appropriate, say, Navajo religious symbols to express his own feelings of psychic dread and then pass those expressions off to students as Navajo religion raises some serious intellectual and ethical questions. While it is probably true that none of us can entirely avoid such trespassing, Tillich's approach to religion encouraged open hunting without any limit or second thought. The same might be said of Eliade's theory of sacred space, Campbell's hero myth, and Jung's archetypes. These were enormously helpful in conveying the universal nature of religion and in uprooting the old idea that Christianity was the only true religion. But they also carried a predatory dimension as self-serving as any missionary endeavor.

With the passage of time, it becomes easier to appreciate the popularity of religious theories advanced by Tillich, Eliade, Campbell, and Jung as part of a particular historical era in American religious thought. These theories created enthusiasm for religious studies in a time of crisis in American culture. Recognizing their role in stimulating the growth of religious studies may be part of a larger process of clarifying the primary function of religious studies as a descriptive and comparative enterprise. The subjective idealism that turned some pockets of religious studies into personality cults can perhaps be viewed as temporary mistakes in the ultimately healthy process of testing ideas and learning from error associated with the growth and maturation of the field.

To borrow the smile from the American philosopher William James quoted at the beginning of this chapter, religious studies at its most useful may be like a corridor in a hotel through which exemplars of different religious persuasions pass through on their way to and from their respective rooms. As an open corridor of public discourse, religious studies is accessible and useful to every faith. As a form of public discourse about one of the most complicated and cherished aspects of human life, religious studies contributes significantly to the democratic spirit of American public life and to the development of an educated citizenry. And as a means of comparing different religions and analyzing their respective effects, religious studies not only contributes to greater understanding of both the diversity and ubiquity of religion in human culture, but also to the improvement of religious thought and practice.

CONCLUSION

❧❧

The Great Awakening of the Late Twentieth Century

To recall Jonathan Edwards, in *Some Thoughts Concerning the Present Revival* in 1742,

[The Revival Not to Be Judged A Priori]

They have greatly erred in the way in which they have gone about to try this work, whether it be work of the Spirit of God or no, viz. In judging of it a priori; from the way that it began, the instruments that have been employed, and means that have been made use of, and the methods that have been taken and succeeded in carrying it on. Whereas, if we duly consider the matter, it will evidently appear that such a work is not to be judged of a priori, but a posteriori: we are to observe the effect wrought.

[The Need for Discrimination]

The weakness of human nature has always appeared in times of great revival of religion, by a disposition to run to extremes and get into confusion . . . And let any wise persons that han't, in the midst of the disputes of the present day, got beyond the calmness of consideration, impartially consider to what lengths, we may reasonably suppose, many of the primitive Christians, in their heat of zeal and under their extraordinary impressions, would soon have gone if they had no inspired guides; and whether or no 'tis not probable that the church of Corinth in particular, by an increase of their irregularities and contentions, would not in a little time have broke to pieces, and dissolved in a state of the utmost confusion? And yet this would have been no evidence that there had not been a most glorious and re-markable outpouring of the Spirit in that city. But as for us, we have no infallible apostle to guide and direct us, to rectify disorders, and reclaim us when we are wandering; but everyone does what is right in his own eyes [Judges 21 25]; and they that err in judgment, and are got into a wrong path, continue to wander, till experience of the mischievous issue convinces them of their error.[1]

American religious history has sometimes been periodized in terms of revivals or "awakenings," beginning with the Great Awakening, which peaked in New England between 1740 and 1742. In concluding this book, it seems fitting to raise the question of whether the transfor-mation of American religious life in the late twentieth century might be appropriately described as another Great Awakening analogous to periods of religious revival that mark the past. More specifically, it may be useful to identify some of the similarities between the flourishing of new forms of spirituality in the second half of the twentieth century and the flourishing of religious enthusiasm in the past. It may also be useful to identify some of the ways in which the recent enthusiasm for new forms of spirituality is unlike anything that came before.

Like great revivals of the past, enthusiasm for religion in the late twentieth century involved widespread intensity of religious feeling and interest in religious ideas. As in earlier awakenings, a significant portion of the American populace was caught up in spiritual matters. And this spiritual enthusiasm had a transforming effect on many religious in-stitutions. As in the past, new ways of speaking about religion and encouraging religious experience came into vogue, new sects and in-terest groups arose, and advances in religious learning were promoted.

Recent enthusiasm for spirituality was also similar to that of the past in its democratization of religious authority and especially in its exten-sion of greater religious authority to women. As Catherine A. Brekus showed, one of the most remarkable aspects of the Great Awakening in eighteenth-century America was the upsurge in female voices speak-ing critically, authoritatively, and inspirationally about religious life. The same might be said of the enthusiasm for spirituality in the late twen-tieth century.

The Great Awakening of the 1740s worked to break down barriers between an elite corps of educated ministers and religiously inspired common folk. In the context of this revolutionary process, "New Light" ministers railed against the complacency of established religion and they, in turn, were castigated for their arrogant, unseemly behavior. James Davenport was deported from Connecticut, declared *non compos mentis* in Boston, and expelled from Massachusetts for disrespect for established religious authority and unruly displays of religious zeal. Similarly in the late twentieth century, criticism of established religion was sometimes extreme and divisive. In addition, the radical idealism of some of the leading exponents of subjective idealism conflated spirituality with narcissism and other personality disorders. But as Jonathan Edwards argued about the awakening he observed, the presence of religious extremists did not disprove the existence of a widespread and concurrent breakthrough in genuine religious insight. In both the eighteenth and twentieth centuries, thoughtful reformers applied themselves to the work of sifting through new forms of religious expression in order to lift out and carry forward their most salutary aspects.

As in the past, rationalists objected to the weight given to individual religious experience. Rationalists of both liberal and conservative persuasion resisted the tendencies to place bliss and beauty above rule and authority, arguing that such tendencies create social disorder. In the late twentieth century, liberal rationalists such as Robert Bellah and Christopher Lasch held up the sense of moral obligation to society as the essence of religion, while conservative religious rationalists such as William Bennett and Pat Buchanan emphasized obedience to orthodox rules. Bellah and Lasch here might be compared to Charles Chauncy, the famous liberal critic of the Great Awakening, who denounced the emotionalism of the revivals, while Bennett and Buchanan might be compared to "Old Light" preachers who defined religious virtue in terms of a return to the orthodoxy they believed once existed in the past.

Despite these remarkable similarities in the transformations of religion in the mid-eighteenth and late twentieth centuries, however, no one can fail to see that many of the changes that occurred in American religious life since the 1960s were unprecedented. Roman Catholic forms of spirituality came to the fore and outmoded Protestant assumptions about the rightful domination of their religious tradition in

American religious life. Buddhist ideas filtered into so many aspects of American culture that the landscape of religious life, while still predominantly Judeo-Christian, was nevertheless deeply altered. And self-consciousness about the role of gender and the body in religious life escalated so dramatically that the differences between American religious ideas about gender and the body before and after the sixties seem to overwhelm the similarities.

Most important, the profound transformation that occurred in American religious life since the sixties involved heightened awareness of the human nature of religion. This was an awakening *to* the social and psychological construction of religion as much as an awakening *of* religious feeling. Religious thought in the late twentieth-century made many people aware of just how subject religion was to human manipulation and how closely it was tied to larger processes of social construction. This awakening put new pressure on people to define their religious traditions in terms of humane standards and human flourishing. It also brought new awareness of religion's universality. As the idea took hold that different traditions were variants of a common human phenomenon, the barriers between traditions seemed lower, and people crossed into other poeple's religious territories with remarkable ease and frequency. If obedience to religious authority declined in this process, respect for religious difference increased as American became more knowledgeable about the characteristics of religious traditions other than their own. And new interest in the spiritual wealth contained in a multitude of particular traditions continued to feed new forms of religious experimentation and cross-fertilization.

The new religious world that emerged in American culture in the late twentieth-century was a post-Protestant one. The Reformed Protestant tradition lost the status and privileges of a de facto established religion. At the same time, religious ideas and attitudes derived from that tradition shaped the character of other American religions. The pragmatism of the Reformed Protestant tradition persisted in shaping the larger culture of American religious life, as did the tendency to invest the individual with religious authority. As in the past, people wrangled over the strong American tendency to define religion in terms of morality, which was a legacy of the Puritans' move to shift control of religious life from external authorities to individuals, families, and local communities. As in the past, an equally strong emphasis on religion as responsiveness to the larger currents of life took shape in reaction to this moralism and led to an upsurge of esthetic, mystical, and nonrational expressions of religion.

Previous awakenings have been framed as reviving the piety and moral conscience of the first generation of American Puritans. If it is true, as this book contends, that some of the underlying dynamics of American religious life in recent years can be traced to the Puritans, it is important to acknowledge that none of the promoters of new forms of spirituality has rushed to point this out. If anything, Puritanism and its association with harsh moralism, Protestant hegemony, and victory culture has a bad reputation, with which few advocates of new forms of spirituality would want to be identified.

Only when one recognizes the New England Transcendentalists as heirs of American Puritanism does the connection between contemporary American spirituality and Puritanism begin to make sense. It was not primarily the moralism of the Puritan tradition that was revived in the late twentieth century—although echoes of that could certainly be found, especially among rationalist critics of the spirituality movement—but rather its esthetic responsiveness to life. The identification of spiritual life with recognition of the beauty of being, expressed in the work of the eighteenth-century Puritan theologian Jonathan Edwards, would be endorsed by many recent proponents of spirituality.

As we have seen, this appreciation of the powerful beauty of life, which runs from Edwards through the New England Transcendentalists to many recent proponents of spirituality, is not without moral force. The expectation that spirituality should result in social and therapeutic benefit is a common one and reflects the pragmatic orientation of American religion, as does the willingness on the part of many Americans to try out new forms of religious experience. Exercising a new freedom to depart from conventional forms of religious belief and practice, many Americans have justified their religious reachings by laying aside some of the qualms that rationalist and rule-oriented religious authorities have had about unorthodoxy and unconventionality. For today's spiritual enthusiasts, as for many of those in the past, the salutary benefits of new forms of spirituality justify their practice.

Notes

Introduction

1. See William R. Hutchinson, *The Modernist Impulse in American Protestantism* (Durham: Duke University Press, 1992), 243–87. Also see Harry Emerson Fosdick, *Christianity and Progress* (New York: Fleming H. Revell Company, 1922); Harry Emerson Fosdick, *Twelve Tests of Character* (New York: Association Press, 1923); Harry Emerson Fosdick, *The Living of These Days: An Autobiography*, 2nd ed. (New York: Harper and Row, 1967).

2. Carl F. H. Henry, "Dare We Renew the Controversy? The Evangelical Responsibility," *Christianity Today* 1 (June 22, 1957): 23–26, 38.

3. H. Richard Niebuhr parodied the optimism of liberal Protestants with the quip "A God without wrath brought men without sin into a kingdom without judgment through the ministrations of a Christ without a cross." See H. Richard Niebuhr, *The Kingdom of God in America* (New York: Harper, 1937), 193. To a considerable extent, however, the critique of religious liberalism and its embrace of the openness and freedom of modern culture was an expression of the very thing being critiqued. Thus, for example, in his famous book *Moral Man and Immoral Society* (New York: Charles Scribner's Sons, 1960; orig. 1932), Reinhold Niebuhr criticized the naive optimism of certain forms of religious and secular liberalism without questioning many of the fundamental assumptions of liberal theology.

4. Quoted in Daniel A. Poling, "Preface," in Lowell R. Ditzen, *The Storm and the Rainbow* (New York: Henry Holt, 1959), x.

5. Ibid., 8. Josiah Royce defined God as the Absolute and argued that this Absolute comes into being through the life of the individual. With regard to the moral implications of this idealist philosophy, Royce wrote, "The soul of goodness in things evil

I shall not merely assume, but shall try actively to find out, though my very effort either to cooperate in removing this natural ill, or so to face it, that I shall come to work all the more serviceably and loyally because of its very presence in my life." Josiah Royce, *The World and the Individual,* second series [i.e., vol. 2], *Nature, Man, and the Moral Order* (Gloucester, Mass.: Peter Smith, 1976; orig. 1901), 391.

6. Robert N. Bellah et al., *Habits of the Heart: Individualism and Commitment in American Life* (Berkeley: University of California Press, 1985), 221.

7. Amanda Porterfield, *Female Piety in Puritan New England: The Emergence of Religious Humanism* (New York: Oxford University Press, 1992), 95–106.

8. Geoffrey F. Nuttall, *The Holy Spirit in Puritan Faith and Experience* (Oxford: Basil Blackwell, 1946).

9. At an earlier moment in the evolution of this American-style freedom, James Madison addressed the problem of factionalism that was inevitably a concomitant of religious freedom and other forms of civil liberty. In a discussion of this issue in *The Federalist Papers,* Madison wrote,

> There are two methods of curing the mischiefs of faction: the one, by removing its causes; the other, by controlling its effects. There are again two methods of removing the causes of faction: the one by destroying the liberty which is essential to its existence; the other, by giving to every citizen the same opinions, the same passions, and the same interest.
>
> It could never be more truly said than of the first remedy, that it is worse than the disease. Liberty is to faction, what air is to fire, an aliment without which it instantly expires. But it could not be a less folly to abolish liberty, which is essential to political life, because it nourishes faction, than it would be to wish the annihilation of air, which is essential to animal life, because it imparts to fire its destructive agency. The second expedient is as impracticable, as the first would be unwise.

Quotation from Alexander Hamilton, James Madison, and John Jay, "The Federalist No. 10: Madison" (orig. 1787), *The Federalist Papers,* ed. Garry Wills (New York: Bantam, 1982), 43.

10. William A. Clebsch, *American Religious Thought: A History* (Chicago: University of Chicago Press, 1973), 1.

11. For further discussion of these points, see William A. Clebsch, *England's Earliest Protestants, 1520–1535* (New Haven: Yale University Press, 1964).

12. See Edmund S. Morgan, *The Puritan Family: Religion and Domestic Relations in Seventeenth-Century New England* (New York: Harper and Row, 1966; orig. 1944); Porterfield, *Female Piety* (New York: Oxford University Press, 1992).

13. James P. Wind and James W. Lewis, eds., *American Congregations,* vol 1., *Portraits of Twelve Religious Communities* (Chicago: University of Chicago Press, 1994), 9. Also see R. Stephen Warner, "The Place of the Congregation in the Contemporary American Religious Configuration," in James P. Wind and James W. Lewis, eds., *American Congregations,* vol. 2, *New Perspectives in the Study of Congregations,* 54.

Chapter 1

1. As Glassman explained in an interview, "You can't get the best part of a teacher and deny who he is at the same time." Emphasizing that Buddhism is based on the insight embodied and transmitted through a teacher, Glassman responds to criticism by reaffirming the authority transmitted to him. As he explained, "[I]t felt like the best thing to do," in response to criticism, "was to be much more expressive of who I am, if I can. It's up front." Quoted in Helen Tworkov, *Zen in America: Five teachers and the Search for an American Buddhism* (New York: Kodansha International, 1994, orig 1989), 148. Some of Glassman's students have complained about his effort to make bakery work the sole context of Zen practice. Others have complained that Glassman's spiritual approach to bakery work is neither good business nor true Zen. But profitability is an important concept for Glassman, who believes that without it social service tends to result in romantic schemes that help no one. He also believes that investment in the people of a community makes good business sense and the effective outreach to people in need makes good customers. And with regard to the authenticity of his Zen, Glassman takes his responsibility as a lineage holder very seriously. See 108–51 in Tworkov, *Zen in America*, and also Bernard Glassman and Rick Fields, *Instructions to the Cook: A Zen Master's Lessons in Living a Life that Matters* (Boston: Shambhala Publications audio, 1996).

2. See William R. Hutchison's important book *The Modernist Impulse in American Protestantism* (New York: Oxford University Press, 1976).

3. M. Richard Shaull, *Encounter with Revolution* (New York: Association Press, 1955), 120, 122.

4. Ibid., 62, 144.

5. Ibid., 25.

6. Ibid., 77.

7. Christian Smith, *The Emergence of Liberation Theology: Radical Religion and Social Movement Theory* (Chicago: University of Chicago Press, 1991), 115–17; quotation from 117.

8. Paul E. Sigmund, *Liberation Theology at the Crossroads: Democracy or Revolution?* (New York: Oxford University Press, 1990), 35.

9. Ibid., 28–39.

10. Ibid, 9. During the 1960s, the Catholic Church in Latin America had moved to the left partly in response to the calls to transform the Church issued during the second Vatican Council, beginning in 1962, especially Pope John XXIII's call for *aggiornamento*, bringing the Church up to date in its ministry to the modern world. The Cuban revolution of 1959 was also a major event in the transformation of Latin American Catholicism in the 1960s. As one observer summarized the impact of this event, Cuba "propelled the anticommunist Latin American Church to go to the poor." See Smith, *Emergence of Liberation Theology*, 90–93, quotation from 93.

11. Gustavo Gutiérrez, *A Theology of Liberation* (Maryknoll: Orbis, 1973), 89.

12. In this regard, Leo XIII's 1891 *Rerum Novarum* functioned as an especially important landmark. But while the concern for the poor expressed in this document did

mark an important development in Catholic social teaching, it emerged as part of an effort to return Europe to a medieval society in which the Church regained its paternal authority. Before Vatican II, *Rerum Novarum* served the Church in its fight *against* socialism and even contributed to its support of paternalistic fascist regimes. See Gene Burns, *The Frontiers of Catholicism: The Politics of Ideology in a Liberal World* (Berkeley: University of California Press, 1992), 40–44.

13. Quotations from Michael Novak, "Liberation Theology and the Pope" (orig. 1979), in *Liberation Theology: A Documentary History*, ed. Alfred T. Hennelly, S. J. (Maryknoll Orbis, 1990), 275; Smith, *Emergence of Liberation Theology*, 254 n. 41.

14. Quotation from "South African Deputation Papers," in Johannes Du Plessis, *A History of Christian Missions in South Africa* (Cape Town: C Struik, 1965; orig. 1911), 306.

15. Quotations from Lord Balfour, "Opening Address," and John Mott, "Closing Address," cited in Rodger C. Bassham, *Mission Theology, 1948–1975: Years of Worldwide Creative Tension—Ecumenical, Evangelical, and Roman Catholic* (Pasadena: William Carey Library, 1979), 16, 17.

16. Konrad Raiser, *Ecumenism in Transition: A Paradigm Shift in the Ecumenical Movement*, trans. Tony Coates (Geneva World Council of Churches Publications, 1991), 35.

17. Quotation from William R. Hutchinson, "Modernism and Missions: The Liberal Search for an Exportable Christianity, 1875–1935," in John K. Fairbank, ed., *The Missionary Enterprise in China and America* (Cambridge: Harvard University Press, 1974), 130.

18. Bassham, *Mission Theology*, 81.

19. John F. McDonnell, *The World Council of Churches and the Catholic Church* (New York: Edwin Mellen, 1985), 171, 145, 146, also see ix, 61.

20. *Lumen Gentium*, no. 16, *The Documents of Vatican II*, ed. Walter M. Abbott, trans. Joseph Gallagher (New York: Geoffrey Chapman, 1966), quoted in Bassham, *Mission Theology*, 351.

21. Raiser, *Ecumenism in Transition*, 54–57.

22. Ibid., 13.

23. *Breaking Barriers, Nairobi 1975: The Official Report of the Fifth Assembly of the World Council of Churches* (Grand Rapids, Mich.: Eerdmans, 1976), 73; quoted in Bassham, *Mission Theology*, 353.

24. See Jonathan Edwards, *The Nature of True Virtue*, ed. William K. Frankena (Ann Arbor: University of Michigan Press, 1960).

25. Joseph A. Conforti, *Samuel Hopkins and the New Divinity Movement: Calvinism, the Congregational Ministry, and Reform in New England Between the Great Awakenings* (Grand Rapids, Mich.: Eerdmans, 1981); Amanda Porterfield, *Mary Lyon and the Mount Holyoke Missionaries* (New York: Oxford University Press, 1997), 11–19. Throughout the nineteenth century and the early decades of the twentieth century, mainline Protestant churches in the United States were firmly committed to the evangelical aspect of Christianity, and many pious Protestants were deeply invested in missionary work. Although the number of individuals who actually left home to serve as missionaries in foreign lands or dangerous territories was relatively small, they enjoyed

high status among their supporters—as well as among the people they baptized, who often treated them like royalty. In the eyes of a significant portion of the American population at that time, missionaries were exemplary models of Christian life. They were the ones with the courage and commitment to undertake the kind of service to others that God called upon every true Christian to perform. The best-known missionaries were religious celebrities whose dedication and accomplishments many American Protestants admired.

26. For an influential treatment of these themes, see Ernest Lee Tuvenson, *Redeemer Nation: The Idea of America's Millennial Role* (Chicago: University of Chicago Press, 1968). Also see Richard Hughes Seager, *The World's Parliament of Religions: The East/West Encounter, Chicago, 1893* (Bloomington: Indiana University Press, 1995).

27. Quotation from Andrew F. Walls, "The American Dimension in the History of the Missionary Movement," in Joel Carpenter and Wilbert R. Shenk, eds, *Earthen Vessels: American Evangelicals and Foreign Missions, 1880–1980* (Grand Rapids, Mich.: Eerdmans, 1990), 2.

28. Kanzo Uchimua, "Can Americans Teach Japanese in Religion?" *Japanese Christian Intelligencer* 1 (1926): 357–61, quoted in Walls, "American Dimension," 2. Second quotation from Walls, "American Dimension," 18.

29. Roland Bainton, *The Reformation in the Sixteenth Century* (Boston: Beacon, 1952), 255.

30. See Porterfield, *Mary Lyon*, 87–143.

31. For an excellent overview, see William R. Hutchison, *Errand to the World: American Protestant Thought and Foreign Missions* (Chicago: University of Chicago Press, 1987).

32. Jonathan Edwards, *A History of the Work of Redemption: Comprising an Outline of Church History* (Boston: American Tract Society, 1774), 22, 128, 474, 479.

33. Arthur Tappan Pierson, *George Muller of Bristol and His Witness to a Prayer-Hearing God* (New York: Loizeaux Bros., Bible Truth Depot, 1899), 261, quoted in Dana L. Robert, "The Crisis of Missions' Premillennial Mission Theory and the Origins of Independent Evangelical Missions," in Carpenter and Shenk, eds., *Earthen Vessels*, 34. Also see Dana L. Robert, "The Legacy of Arthur Tappan Pierson," *International Bulletin of Missionary Research* 8 (July 1984): 120–25.

34. As one analyst of the social gospel observed, Rauschenbush still retained "the definition of sin as selfishness," which was tied to middle-class Protestant culture and its tendency to define morality in terms of self-denial. Nevertheless, Rauschenbusch's reformulation of unselfishness in terms of solidarity with others "poses a profound challenge to the way conventional morality had bifurcated self-denial into a secular work ethic that ultimately justified selfish acquisitiveness and a religious ideal of service that isolated the servant from the organic life of the society he served." See Paul William Harris, "Missionaries, Martyrs, and Modernizers: Autobiography and Reform Thought in American Protestant Missions," Ph.D. dissertation, University of Michigan, 1986, 489.

35. Adoniram Judson Gordon, *The Holy Spirit in Missions: Six Lectures* (New York: Fleming H. Revell Co., 1893), 213; quoted in Harris, "Missionaries," 490.

36. For discussion of Emma Rauschenbusch Clough's *While Sewing Sandals: Tales*

of a Telegu Pariah Tribe and of *Social Christianity in the Orient*, which Emma mostly wrote but published jointly with her husband, John E. Clough, and for discussion of Walter Rauschenbusch's connections to missionary work, see Harris, "Missionaries," 377–500.

37. As William R. Hutchinson showed, the ideas advanced in *Re-Thinking Missions* had been even more cogently articulated in the 1920s by Daniel Johnson Fleming and R. C. Hutchison. See *Errand to the World*, 146–64.

38. Quoted in Grant Wacker, "Second Thoughts on the Great Commission: Liberal Protestants and Foreign Missions, 1890–1940," in Carpenter and Shenk, eds., *Earthen Vessels*, 297. For an example of the influence of liberal Protestant thought in United States foreign policy debate, see George F. Kennan, *Foreign Policy and Christian Conscience* (Philadelphia: American Friends Service Committee, 1959).

39. F. Max Muller, "Greek Philosophy and the Christian Religion," quoted in Seager, *World's Parliament*, 70.

40. Quoted in Wacker, "Second Thoughts," 299 n. 28.

41. Figures quoted in Carpenter and Shenk, "Preface," *Earthen Vessels*, xii. Also see Steve Brouwer, Paul Gifford, and Susan D. Rose, *Exporting the American Gospel: Global Christian Fundamentalism* (New York: Routledge, 1996).

Chapter 2

1. See Anne C. Rose, *Transcendentalism as a Social Movement, 1830–1850* (New Haven: Yale University Press, 1981), 144–45 n. 94, 196–97 n. 110.

2. Orestes A. Brownson, "The Mediatorial Life of Jesus" (1842), in *The Works of Orestes A. Brownson*, ed. Henry F. Brownson (Detroit: H. F. Brownson and Thorndike Nourse, 1882–1887), 4: 154–56, quoted in Rose, *Transcendentalism*, 210–11.

3. Orestes A. Brownson, "Rights of the Temporal," *Brownson's Quarterly Review* 22 (October 1860): 496, quoted in Joseph P. Chinnici, ed., *Devotion to the Holy Spirit in American Catholicism* (New York: Paulist, 1985), 8.

4. Geoffrey F. Nuttall, *The Holy Spirit in Puritan Faith and Experience* (Oxford: Basil Blackwell, 1946).

5. See James F. MacLear, "Anne Hutchinson and the Mortalist Heresy," *New England Quarterly* 54, 1 (1981): 74–103.

6. Like both Aquinas and Hutchinson, Edwards emphasized the infusion of grace into the believer's soul and the supernatural transformation it produced. See, for example, Jonathan Edwards, *Treatise on the Religious Affections* (orig. 1746), in *The Works of Jonathan Edwards* (New Haven: Yale University Press, 1959), 2: 197–205. For discussion of the human race as an organic whole, see Jonathan Edwards, *Original Sin* (orig. 1758), in *The Works of Jonathan Edwards*, vol. 3 (New Haven: Yale University Press, 1970). For his vision of God's kingdom as a building constructed over the course of human history, see Jonathan Edwards, *A History of the Work of Redemption: Comprising an Outline of Church History* (Boston: American Tract Society, 1774).

7. Chinnici, *Devotion to the Holy Spirit*, 25–34. Also see *Isaac T. Hecker, the Diary:*

Romantic Religion in Ante-Bellum America, ed. John Farina (New York: Paulist, 1988), John Farina, ed., *Hecker Studies: Essays on the Thought of Isaac Hecker* (New York: Paulist, 1983).

8. Richard Hughes Seager, *The World's Parliament of Religions: The East/West Encounter, Chicago, 1893* (Bloomington: Indiana University Press, 1995), 119, 133–34, quotation from 134.

9. Seager, *The World's Parliament,* 133, 132, 111, 133.

10. Chinnici, *Devotion to the Holy Spirit,* 76–77.

11. Jay P. Dolan, *The American Catholic Experience: A History from Colonial Times to the Present* (Garden City, N.Y.: Doubleday, 1985), 425.

12. R. Scott Appleby, "The Triumph of Americanism: Common Ground for U.S. Catholics in the Twentieth Century," in Mary Jo Weaver and R. Scott Appleby, eds. *Being Right: Conservative Catholics in America* (Bloomington: Indiana University Press, 1995), 37–62. Appleby argues that despite enormous conflict between conservative and liberal Catholics in the United States after Vatican II, both sides (with the exception of extremists at either end) endorsed the Americanist principle of separation of church and state.

13. Speaking on behalf of the need for greater obedience, representatives of several conservative subcultures within American Catholicism have complained that the innovations introduced by progressives are, in essence, not Catholic. As the Catholic historian Mary Jo Weaver describes the thoughts of many conservative Catholics she interviewed, these religious people remember being "brought up in a church that was alive with the supernatural." Weaver heard many conservative Catholics say, in essence, "God was present in the tabernacle, the saints were part of my life, the mystical body of Christ defined my place in the universe." No less important, "the church then was an unambiguous source of authority and moral guidance at every stage of my life. The family, the church, and the school worked together to see to it that we all kept the faith." Conservative Catholics respected the renewal of Catholicism promoted by the second Vatican Council and were even enthusiastic about it. But they were dismayed by the liberal and radical interpretations of the council that seem to them to have come to dominate American Catholic thinking. From the conservative perspective, "the core of Catholic identity has been lost." The Church has become full of dissenters who no longer define themselves in terms of obedience to Church teachings, but "who have adopted other sources of authority as their guide for moral life and liturgical consciousness." Mary Jo Weaver, "Who Are the Conservative Catholics," in Weaver and Appleby, eds., *Being Right,* 2–3, 4.

14. Thomas J. Sheeran, "Group Looks to Expand Priesthood," *Casper* (Wyo.) *Star-Tribune,* November 21, 1998, A9.

15. Amanda Porterfield, "East University," in Conrad Cherry, Betty DeBerg, and Amanda Porterfield, *Religion on Campus: An Ethnographic Study of Teaching and Practice* (Chapel Hill: University of North Carolina Press, forthcoming in 2001).

16. Thomas Merton, *The Seven Storey Mountain* (New York: Harcourt Brace, 1948), 325.

17. Ibid., 224–25.

18. Letter from Father Charles Aho to author, December 5, 1998. For further discussion of Merton's life and influence, see Thomas M. King, *Merton: Mystic at the Center of America* (Collegeville, Minn.: Liturgical Press, 1992).

19. Thomas Merton, *The Geography of Lograire* (New York: New Directions, 1968), 123.

20. Sebastian Painadath, "Ashrams: A Movement of Spiritual Integration," in Christian Duquoc and Gustavo Gutiérrez, eds., *Mysticism and the Institutional Crisis* (Maryknoll, N.Y.: Orbis, 1994), 38; C. Murray Rogers, "Hindu Ashram Heritage: God's Gift to the Church," *Concilium* 1 (1965): 73; Duquoc and Gutiérrez, "Introduction," *Mysticism and the Institutional Crisis*, vii; Sebastian Kappen, "Spirituality in the New Age of Recolonization," in Duguoc and Gutiérrez, eds., *Mysticism and the Institutional Crisis*, 32.

21. William Johnston, *Christian Zen* (New York: Fordham University Press, 1997; orig. 1970); William Johnston, *The Mirror Mind: Zen-Christian Dialogue* (New York: Fordham University Press, 1981), 23.

22. Donald W. Mitchell, "God, Creation and Spiritual Life," in, Donald W. Mitchell and James A. Wiseman, eds., *The Gethsemani Encounter: A Dialogue on the Spiritual Life by Buddhist and Christian Monastics* (New York: Continuum, 1997), 32. This concept of the Spirit was so fundamental to the language of the Christian ecumenists at the conference that Dianna Eck, a Methodist laywoman and professor of religion specializing in Hinduism, expressed the following reservation: "When I observe the lightening countenance of people who are *not* Christians, it seems strange to say that their lives are filled with what I call the Holy Spirit." Eck called for "a new theological language that is forged out of *this* dialogue situation so that Christians do not go on discussing the whole world of spiritual reality using just Christian terms" (202).

23. Gene R. Thursby, "Hindu Movements Since Mid-Century: Yogis in the States," in Timothy Miller, ed., *America's Alternative Religions* (Albany: State University of New York Press, 1995), 193, 209 n. 9.

24. James F. White, "Roman Catholic and Protestant Worship in Relationship," in *Christian Worship in North America: A Retrospective, 1955–1995* (Collegeville, Minn.: Liturgical Press, 1997), 3–15, 38–39.

Chapter 3

1. Allen Ginsberg, quotations from back cover of Bob Dylan, *Desire: Songs of Redemption* (New York: Columbia Records, 1975).

2. Max Weber, *The Sociology of Religion*, trans. Ephraim Fischoff (Boston: Beacon, 1963), 207, 217. This work was first published in German in 1922, two years after Weber's death, under the title *Religionssoziologie*, as part of the larger work, *Wirtschaft und Gesellschaft*. The 1963 book cited here was the first English translation.

3. Quoted in David Obst, *Too Good to Be Forgotten: Changing America in the '60s and '70s* (New York: John Wiley and Sons, 1998), 163.

4. As Haeberle described that particular shot: "Guys were about to shoot these

people. I yelled, 'Hold it,' and shot my picture. As I walked away I heard M16s open up. From the corner of my eye I saw bodies falling, but I didn't turn to look." *Life,* December 5, 1969, quoted in Richard Drinnon, *Facing West: The Metaphysics of Indian-Hating and Empire-Building* (New York: New American Library, 1980), 453.

5. Obst, *Too Good,* 172.

6. Perry Miller, "Foreword" and "Epilogue," in *Roger Williams: His Contribution to the American Traditions,* ed. Perry Miller (New York: Atheneum, 1970; orig. 1953), v, 253.

7. See Paul Tillich, *The Religious Situation,* trans. H. Richard Niebuhr (Cleveland: World, 1956; orig. [German] 1932); H. Richard Niebuhr, *Christ and Culture* (New York: Harper and Brothers, 1951). See Chapter 6 for discussion of Tillich's influence in religious studies. For discussion of Niebuhr's influence in American religious thought, see Ronald F. Thiemann, ed., *The Legacy of H. Richard Niebuhr* (Minneapolis: Fortress, 1991).

8. Martin Luther King Jr., quoted in David J. Garrow, *Bearing the Cross: Martin Luther King, Jr., and the Southern Christian Leadership Conference: A Personal Portrait* (New York: William Morrow, 1986), 57–58.

9. According to Pappas, "[Q]uestions about [King's] academic work surfaced in late 1987, nearly 20 years after his death." In December 1990 an article on King's plagiarism appeared in The *Wall Street Journal* two weeks after Pappas's more detailed article on the subject for the *Chronicle of Higher Education* had gone to press. Theodore Pappas, *Plagiarism and the Culture War: The Writings of Martin Luther King, Jr., and Other Prominent Americans* (Tampa: Hallberg, 1998; abbreviated 1st ed., 1994), 85–103; quotations from 88 and 91.

10. Paul Deats, "Introduction to Boston Personalism," in Paul Deats and Carol Robb, eds., *The Boston Personalist Tradition in Philosophy, Social Ethics, and Theology* (Macon, Ga.: Mercer University Press, 1986), 4–5.

11. See Peter A. Bertocci, "Reflections on the Experience of 'Oughting,'" in Deats and Robb, eds., *Boston Personalist Tradition,* 209–19.

12. Niebuhr's critique of social gospel idealism and his famous distinction between ethical capacities of persons and institutions can be found in Reinhold Niebuhr, *Moral Man and Immoral Society* (New York: Charles Scribner's Sons, 1932).

13. Walter G. Muelder, "Edgar S. Brightman: Person and Moral Philosopher," in Deats and Robb, eds., *Boston Personalist Tradition,* 117–20; L. Harold DeWolf, "Ethical Implications for Criminal Justice," in Deats and Robb, eds., *Boston Personalist Tradition,* 223; Walter G. Muelder, "Communitarian Dimensions of the Moral Laws," in Deats and Robb, eds., *Boston Personalist Tradition,* 241.

14. David Halberstam, *The Children* (New York: Random House, 1998).

15. James J. Farrell, *The Spirit of the Sixties: The Making of Postwar Radicalism* (New York: Routledge, 1997), esp. 21–22.

16. Quotations from William D. Miller, *Dorothy Day: A Biography* (San Francisco: Harper and Row, 1982), 184.

17. Jay Dolan, *The American Catholic Experience: A History from Colonial Times to the Present* (Garden City: Doubleday, 1985), 451; Farrell, *Spirit of the Sixties,* 246–47.

18. Paul Giles, *American Catholic Arts and Fictions: Culture, Ideology, Aesthetics* (New York: Cambridge University Press, 1992), 492–503, quotations from 499 and 501–2.

19. Norman Mailer, "The Hip and the Square," in *Advertisements for Myself* (New York: Putnam, 1959), 424–28, *Farrell, Spirit of the Sixties*, 22, 69.

20. Norman Mailer, *Armies of the Night: History as Novel, Novel as History* (New York: New American Library, 1968), 139–41.

21. Ibid, 143.

22. Mary Daly, "Autobiographical Preface to the 1975 Edition," *The Church and the Second Sex* (Boston: Beacon, 1975; orig. 1968), 10.

23. Ibid, 12, 13. Also see Mary Daly, *Beyond God the Father: Toward a Philosophy of Women's Liberation* (Boston: Beacon, 1973); Mary Daly, *Pure Lust: Elemental Feminist Philosophy* (Boston: Beacon, 1984), esp. 82–83.

24. Tom Engelhardt, *The End of Victory Culture: Cold War America and the Disillusioning of a Generation* (New York: Basic Books, 1995), 37.

25. Roger Williams, *A Key into the Language of America: or, Help to the Language of the Natives in that Part of America, Called New-England* (London: G. Dexter, 1643), quoted in Perry Miller, *Roger Williams: His Contribution to the American Tradition* (New York: Atheneum, 1970), 64.

26. See Albert Keiser, *The Indian in American Literature* (New York: Oxford University Press, 1933). Also see Roy Harvey Pearce, *Savagism and Civilization* (Baltimore: Johns Hopkins University Press, 1965; first published in 1953 as *The Savages of America: A Study of the Idea of Civilization*).

27. Henry David Thoreau, April 21, 1852, *Journal*, ed. Bradford Torrey (Boston: Houghton Mifflin, 1906), quoted in Robert F. Sayre, *Thoreau and the American Indians* (Princeton: Princeton University Press, 1977), 97.

28. Quotation from Robert F. Berkhofer, Jr., "Introduction," *Salvation and the Savage: An Analysis of Protestant Missions and American Indian Response, 1987–1862* (New York: Atheneum, 1976; orig. 1965), n.p.

29. Drinnon, *Facing West*, 368. Also see Richard Slotkin, *Regeneration Through Violence: The Mythology of the American Frontier, 1600–1860* (Middletown: Wesleyan University Press, 1973).

30. Ann Taves, *Fits, Trances, and Visions: Experiencing Religion and Explaining Experience from Wesley to James* (Princeton: Princeton University Press, 1999).

31. *Sun Bear: The Path of Power*, as told to Wabun and Barry Weinstock (Spokane: Bear Tribe Publishing, 1983), 137, 207–8, quoted in Catherine L. Albanese, *Nature Religion in America: From the Algonkian Indians to the New Age* (Chicago: University of Chicago Press, 1990), 160–61.

32. Sam D. Gill, "Hopi Kachina Cult Initiation: The Shocking Beginning to the Hopi's Religious Life," *Journal of the American Academy of Religion* 45, 2, supp. (1977): A447–A64.

33. Victor Turner, *The Forest of Symbols: Aspects of Ndembu Ritual* (Ithaca: Cornell University Press, 1967); Amanda Porterfield, "East University," in Conrad Cherry, Betty DeBerg, in Amanda Porterfield, *Religion on Campus: An Ethnographic Study of Practice and Teaching* (Chapel Hill: University of North Carolina Press, 2001).

Chapter 4

1. Thich Nhat Hanh, *Vietnam: Lotus in a Sea of Fire* (New York: Hill and Wang, 1967), 106; Stephen Batchelor, *The Awakening of the West: The Encounter of Buddhism and Western Culture* (Berkeley: Parallax, 1994), 353–54, David Steindl-Rast, "Foreword," in Thich Nhat Hanh, *Living Buddha, Living Christ* (New York Riverhead, 1995), xv–xvi.

2. Nhat Hanh, *Vietnam*, 1.

3. See Batchelor, *Awakening of the West*, 356.

4. *Asian Religions in America: A Documentary History*, ed. Thomas A. Tweed and Stephen Prothero (New York: Oxford University Press, 1999), 349–51, 335–39, 353–57, 342–45, quotations from 350–51, 353, 343–45. Also see Donald S. Lopez, Jr., *Prisoners of Shangri-La: Tibetan Buddhism and the West* (Chicago: University of Chicago Press, 1998), 1–2.

5. Thomas A. Tweed, *The American Encounter with Buddhism, 1844–1912: Victorian Culture and the Limits of Dissent* (Bloomington: Indiana University Press, 1992), 133–56.

6. Dalai Lama and Howard C. Cutler, *The Art of Happiness: A Handbook for Living* (New York: Riverhead Books, 1998), 13, 14, 15.

7. Rick Fields, "Divided Dharma: White Buddhists, Ethnic Buddhists, and Racism," in Charles S. Prebish and Kenneth K. Tanaka, eds., *The Faces of Buddhism in America* (Berkeley: University of California Press, 1998), 196–206; Catherine L. Albanese, *America: Religions and Religion*, 2nd ed. (Belmont, Calif.: Wadsworth, 1992), 314–18; Jan Nattier, "Who Is a Buddhist? Charting the Landscape of Buddhist America," in Prebish and Tanaka, eds., *Faces*, 189–90.

8. Although the two main groups of evangelical Buddhists in the United States, Nichiren Shoshu and Soka Gakkai, ceased cooperation in 1991 as a result of disputes between the leaders of the two groups, both groups are similar (and quite different from other Buddhists) in their lack of interest in the Eightfold Path or any demanding form of meditation as a means to enlightenment. Members of both groups are intensely pious people devoted to the Buddha-mind and its manifestations. At the same time, they are also practical Buddhists by virtue of being invested in the salutary effects of chanting and evangelical outreach. In other words, the practical investment that members of these groups have made in the salvific power of the *Lotus Sutra* is saturated with devotional piety.

9. Erik Fraser Storlie, *Nothing on My Mind: Berkeley, LSD, Two Zen Masters, and a Life on the Dharma Trail* (Boston: Shambhala, 1996), 145.

10. Karma Lekshe Tsomo, ed., *Buddhism Through American Women's Eyes* (Ithaca: Snow Lion Publications, 1995), 157–58.

11. William A. Clebsch credits the sixteenth-century English theologian and Bible translator William Tyndale with "fashion[ing] the spectacles through which generations of Englishmen read their Bibles. One lens, of theological legalism, made the New Testament look like the Old. The other lens, of religious moralism, made the Bible everyman's book of prudential ethics." Like the Puritans who read the Bible through

his spectacles, Clebsch explained, "Tyndale reconciled the double movements of gospel and law into a two-pronged justification—before God through faith and before man through good works." Thus "the covenant-contract theology crystallized in Tyndale's mind," Clebsch argued. "The Old Testament and the New Testament comprised one covenant, and a covenant was understood as a contract. God had revealed what men may do and may not do." And not only that: "God had furnished personal strength to do and not to do according to his rules." William A. Clebsch, *England's Earliest Protestants, 1520–1535* (New Haven: Yale University Press, 1964), 197, 201, 203.

12. Marsha M. Linehan, *Cognitive-Behavioral Treatment of Borderline Personality Disorder* (New York: Guilford, 1993); Marsha M. Linehan, *Skills Training Manual for Treating Borderline Personality Disorder* (New York: Guilford, 1993).

13. Gil Fronsdal, "Insight Meditation in the United States: Life, Liberty, and the Pursuit of Happiness," in Prebish and Tanaka, eds., *Faces*, 164–80.

14. As Kornfield explained, his book originated as a series of talks in 1986 to a group calling itself the Spiritual Emergency Network, a network of mental health professionals concerned with helping people negotiate "the powerful spiritual transitions that are poorly understood in our culture and often confused with mental illness." Kornfield recognized that personality and mood disorders often interfered with spiritual development and that more than a few of the people who attended meditation retreats needed help with these problems in order to begin meditation work. At the same time, he saw that even advanced meditators could benefit from psychotherapy at certain points in their life. Ultimately, he explained, meditation and psychotherapy were both aimed at the same goal: enabling persons to live fully in both love and work. And "good therapy," he argued, always created "a sense of openness and a more transparent understanding of the self" so that "the truths of spiritual life can be brought into personal practice." See Jack Kornfield, *A Path with Heart: A Guide Through the Perils and Promises of Spiritual Life* (New York: Bantam, 1993), 81, 251–52, 9.

15. Mark Epstein, *Thoughts Without a Thinker: Psychotherapy from a Buddhist Perspective* (New York: Basic Books, 1995), 21, 9, 129–30.

16. Daniel Goleman, *Emotional Intelligence: Why It Can Matter More than IQ* (New York: Bantam, 1995); quotation from Gil Fronsdal, "Insight Meditation," 165, as quoted from the semiannual *vipassana* journal *Inquiring Mind* 2, 1 (1985): 7.

17. Jacques Derrida, *Writing and Difference*, trans. A. Bass (Chicago: University of Chicago Press, 1978); Jacques Lacan, "The Subversion of the Subject and the Dialectic of Desire in the Freudian Unconscious," in *Ecrits: A Selection* (New York: W. W. Norton, 1977), 294, 300.

18. In his essay "Beat Zen, Square Zen and Zen" (1958), Watts criticized the extreme hedonism he associated with some forms of Beat Zen as well as, at the other extreme, the rigid structure of monastic Zen. Despite this criticism of Beat Zen, Watts is often considered an important example of Beat Zen as well as a major influence on others associated with it. See Helen Tworkov, *Zen in America: Five Teachers and the Search for an American Buddhism* (New York: Kodansha International, 1994; orig. 1989), 81.

19. Allen Ginsberg, quotations from *Big Sky Mind: Buddhism and the Beat Gener-*

ation, ed., Carole Tonkinson (New York: Riverhead Books, 1995), 107, 119, 123–24, and 126.

20. Gary Snyder, "On the Road with D. T. Suzuki," in Masao Abe, ed., *A Zen Life: D. T. Suzuki Remembered* (New York: Weatherhill, 1986), 208, 209.

21. Alan Watts, "Prefatory Essay," in D. T. Suzuki, *Outlines of Mahayana Buddhism* (New York: Schocken, 1963; orig. 1907), xv.

22. Tworkov, *Zen in America*, 80, 81.

23. D. T. Suzuki, "Satori," in Abe, ed., *A Zen Life*, 27, 28, 43.

24. Ibid., 141, 150.

25. See Rodger Kamenetz, *The Jew in the Lotus: A Poet's Rediscovery of Jewish Identity in Buddhist India* (New York: HarperCollins, 1994), 7–9, 149, quotation from 9.

Chapter 5

1. Quoted in Rebecca Chopp, *The Power to Speak: Feminism, Language, God* (New York: Crossroad, 1991), 125, 127, 128.

2. Quoted in Debra Renee Kaufman, *Rachel's Daughters: Newly Orthodox Women* (New Brunswick: Rutgers University Press, 1991), 18, 23.

3. Michelle Rosaldo, "Women, Culture and Society: A Theoretical Overview," in Michelle Rosaldo and Louise Lamphere, eds., *Women, Culture and Society* (Stanford: Stanford University Press, 1974), 17–42; also see Michelle Rosaldo, "The Use and Abuse of Anthropology: Reflections On Feminism and Cross-cultural Understanding," *Signs* 5:3 (1980): 398–417.

4. Elizabeth A. Johnson, *She Who Is: The Mystery of God in Feminist Theological Discourse* (New York: Crossroad, 1998), 30–31; Rosemary Radford Reuther, *Sexism and God-Talk: Toward a Feminist Theology* (Boston: Beacon, 1983), 18–19.

5. See Nancy F. Cott, *The Grounding of Modern Feminism* (New Haven: Yale University Press, 1987), 4–6.

6. See Anita Shreve, *Women Together, Women Alone: The Legacy of the Consciousness-Raising Movement* (New York: Fawcett Columbine, 1989).

7. Linda Williams, *Hard Core: Power, Pleasure, and the "Frenzy of the Visible"* (Berkeley: University of California Press, 1999; orig. 1989), xi, 315, 311.

8. See especially Rosemary Radford Reuther, "Motherearth and the Megamachine: A Theology of Liberation in a Feminine, Somatic and Ecological Perspective," in Carol P. Christ and Judith Plaskow, eds., *Womanspirit Rising: A Feminist Reader in Religion* (San Francisco: Harper and Row, 1979), 44–52; Rosemary Radford Reuther, *New Woman, New Earth: Sexist Ideologies and Human Liberation* (New York: Seabury, 1975).

9. As Leacock defined it, the Western myth of male dominance had many variants but always boiled down to the idea that women were subordinate to men because of their biological difference. In Leacock's view, female subordination was not a universal construct but a distinctive aspect of Western culture designed to bolster its male-dominated, nonegalitarian, capitalist structures. But male dominance was so firmly ensconced in Western mythology, Leacock believed, that Western people presumed it

to be a universal reality. Thus many Western observers mistakenly invoked their own myth of male dominance to explain gender roles in non-Western tribal societies. Eleanor Burke Leacock, *Myths of Male Dominance: Collected Articles on Women Cross-Culturally* (New York: Monthly Review Press, 1981), 40, 206, 207; also see 2–3.

10. Sam D. Gill, *Mother Earth: An American Story* (Chicago: University of Chicago Press, 1991); Elisabeth Tooker, "Women in Iroquois Society" (orig. 1984), in W. G. Spittal, ed., *Iroquois Women: An Anthology* (Ohsweken, Ont.: Iroqrafts, 1990), 109–23.

11. Starhawk (Miriam Simos), *The Spiral Dance: A Rebirth of the Ancient Religion of the Great Goddess* (San Francisco: Harper and Row, 1979), 35, 37.

12. Wendy Hunter Roberts, *Celebrating Her: Feminist Ritualizing Comes of Age* (Cleveland: Pilgrim, 1998), 105.

13. Johnson, *She Who Is*, 82–103; quotations from 91.

14. Margaret Lamberts Bendroth, *Fundamentalism and Gender: 1875 to the Present* (New Haven: Yale University Press, 1993), 120–27, quotations from 123; David Harrington Watt, *A Transforming Faith: Explorations of Twentieth-Century American Evangelicalism* (New Brunswick: Rutgers University Press, 1991).

15. Kaufman, *Rachel's Daughters*, especially 10–14, 21–23, 155–67.

16. See Leila Ahmed, *Women and Gender in Islam: Historical Roots of a Modern Debate* (New Haven: Yale University Press, 1992); Gisella Webb, *Windows of Faith: Muslim Women's Scholarship Activism in the United States* (Syracuse: Syracuse University Press, 2000).

17. Mary McClintock Fulkerson, *Changing the Subject: Women's Discourses and Feminist Theology* (Minneapolis: Fortress, 1994), 9, 119.

18. Susan A. Ross, "God's Embodiment and Women—Sacraments," in Catherine Mowry LaCugna, ed., *Freeing Theology: The Essentials of Theology in Feminist Perspective* (New York: HarperCollins, 1993), 185–209, quotations from 195.

19. Paula M. Cooey, *Religious Imagination and the Body: A Feminist Analysis* (New York: Oxford University Press, 1994), 61, 122, 111, 64, 117.

20. Amanda Porterfield, "Shamanism: A Psychosocial Definition," *Journal of the American Academy of Religion* 55, 4 (1987): 721–39; Claude Lévi-Strauss, "The Effectiveness of Symbols," in *Structural Anthropology*, trans. Claire Jacobson and Brooke Grundfest Schoepf (Garden City: Anchor Books, 1967; orig. [English] 1958), 181–201; Knud Rasmussen, *Intellectual Culture of the Hudson Bay Eskimos: Report of the Fifth Thule Expedition, 1921–4* (Copenhagen: Gyldendals Forlagstrykkeri, 1930), 123–29.

21. See, for example, René Girard, *Violence and the Sacred*, trans. P. Gregory (Baltimore: Johns Hopkins University Press, 1977), and René Girard, *The Scapegoat*, trans. Y. Freccero (Baltimore: Johns Hopkins University Press, 1986).

22. David Kinsley, *Health, Healing, and Religion: A Cross-Cultural Perspective* (Upper Saddle River, NJ: Prentice Hall, 1996), especially 151–76; Jerome D. Frank and Julia B. Frank, *Persuasion and Healing: A Comparative Study of Psychotherapy*, 3rd ed. (Baltimore: Johns Hopkins University Press, 1991; orig. 1974); Herbert Benson, *Timeless Healing: The Power of Biology and Belief* (New York: Fireside, 1996).

23. Thanks to my colleague Prof. Sarah Strauss for information on the syncretism of Yogananda's approach to yoga.

24. For helpful discussion of connections between New Thought and New Age,

see Catherine L. Albanese, "The Aura of Wellness: Subtle-Energy Healing and New Age Religion," *Religion and American Culture: A Journal of Interpretation* 10, 1 (2000).

25. Susan Anderson Swedo and Henrietta L. Leonard, *It's Not All in Your Head: Now Women Can Discover the Real Causes of Their Most Commonly Misdiagnosed Health Problems* (San Francisco: HarperSanFrancisco, 1996), 24; also see Edward Shorter, *From Paralysis to Fatigue: A History of Psychosomatic Illness in the Modern Era* (New York: Macmillan, 1992).

26. For discussion of Wesley's influence on psychological thinking about religion, see Ann Taves, *Fits, Trances, and Visions: Experiencing Religion and Explaining Experience from Wesley to James* (Princeton: Princeton University Press, 1999).

Chapter 6

1. William James, "Pragmatism: A New Name for Some Old Ways of Thinking" (orig. 1907), in *Pragmatism and the Meaning of Truth* (Cambridge: Harvard University Press, 1978), 32. James attributed this metaphor of pragmatism as a hotel corridor to "the young Italian pragmatist Papini."

2. Mark C. Taylor, "Unsettling Issues," *Journal of the American Academy of Religion*, special issue: "Settled Issues and Neglected Questions in the Study of Religion," 62, 4 (1994): 953.

3. James Madison, "To the Honorable General Assembly of the Commonwealth of Virginia, A Memorial and Remonstrance," in *James Madison on Religious Liberty*, ed. Robert S. Alley (Buffalo: Prometheus, 1985), 60, 56, 58, 59.

4. *Time*, (March 16, 1959), cover and 46–52, quotations from 46, 51–52; Wilhelm and Marion Pauck, *Paul Tillich: His Life and Thought*, vol. 1; *Life* (New York: Harper and Row, 1976), 273, 283, 252–54; *New York Times*, October 23, 1965, 1, 31.

5. Parker Rossman, "Individualism: The Religion at Harvard," *Religious Education* 55, 1 (1960): 24–30, quotations from 25 and 28.

6. While some of the theological movements that he influenced had important political ramifications, Tillich himself was less interested in politics and public life than he was in the existential reality they sometimes pointed to. In an essay that first appeared in German in 1929, he argued that "the ultimate power of being, the ground of reality, appears in a special moment, in a concrete situation, revealing the infinite depth and the eternal significance of the present. But this is possible only in terms of a paradox," he explained. When a particular historical situation "is seen in the light of the ultimate power," he claimed, "the more it appears as questionable and void of lasting significance." As the first volume of his *Systematic Theology* made clear, Tillich believed that "historical revelation is not revelation *in* history but *through* history." Thus "historical events, groups, or individuals as such are not mediums of revelation," he explained. Rather, "it is the revelatory constellation into which they enter under specific conditions that make them revelatory, not their historical significance."

The condition that made events revelatory, according to Tillich, was ecstasy, which he defined as a state of mind in which reason transcends "its subject-object structure." For Tillich, "revelation can occur through every personality which is transparent (through ecstasy) for the ground of being." Thus political activists and religious visionaries could identify their experiences of ecstasy with revelation and celebrate their freedom from the practical limitations of history. This attitude toward history had important implications for understanding the meaning of Christ. Tillich drew a sharp distinction between the finite, historical Jesus and the eternal, universal Christ, arguing that just as Jesus sacrificed his finitude on the cross, so his followers were "liberated from the authority of everything finite in him, from his speculative traditions, from his individual piety, from his rather conditioned world view, from any legalistic understanding of his ethics."

Tillich's theology was essentially a form of idealism, although he used the term *realism* to describe it. Realism for Tillich had little to do with pragmatism, functionalism, empiricism, or historicism. Rather, it was an offshoot of medieval realism, with earlier roots in Plato's commitment to the reality of eternal ideas. In his doctoral dissertation, Tillich aligned himself with the view of the philosophical idealist Friedrich Wilhelm Joseph von Schelling, who claimed that emotionally passionate responses to nature and art were inherently religious expressions of the Absolute. Thus in embracing "realism," Tillich referred not only to the philosophical tradition that defined reality in terms of ideas, but also to a state of high emotional intensity that he equated with the authentic expression of ideas.

Paul Tillich, "Realism and Faith," in *Paul Tillich, Theologian of the Boundaries*, ed. Mark Kline Taylor (London: Collins Liturgical Publications, 1987), 67–82, quotation from 78; Paul Tillich, *Systematic Theology* (Chicago: University of Chicago Press, 1951), 1: 120–21, 134.

7. Paul Tillich, *Systematic Theology* (Chicago: University of Chicago Press, 1963), 3: 156.

8. William R. Rogers, "Tillich and Depth Psychology," in James Luther Adams et al, eds., *The Thought of Paul Tillich* (San Francisco: Harper and Row, 1985), 102–88, especially 105; Samuel Z. Klausner, "Role Adaption of Pastors and Psychiatrists," *Journal of the Scientific Study of Religion* 4, 1 (1965): 14–39, especially 14–15; and "Autobiographical Reflections of Paul Tillich," in Charles W. Kegley, ed., *The Theology of Paul Tillich* (New York: Macmillan, 1964; orig. 1952), 18–19.

9. Mircea Eliade, "Paul Tillich and the History of Religions," in Jerald C. Brauer, ed., *The Future of Religions: Paul Tillich* (New York: Harper and Row, 1966), 31–36, quotation from 33; Paul Tillich, "The Significance of the History of Religions for the Systematic Theologian," in *Paul Tillich*, 312–23, quotations from 321 and 319.

10. Rudolf Otto, *The Idea of the Holy: An Inquiry into the Non-rational Factor in the Idea of the Divine and Its Relation to the Rational*, trans. John W. Harvey (New York: Oxford University Press, 1958; orig. [German] 1917); Philip C. Almond, *Rudolf Otto: An Introduction to His Philosophical Theology* (Chapel Hill: University of North Carolina Press, 1984). For Eliade's relationship to Otto, see Antonio Barbosa da Silva, *The Phenomenology of Religion as a Philosophical Program: An Analysis of the Theoretical Background of the Phenomenology of Religion, in General, and of Mircea Eliade's Phenomenological Approach, in Particular* (Uppsala: CWK Gleerup, 1983), especially 80. For Tillich on Otto, see "Autobiographical Reflections," 6, and *Systematic Theology*, 1:216.

The ideas of both Tillich and Eliade are, in Tillich's case especially, indebted to ideas that Martin Heidegger developed out of Edmund Husserl's phenomenology of consciousness. Husserl took Kant's term *transcendental* to apply not just to the conditions that made thought possible, such as time and space, but to the essential nature of the human ego. Husserl believed that the logical structures of human consciousness were universal and open to phenomenological analysis. But while Husserl believed it necessary to hold in abeyance questions about the meaning or existence of objects outside their intended meaning in acts of consciousness, Heidegger attributed ontological existence to the transcendental ego and its experiences. Thus for Heidegger, an experience of terror was not just a response to something fearful and threatening, but a terrible reality with transcendental being in itself. In this way, Heidegger and other ontological realists argued that subjective experiences of terror, anxiety, sacredness, and ultimate concern were universal experiences at the heart of human life.

11. See William A. Clebsch, *American Religious Thought: A History* (Chicago: University of Chicago Press, 1973), especially 49–56 and 95–100, for fuller argument along these lines.

12. See Anne C. Rose, *Transcendentalism as a Social Movement, 1830–1850* (New Haven: Yale University Press, 1981); Catherine L. Albanese, ed., *The Spirituality of the American Transcendentalists: Selected Writings of Ralph Waldo Emerson, Amos Bronson Alcott, Theodore Parker, and Henry David Thoreau* (Macon, Ga.: Mercer University Press, 1988).

13. *Systematic Theology* 2:36–37, 45–47; Rollo May, *Paulus: Reminiscences of a Friendship* (New York: Harper and Row, 1973), 26, 29, 49. "I remember," Hannah Tillich wrote in *From Time to Time* (New York: Stein and Day, 1974; orig. 1973), "how you pretended you did not know you were caressing a woman friend who was sitting on one side of you, while I sat on the other" (20).

14. Christopher Lasch, *The Culture of Narcissism: American Life in An Age of Diminishing Expectations* (New York: W. W. Norton, 1979), 85.

15. Valerie Saiving, "The Human Situation: A Feminine View," in Carol Christ and Judith Plaskow, eds., *Womanspirit Rising: A Feminist Reader in Religion* (San Francisco: Harper and Row, 1979; orig. 1978), 25–42; Judith Plaskow, *Sex, Sin and Grace: Women's Experience and the Theologies of Reinhold Neibuhr and Paul Tillich* (Washington, D.C.: University Press of America, 1980); Mary Daly, *Pure Lust: Elemental Feminist Philosophy* (Boston: Beacon Press, 1984), 29 n., 30.

16. Pythia Peay, "Campbell and Catholicism," *Common Boundary*, March-April 1992, 28–33, quotations from 30, 31, 32, and 33.

17. C. G. Jung, *The Collected Works of C. G. Jung*, vol. 8, *The Structure and Dynamics of the Psyche*, 2nd ed., trans. R. F. C. Hull (Princeton: Princeton University Press, 1969), 156–57.

Conclusion

1. Reproduced in Jonathan Edwards, *The Great Awakening*, ed., C. C. Goen (New Haven: Yale University Press, 1972), 293, 320.

Index

ABCFM. *See* American Board of
    Commissioners for Foreign Missions
Activism
    in Catholicism, after Vatican II, 73–74
    of Dorothy Day, 106–107
    grace and, 47–48
    idealism and, 48
    in missionary evangelicalism, 26–27, 47–48
    pluralism and, 25–27
Agape, and justice, 76–77
Albanese, Catherine L., 135
Alpert, Richard (Ram Dass), 144
Alves, Rubem, 30–31
American Board of Commissioners for
    Foreign Missions (ABCFM), 34
American Indians. *See* Native Americans
Americanism, 69–70, 72
Antiwar protests, Catholic sacraments in
    by Catonsville Nine, 107–108
    at Pentagon exorcism, 110–112
Appleby, R. Scott, 70
Armies of the Night (Mailer), 110–112
The Art of Happiness (Dalai Lama), 133
Asian immigration, and growth of
    Buddhism, 134
Asian thought. *See* Eastern religions
Auclert, Hubertine, 169
Authority, religious
    of Bible, 52

in Catholicism, 59, 68, 73–75
family as, 19
individual as, 13–14, 18–19
monarchy vs. morality as, 17
of monks, 59

Balfour, Arthur James, 35
Basic Education Movement, 30
"Battle Hymn of Lieutenant Calley" (song),
    93
Bear Tribe Medicine Society, 120
Beastie Boys, 129–130
Beat Zen, 151–154
Bellah, Robert, 12–13, 17–18, 229
Bendroth, Margaret Lamberts, 182
Benevolence, 42–57
    biblical interpretation and, 48–53
    from grace, 42–44
    humanitarian vs. evangelical, 52–55
    pragmatism of, 47–48
    progressivism and, 48–52
    in Puritanism, 43
    republican idealism in, 45–46
    results of, 44–45
    and salvation, 44
    source of, 43–44
Bennett, William, 229
Benson, Herbert, 192
Berdyaev, Nicolas, 105